"You are the perfect weapon—
the perfect killing machine.
You've toppled empires with a
single shot...

...You just don't know it yet."

Written by: **Dave Wohl**

Pencils: **Dave Finch**
Clarence Lansang, Brian Ching

Inks: **Joe Weems V, Jason Gorder,**
Jay Leisten, Victor Llamas, Marco Galli,
D-Tron, Matt "Batt" Banning

Colors: **Steve Firchow,**
John Starr, Beth Sotelo,
Tyson Wengler, Matt Nelson

Lettering and Design by: **Robin Spehar &**
Dreamer Design's Dennis Heisler

Associate Collections Editor: **Phil Smith**

Collected Edition Cover by: **Dave Finch**

APHRODITE IX ISBN#: 1-58240-372-4

Published by Image Comics®
Aphrodite IX: Time Out of Mind JUNE 2004. FIRST PRINTING.
Office of Publication: 1071 North Batavia Street Suite A. Orange, California 92867. Originally
published as Aphrodite IX Vol. 1 issue 1-4, and Aphrodite IX issue #0. Aphrodite IX®, its logos,
all related characters and their likenesses are ®,™ & © 2004 Top Cow Productions Inc. All rights
reserved. The entire contents of this book are © 2004 Top Cow Productions Inc. Any similarities
to persons living or dead is purely coincidental. With the exception of artwork used for review
purposes, none of the contents of this book may be reprinted in any form without the express
written consent of Marc Silvestri or Top Cow Productions Inc. PRINTED IN THE USA

To order by telephone call **1-888-TOPCOW1**
(1-888-867-2691) or go to a comics shop near you.

To find the comics shop nearest you call:
1-888-COMICBOOK (1-888-266-4226)

What did you think of this book? We love to hear from
our readers. Please e-mail us at: **fanmail@topcow.com**
Or write us at:
Aphrodite IX c/o Top Cow Productions Inc.
10350 Santa Monica Blvd., Suite #100
Los Angeles, CA 90025

Marc Silvestri—chief executive officer
Matt Hawkins—president/chief operating officer
Jim McLauchlin—editor in chief
Renae Geerlings—vp of publishing/managing editor
Chris Carlisle—vp of creative affairs
David Wohl—consulting editor
Joel Elad—director of sales and marketing
Scott Tucker—editor
Chaz Riggs—production manager
Phil Smith—associate editor
Peter Lam and Rob Levin—editorial assistants

For **image** Comics:
Erik Larsen—publisher

visit us on the web at
www.topcow.com

Contents

Introduction pg 4

Prelude   pg 7

Chapter 1   pg 20

Chapter 2   pg 49

Chapter 3   pg 75

Chapter 4   pg 99

Sketchbook pg 142

Cover Credits

Issue #2, Dynamic Forces & Graham Cracker variant:
Dave Finch, Victor Llamas, Steve Firchow pg 6

Issue #1, Cover A:
Dave Finch, Joe Weems V, Steve Firchow pg 19

Issue #1, Cover C:
Marc Silvestri, Joe Weems V, Steve Firchow pg 27

Issue #1, Cover B:
Michael Turner, John Livesay, Steve Firchow pg 33

Issue #1, Cover D:
Joe Benitez, Victor Llamas, Dan Kemp pg 43

Issue #1, Tower.com variant:
Dave Finch, Joe Weems V, Steve Firchow pg 47

Issue #2, Graham Cracker exclusive variant:
Dave Finch, Victor Llamas, Steve Firchow pg 48

Issue #2:
Dave Finch, Joe Weems V, Steve Firchow pg 57

Issue #0 Wizard Edition:
Dave Finch, Joe Weems V, Liquid pg 67

Issue #3:
Dave Finch, Victor Llamas, Steve Firchow pg 74

Issue #2, Dynamic Forces variant:
Dave Finch, Victor Llamas, Steve Firchow pg 97

Issue #4:
art by **Dave Finch** pg 98

Issue #1, Black and white sketch variant:
Dave Finch pg 111

Issue #0, Top Cow edition cover:
Dave Finch, Victor Llamas, Steve Firchow pg 133

Issue #1, Wizard World/Fandom variant:
art by **Dave Finch** pg 137

Foreword

I'm writing this under deadline pressure (what else is new?), so bear with me a little bit. I've read so many very eloquent things from artists about their work, but nothing clever is coming to mind. I suppose that's appropriate though, given that Aphrodite IX was never meant to be subtle or clever when it was created. That's just not the sort of work that I do. I like straightforward, unnuanced, visceral fun in a comic book. It seems like books of that sort have become a bit of an endangered species nowadays, which is a real shame. So it puts a real smile on my face to look back on the work we did with Aphrodite IX. We put together a comic book by the seat of our pants; all based upon what we thought would be fun at the time. There were no story meetings, or pitches, or character design sessions. Aphrodite wasn't so much created, conceptualized and honed, as it was just shot-gunned onto the page. That had some drawbacks, I'll admit! But I think some good things came out of that too. We took quite a few lumps, but I'm proud of the result.

Aphrodite was Joe Benitez's idea initially, but he has so many ideas that he'll never get to them in a dozen lifetimes, so he let me have it when I asked. Shortly after, I needed to draw something for a poster we were putting out, and so I drew the original character in a cheerleader costume, which really, really didn't work for me the way I intended. I wanted a much more mature, strong, and world-wise woman to lead the book. Besides, I really felt like I had a good template in mind, and the original drawing just didn't fit. Anyway, fast forward a few weeks, and I was behind on yet another deadline, and I had to draw her again for a preview cover. I hadn't put too much thought into her outfit, but for me, if I feel like I know the character, all the rest just falls into place. I knew that I had what I wanted right away.

Dave Wohl had a lot of ideas about how to create a context for her, which was great, because I was sure drawing a blank! I got his plots, and we were rolling, er, slowly rolling, which is my only regret looking back, not only on Aphrodite, but my whole Top Cow career. There were so many things we could have done with Aphrodite if only I could have appreciated what I had at the time. I had a bit of a tendency to feel trapped the minute pressure started to build, and that urge pushed me off the book prematurely, and eventually it pushed me away from Top Cow completely.

A few weeks ago I was back in California working in the Top Cow studio with Marc Silvestri, Renae Geerlings and the crew again, and it was a great feeling. It really reminded me of what I took for granted when I worked there. It's a special place, full of creative, driven people. I learned everything I know from my days in the studio, and now that I'm off working on other things, their influence will always be with me.

Thanks for reading,

Dave Finch

Issue #2, Dynamic Forces & Graham Cracker variant:
Dave Finch, Victor Llamas, Steve Firchow

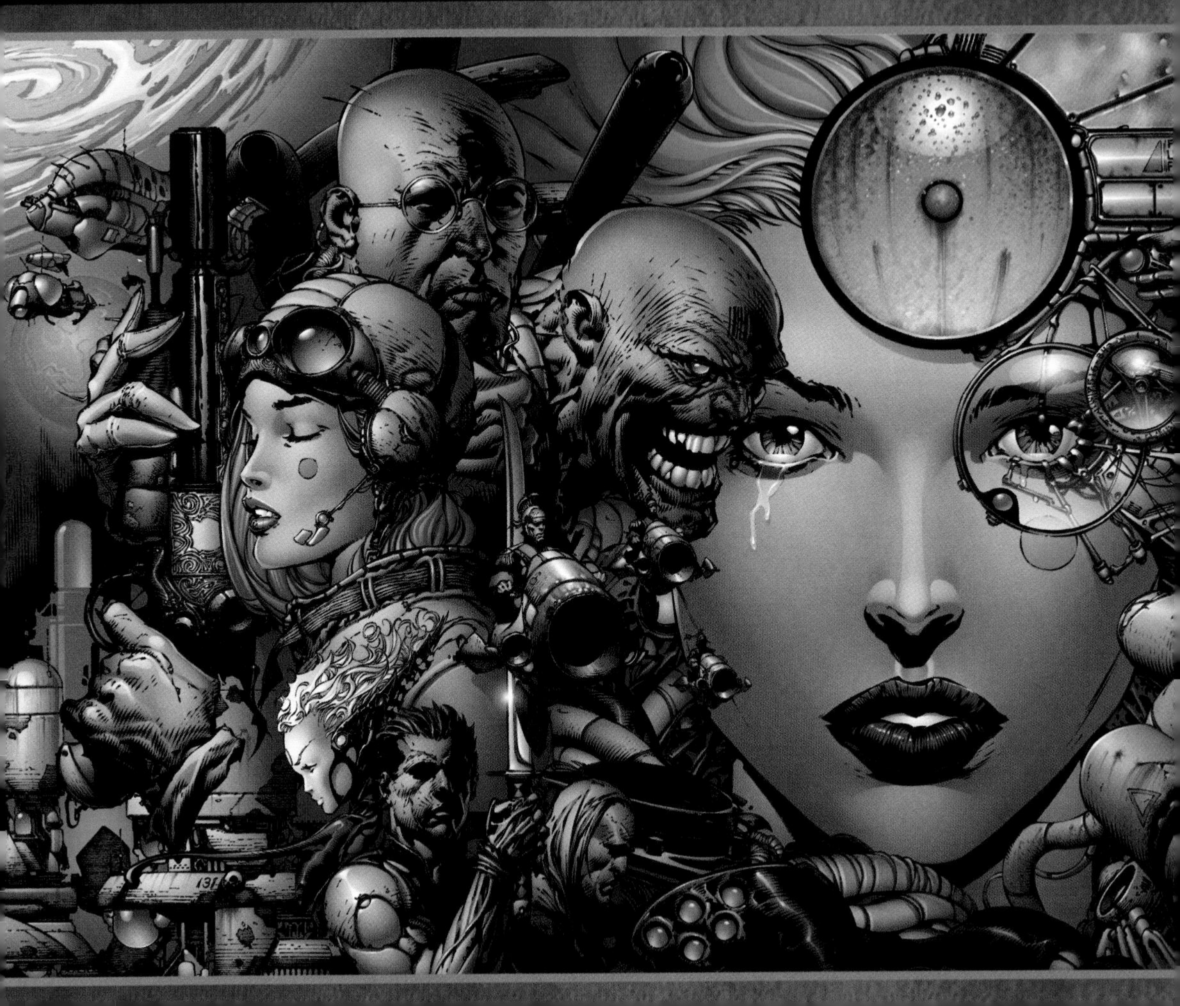

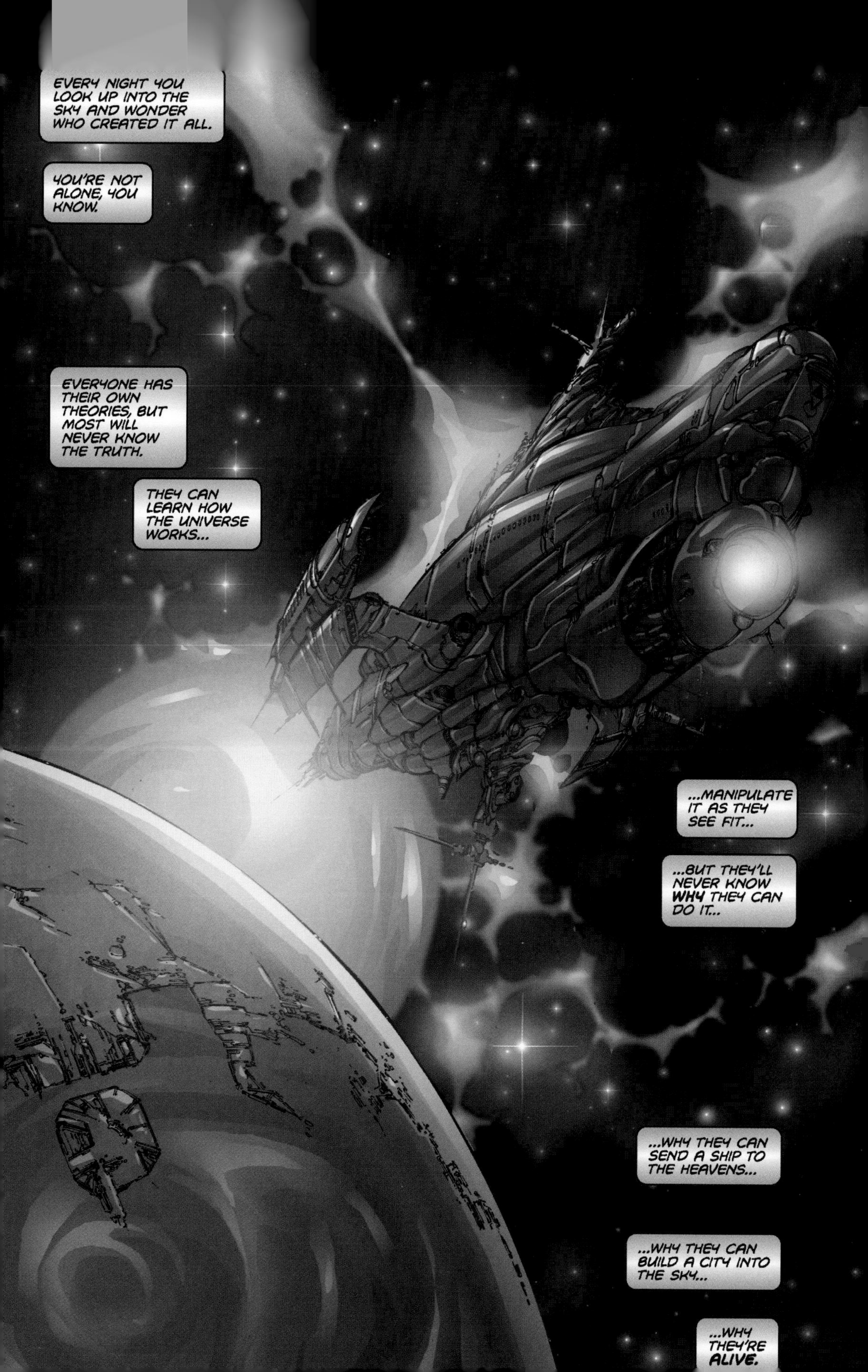
EVERY NIGHT YOU LOOK UP INTO THE SKY AND WONDER WHO CREATED IT ALL.
YOU'RE NOT ALONE, YOU KNOW.
EVERYONE HAS THEIR OWN THEORIES, BUT MOST WILL NEVER KNOW THE TRUTH.
THEY CAN LEARN HOW THE UNIVERSE WORKS...
...MANIPULATE IT AS THEY SEE FIT...
...BUT THEY'LL NEVER KNOW WHY THEY CAN DO IT...
...WHY THEY CAN SEND A SHIP TO THE HEAVENS...
...WHY THEY CAN BUILD A CITY INTO THE SKY...
...WHY THEY'RE ALIVE.

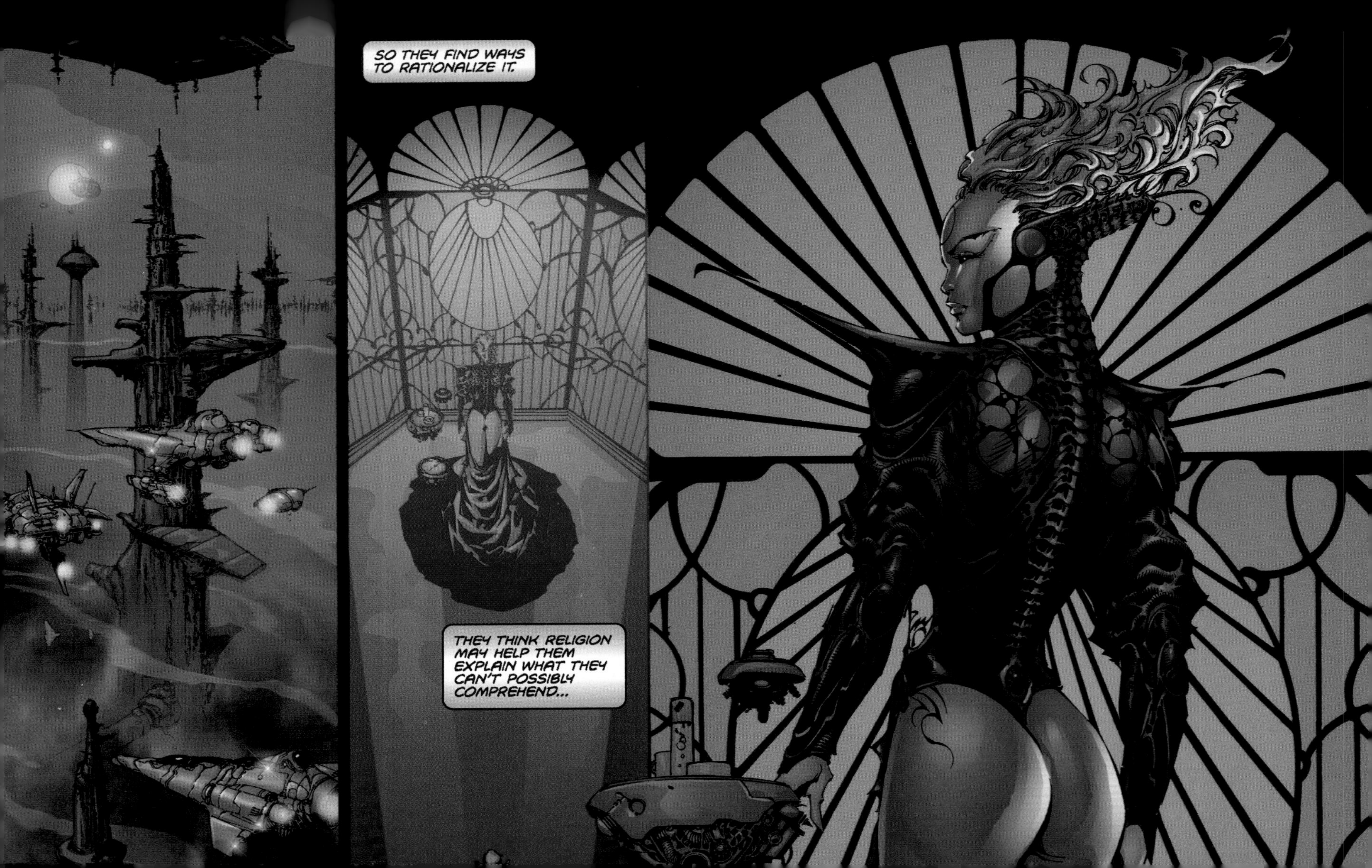
SO THEY FIND WAYS TO RATIONALIZE IT.
THEY THINK RELIGION MAY HELP THEM EXPLAIN WHAT THEY CAN'T POSSIBLY COMPREHEND...

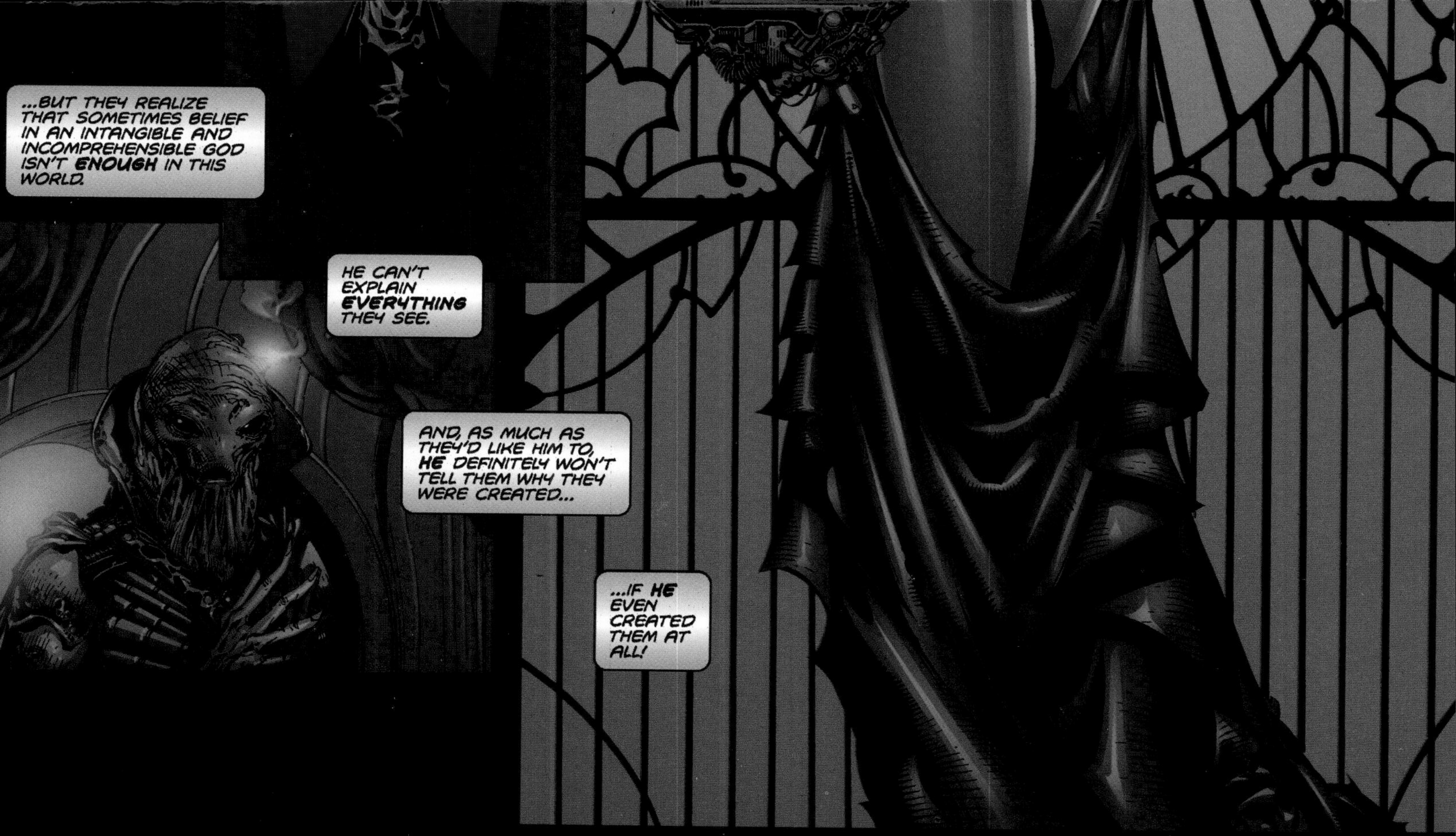
...BUT THEY REALIZE THAT SOMETIMES BELIEF IN AN INTANGIBLE AND INCOMPREHENSIBLE GOD ISN'T ENOUGH IN THIS WORLD.
HE CAN'T EXPLAIN EVERYTHING THEY SEE.
AND, AS MUCH AS THEY'D LIKE HIM TO, HE DEFINITELY WON'T TELL THEM WHY THEY WERE CREATED...
...IF HE EVEN CREATED THEM AT ALL!

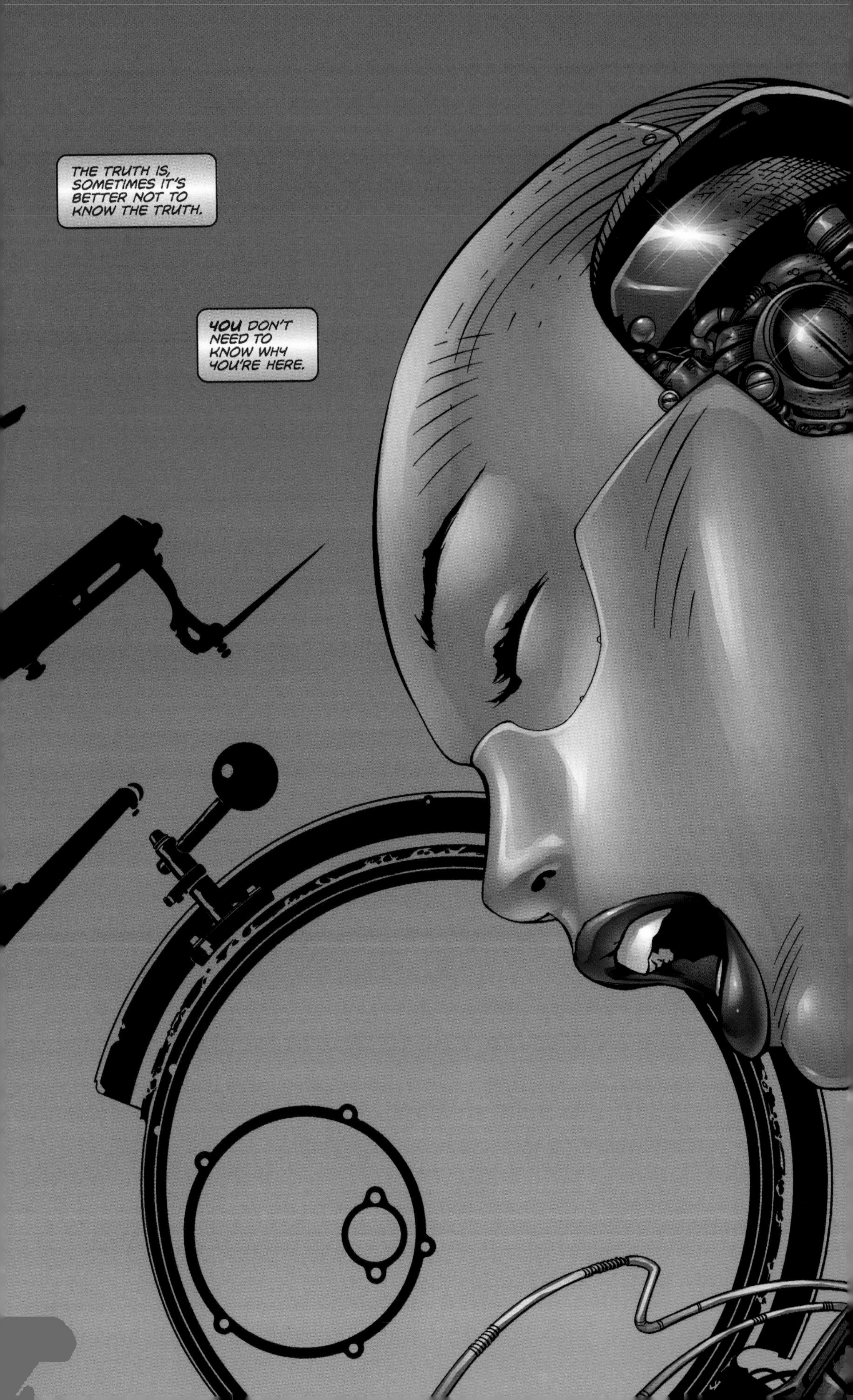
THE TRUTH IS, SOMETIMES IT'S BETTER NOT TO KNOW THE TRUTH.
YOU DON'T NEED TO KNOW WHY YOU'RE HERE.

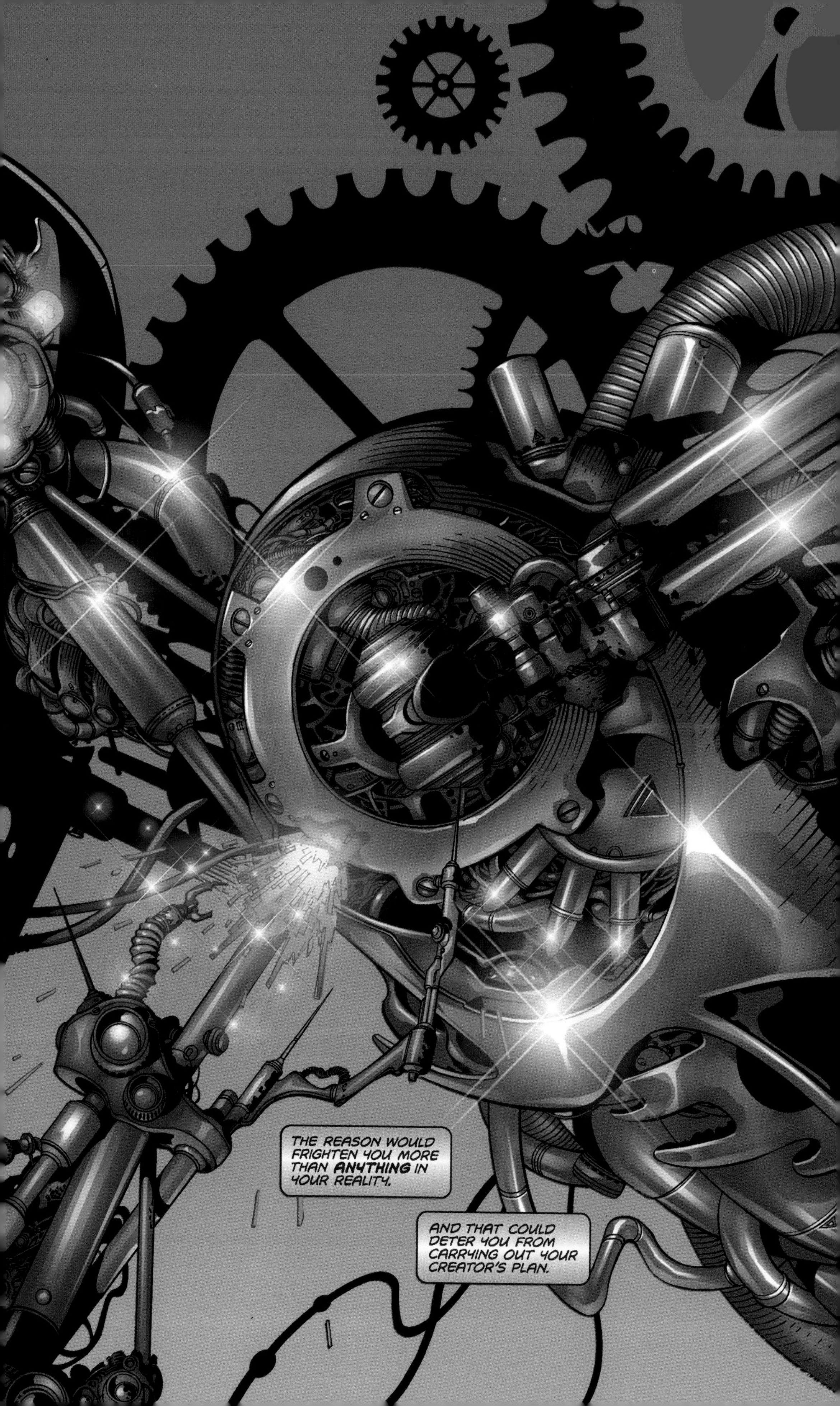
THE REASON WOULD FRIGHTEN YOU MORE THAN ANYTHING IN YOUR REALITY.
AND THAT COULD DETER YOU FROM CARRYING OUT YOUR CREATOR'S PLAN.

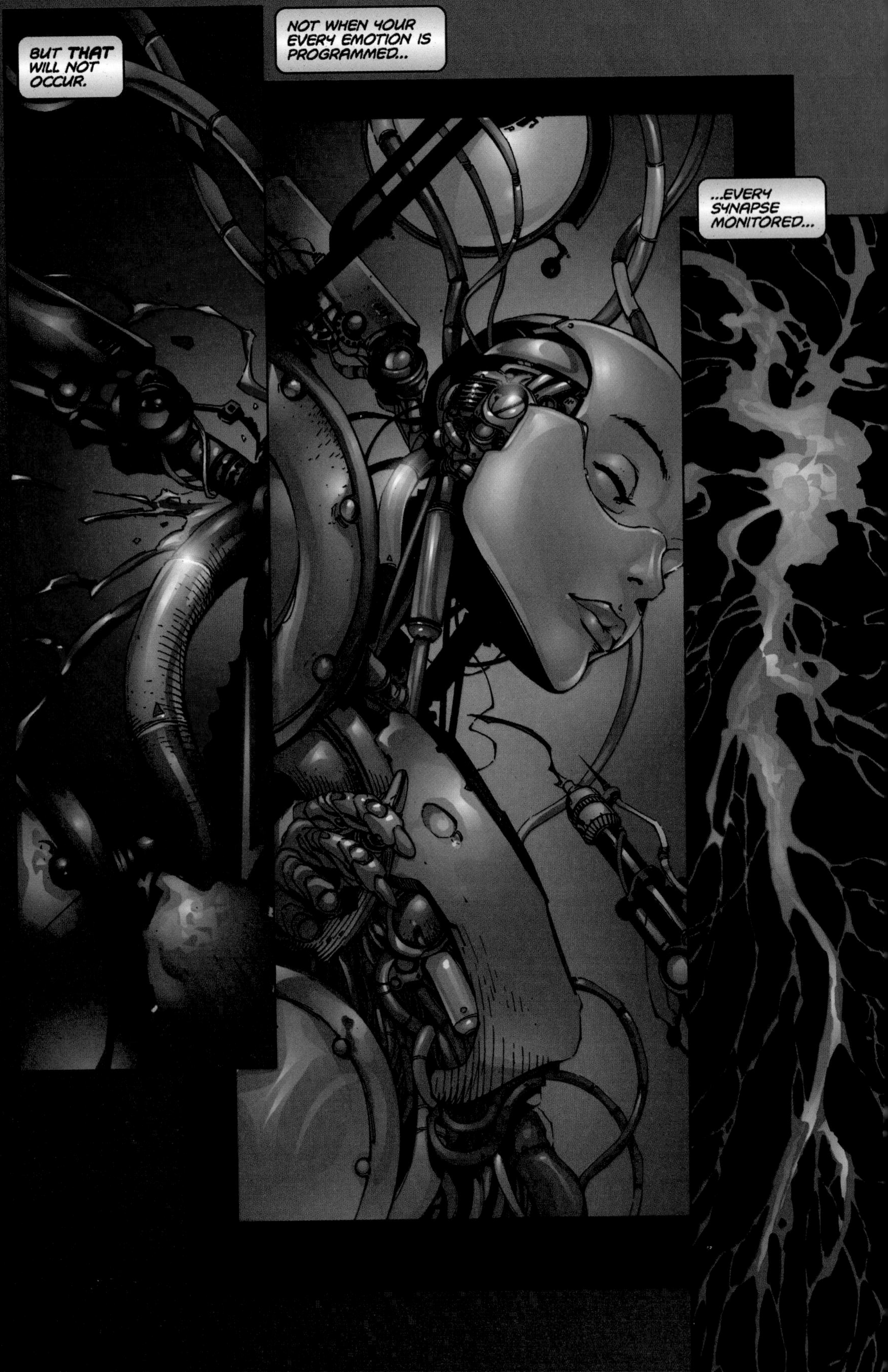
BUT THAT WILL NOT OCCUR.
NOT WHEN YOUR EVERY EMOTION IS PROGRAMMED...
...EVERY SYNAPSE MONITORED...

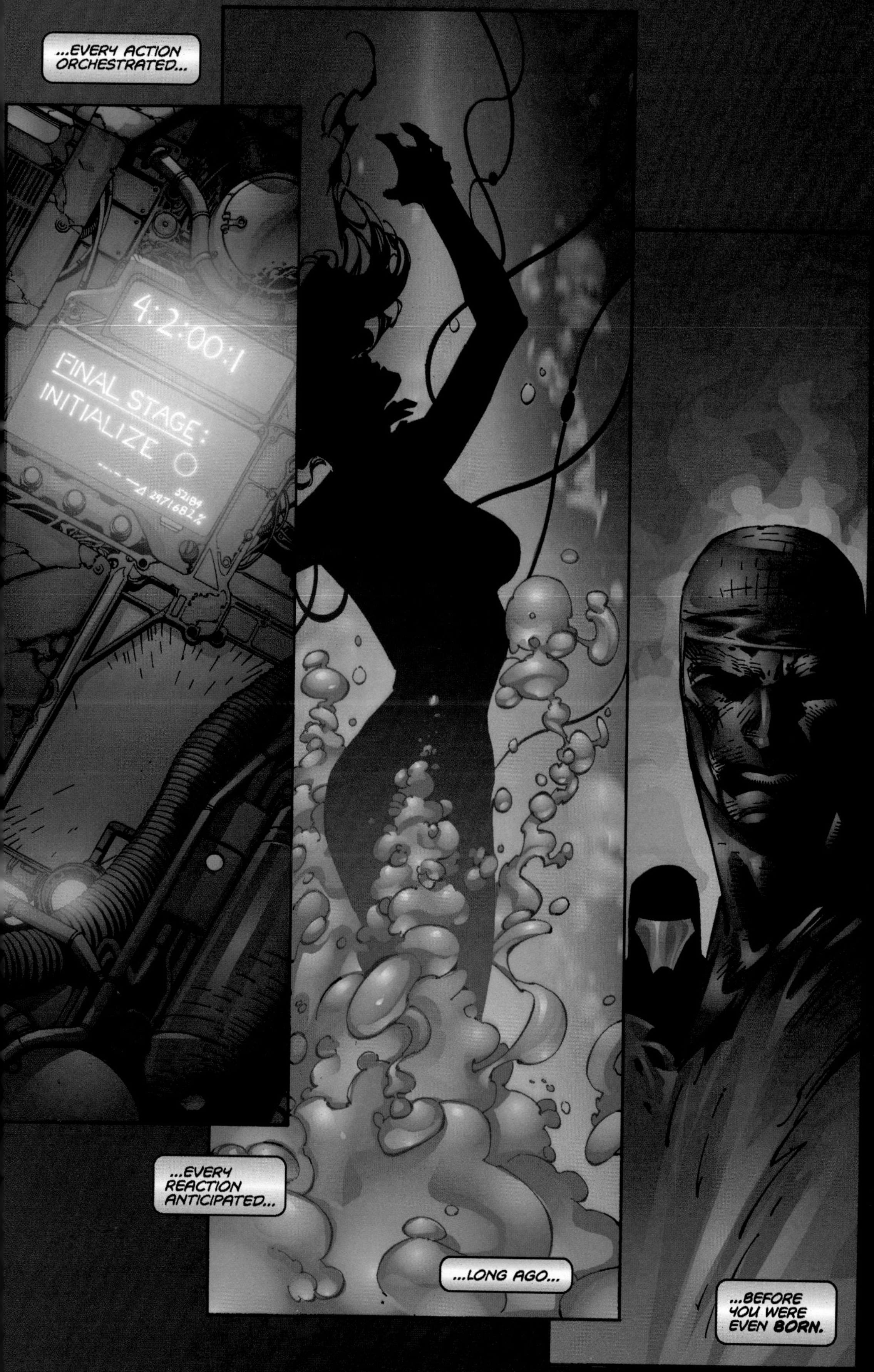
...EVERY ACTION ORCHESTRATED...
4:2:00:1
FINAL STAGE: INITIALIZE
...EVERY REACTION ANTICIPATED...
...LONG AGO...
...BEFORE YOU WERE EVEN BORN.

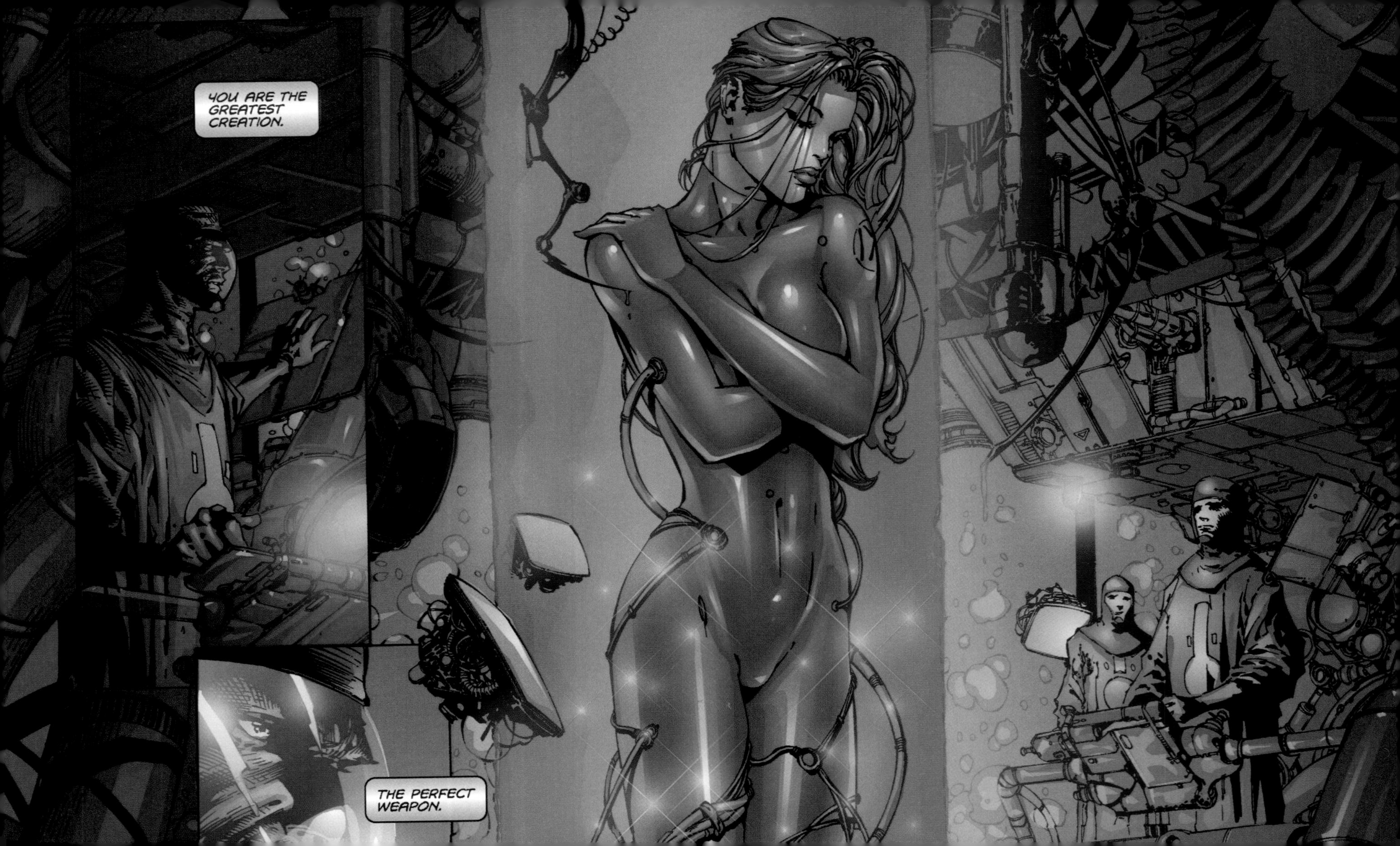
YOU ARE THE GREATEST CREATION.
THE PERFECT WEAPON.

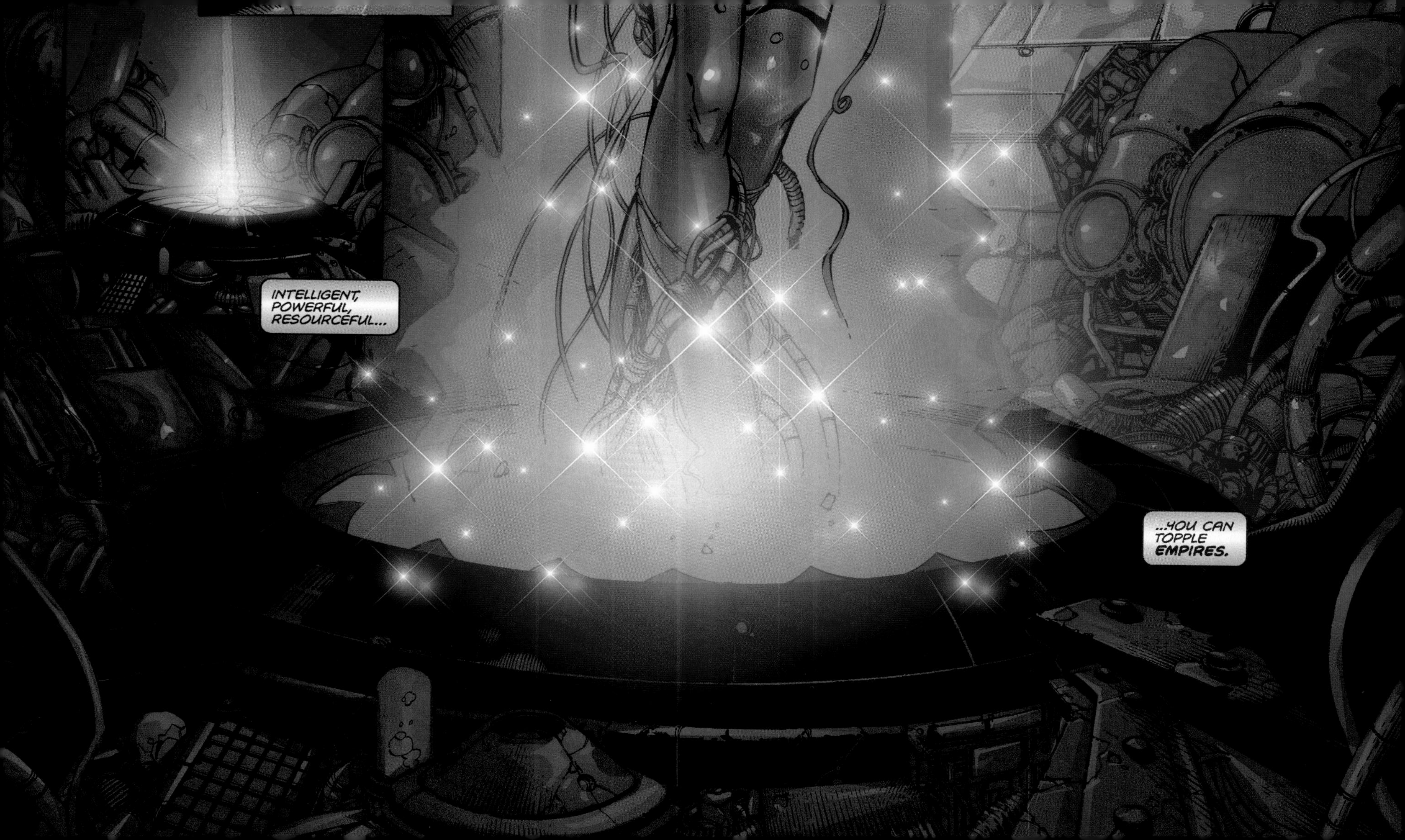
INTELLIGENT, POWERFUL, RESOURCEFUL...
...YOU CAN TOPPLE EMPIRES.

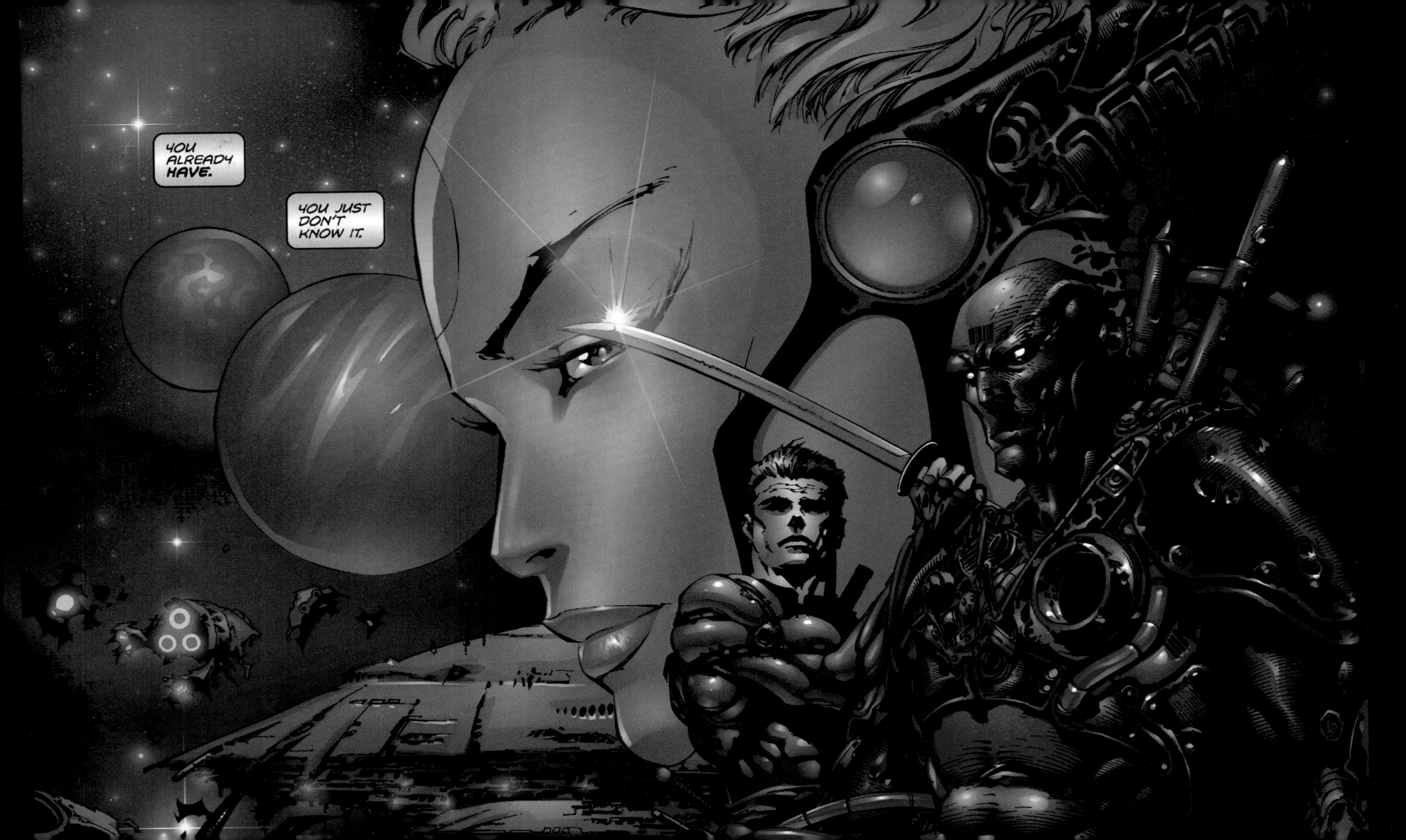
YOU ALREADY HAVE.
YOU JUST DON'T KNOW IT.

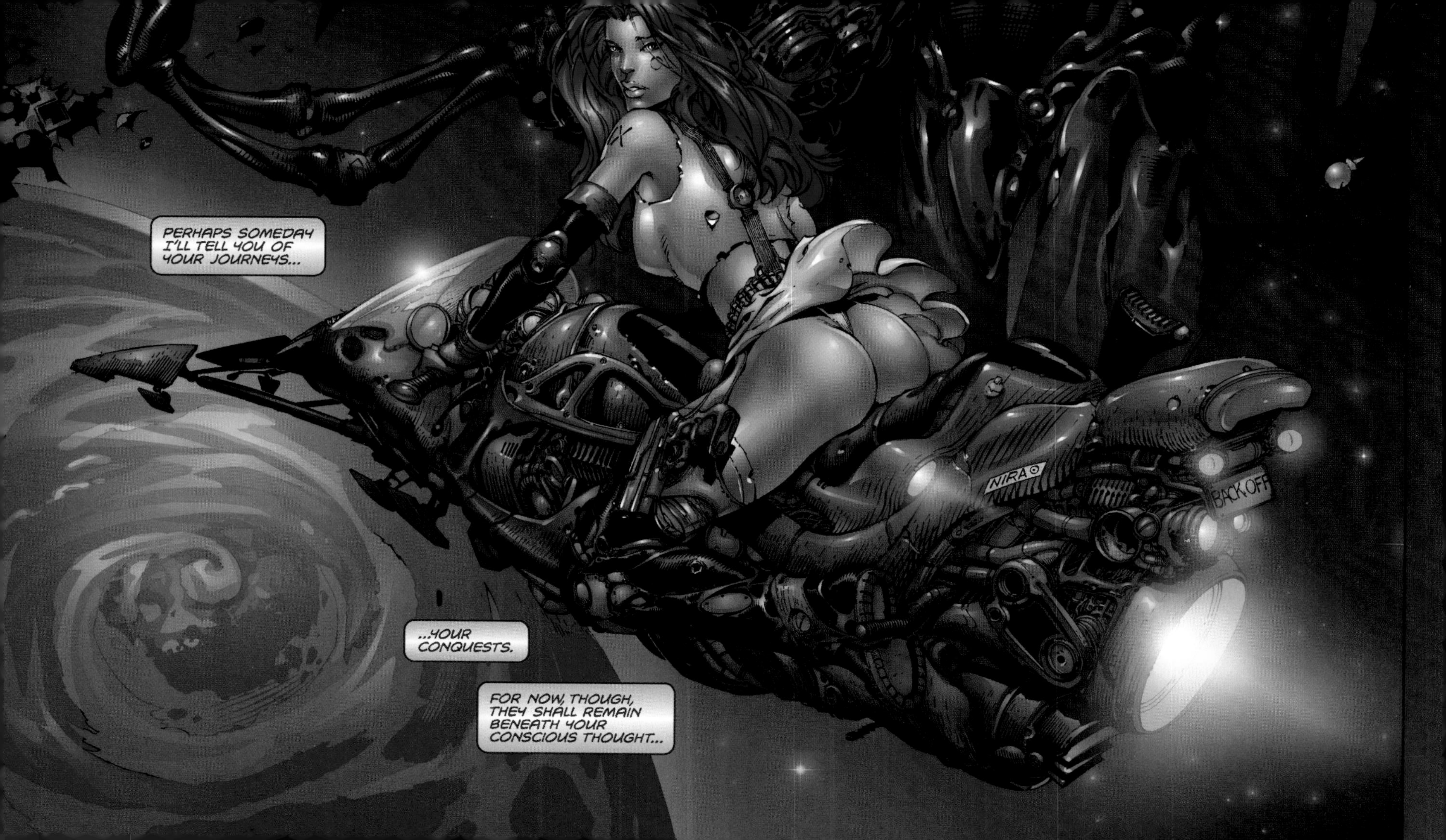
PERHAPS SOMEDAY I'LL TELL YOU OF YOUR JOURNEYS...
...YOUR CONQUESTS.
FOR NOW, THOUGH, THEY SHALL REMAIN BENEATH YOUR CONSCIOUS THOUGHT...
NIRA
BACK OFF

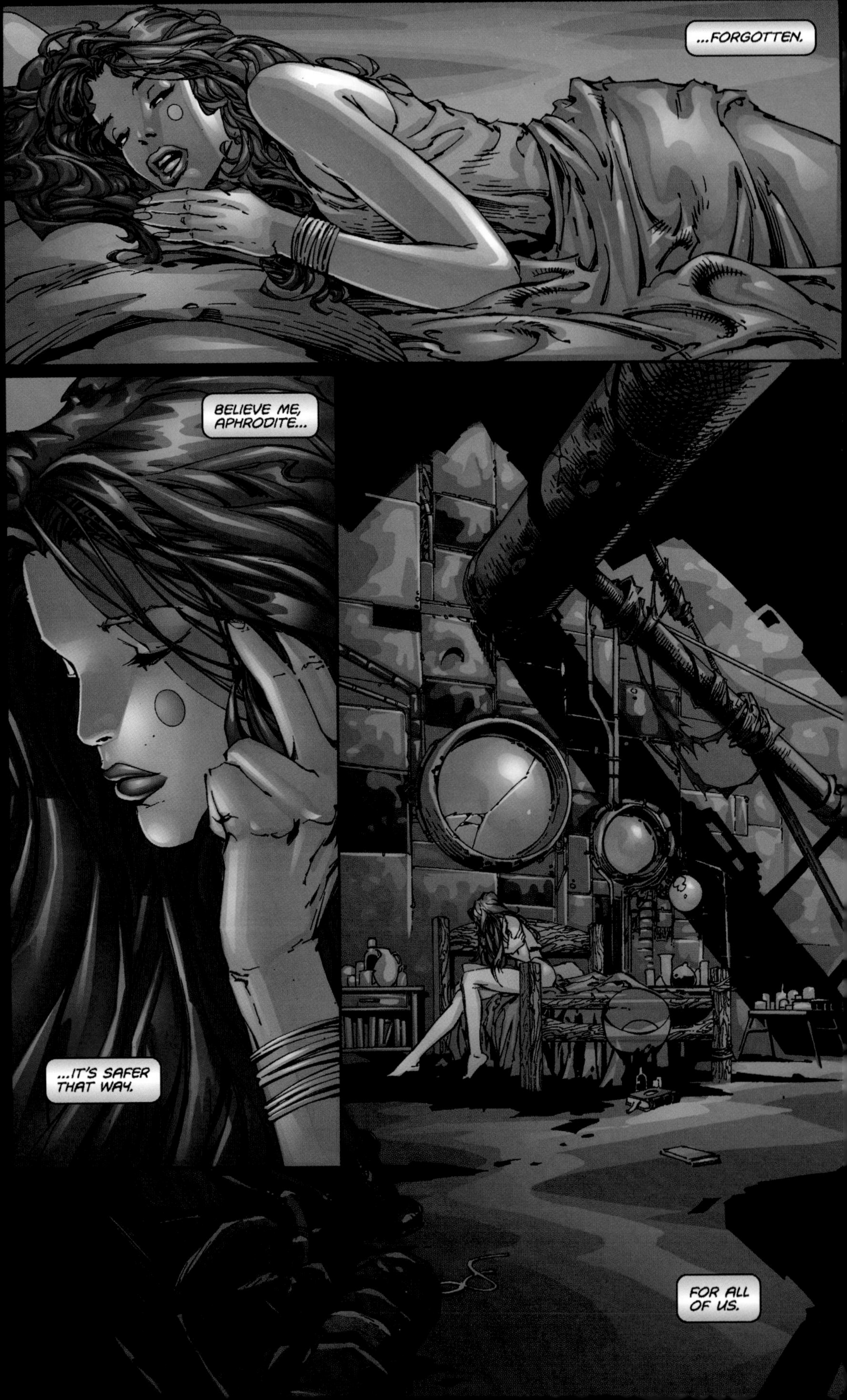
...FORGOTTEN.
BELIEVE ME, APHRODITE...
...IT'S SAFER THAT WAY.
FOR ALL OF US.

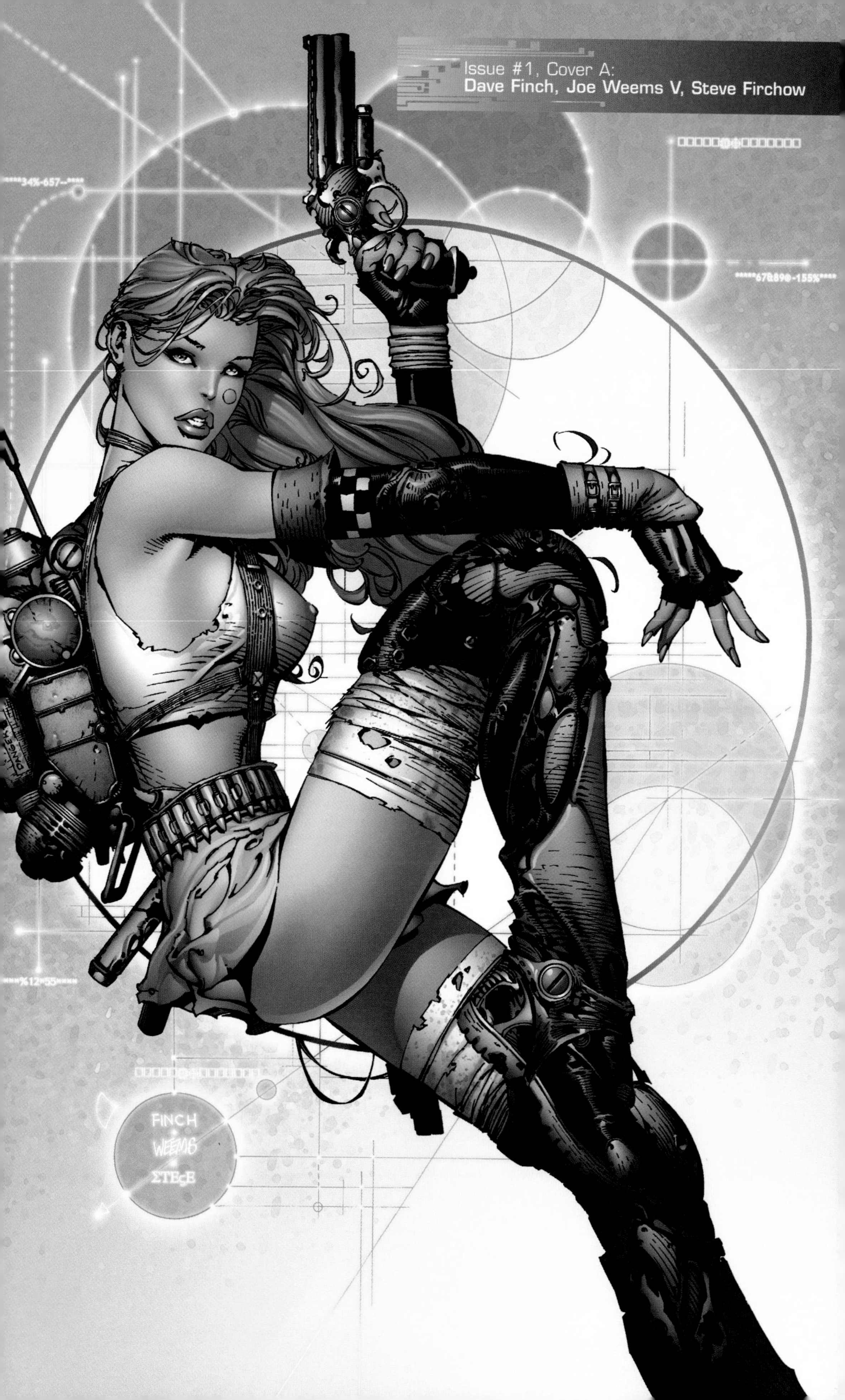
FINCH
WEEMS

Issue #1, Cover A:
Dave Finch, Joe Weems V, Steve Firchow

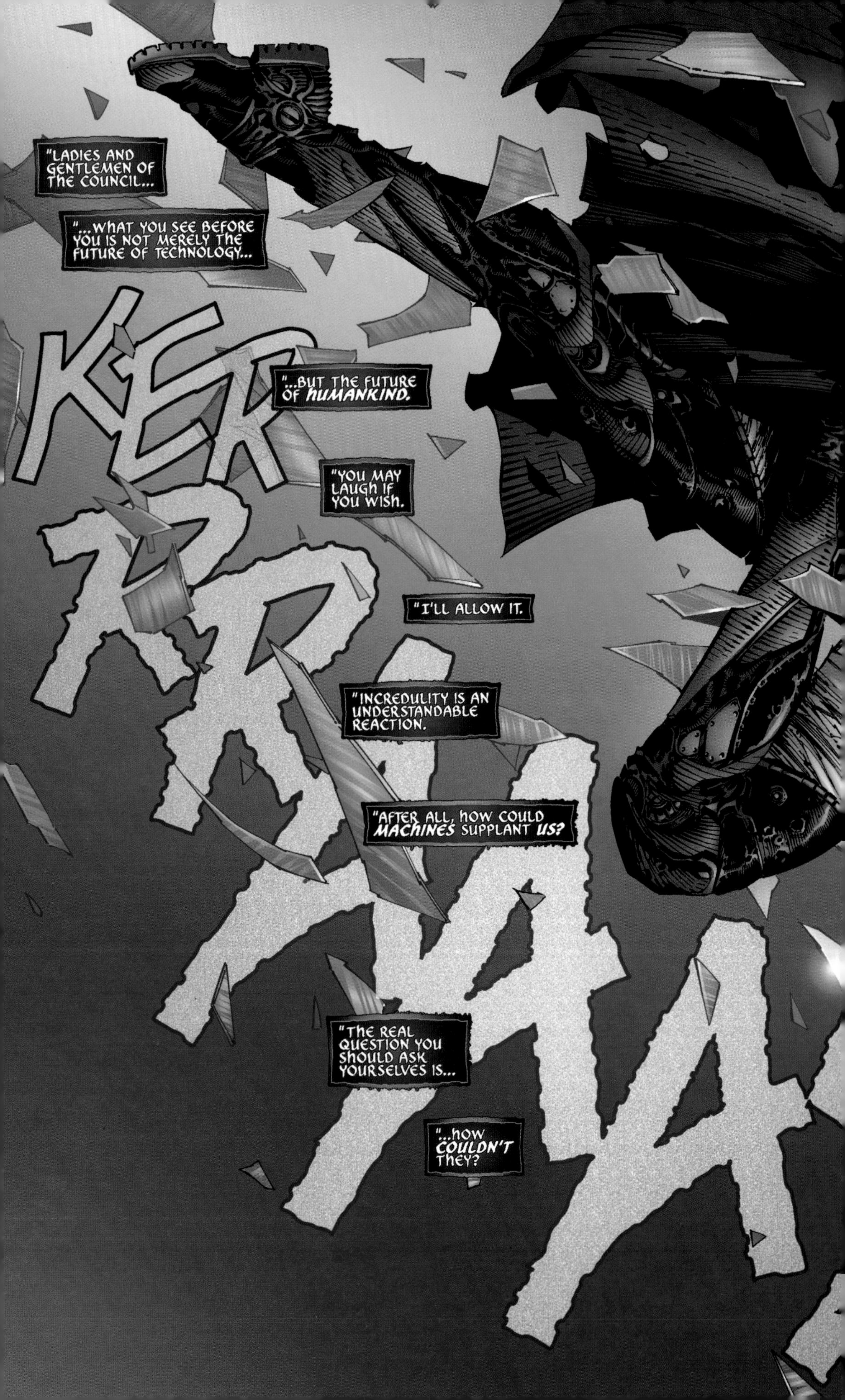
"LADIES AND GENTLEMEN OF THE COUNCIL...
"...WHAT YOU SEE BEFORE YOU IS NOT MERELY THE FUTURE OF TECHNOLOGY...
KER
"...BUT THE FUTURE OF HUMANKIND.
"YOU MAY LAUGH IF YOU WISH.
"I'LL ALLOW IT.
"INCREDULITY IS AN UNDERSTANDABLE REACTION.
"AFTER ALL, HOW COULD MACHINES SUPPLANT US?
"THE REAL QUESTION YOU SHOULD ASK YOURSELVES IS...
"...HOW COULDN'T THEY?

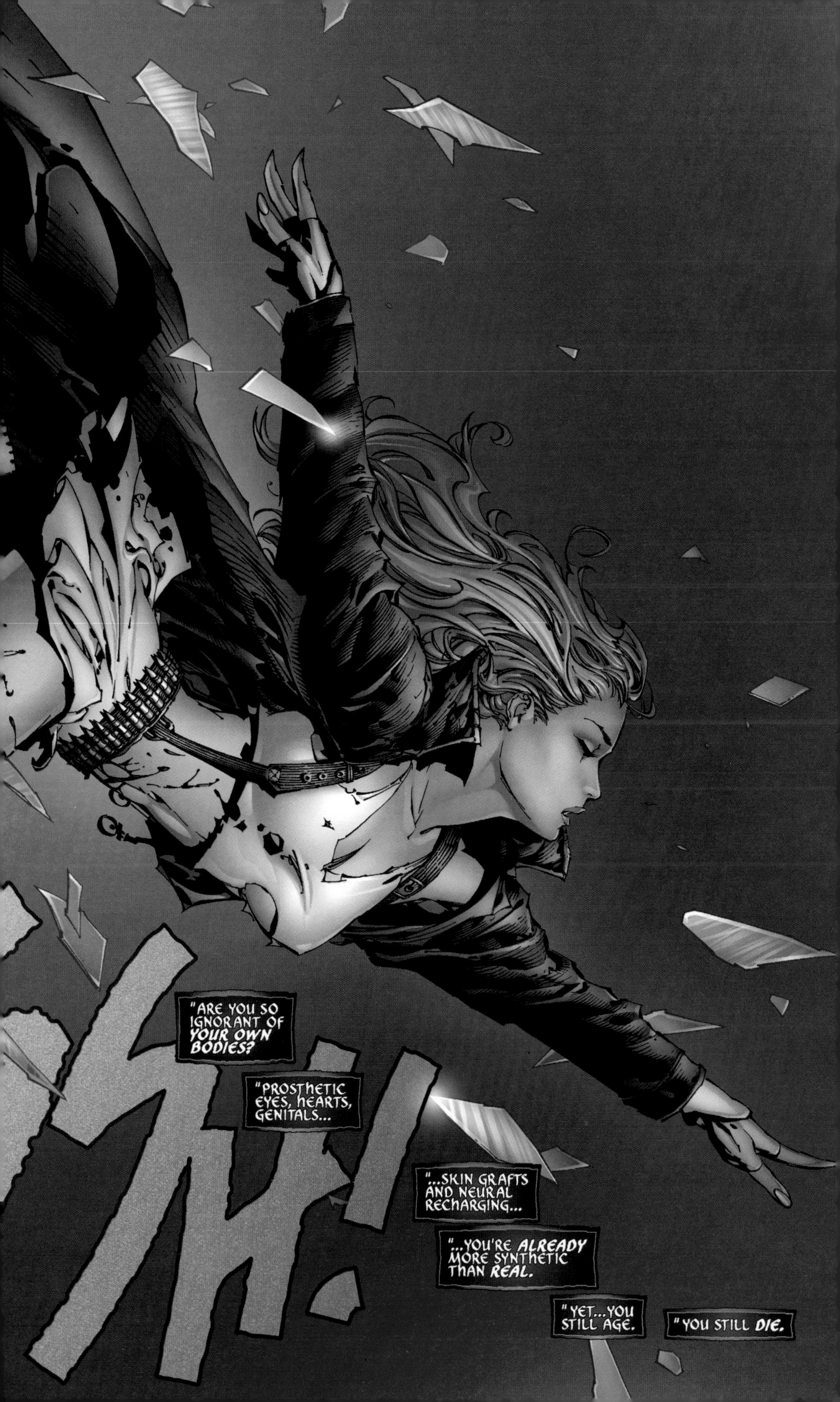
"ARE YOU SO IGNORANT OF YOUR OWN BODIES?
"PROSTHETIC EYES, HEARTS, GENITALS...
"...SKIN GRAFTS AND NEURAL RECHARGING...
"...YOU'RE ALREADY MORE SYNTHETIC THAN REAL.
"YET...YOU STILL AGE.
"YOU STILL DIE.

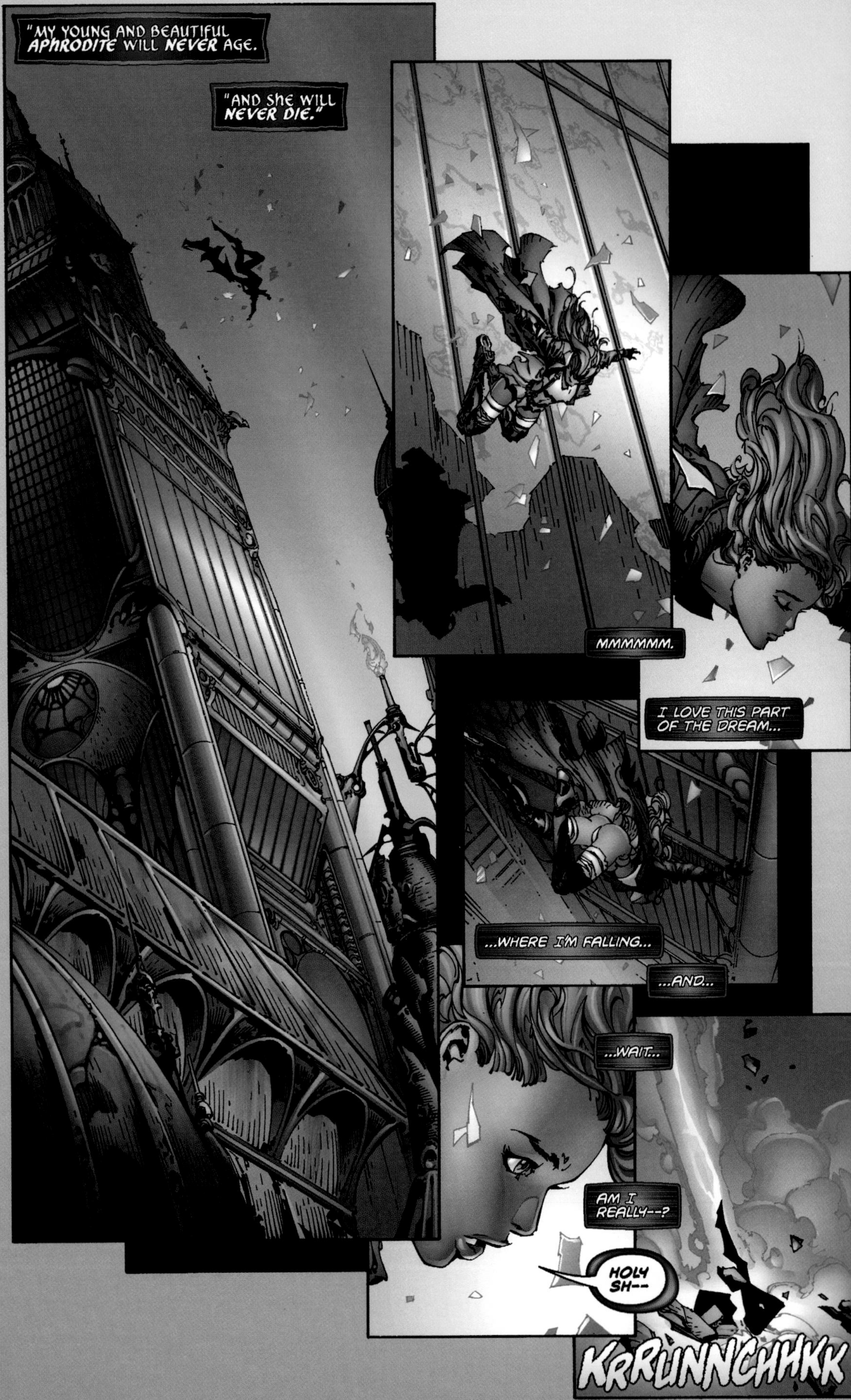
"MY YOUNG AND BEAUTIFUL APHRODITE WILL NEVER AGE.
"AND SHE WILL NEVER DIE."
MMMMMM.
I LOVE THIS PART OF THE DREAM...
...WHERE I'M FALLING...
...AND...
...WAIT...
AM I REALLY--?
HOLY SH--
KRRUNNCHHKK

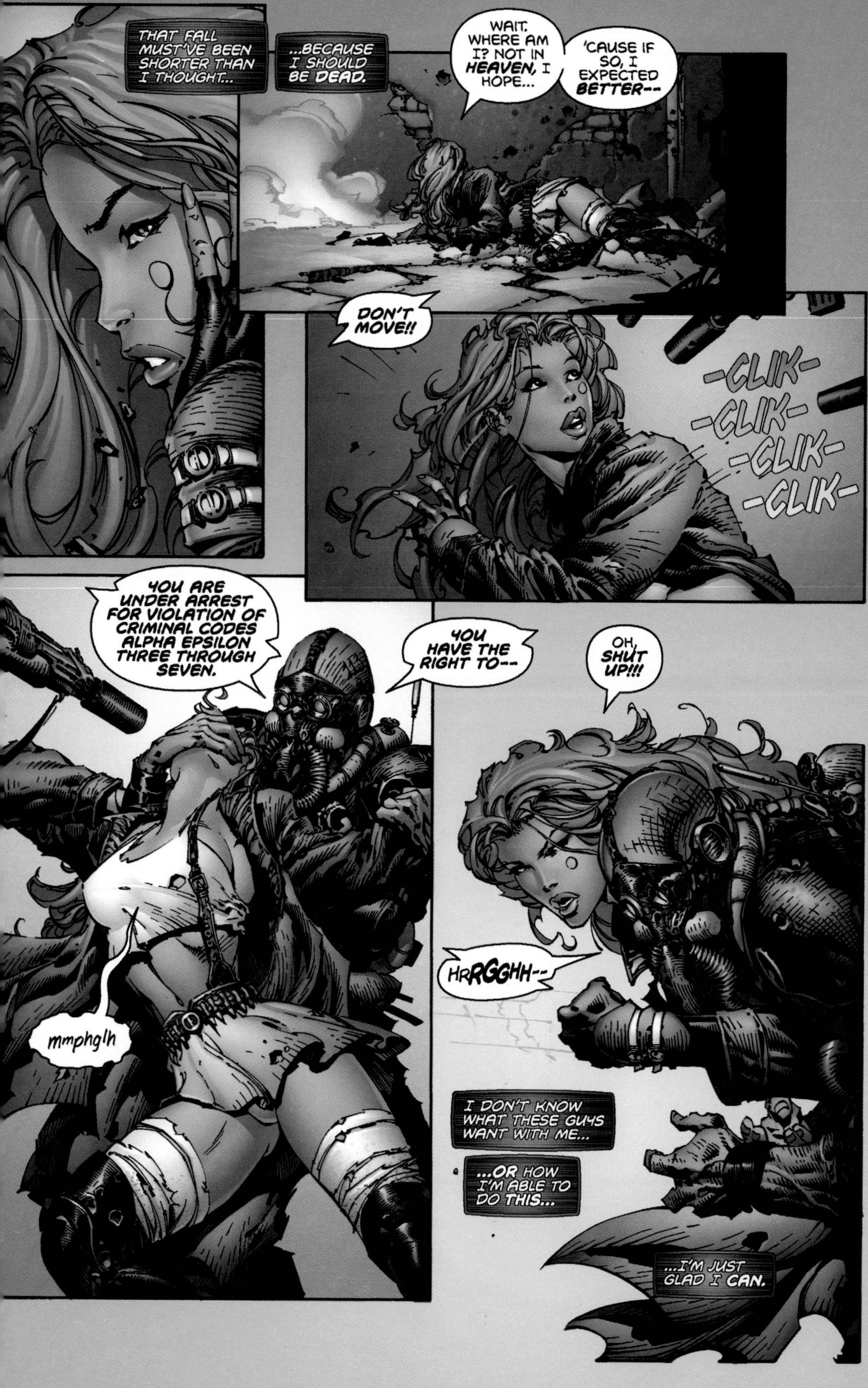
THAT FALL MUST'VE BEEN SHORTER THAN I THOUGHT...
...BECAUSE I SHOULD BE DEAD.
WAIT. WHERE AM I? NOT IN HEAVEN, I HOPE...
'CAUSE IF SO, I EXPECTED BETTER--
DON'T MOVE!!
-CLIK-
-CLIK-
-CLIK-
-CLIK-
YOU ARE UNDER ARREST FOR VIOLATION OF CRIMINAL CODES ALPHA EPSILON THREE THROUGH SEVEN.
YOU HAVE THE RIGHT TO--
mmphglh
OH, SHUT UP!!!
HRRGGHH--
I DON'T KNOW WHAT THESE GUYS WANT WITH ME...
...OR HOW I'M ABLE TO DO THIS...
...I'M JUST GLAD I CAN.

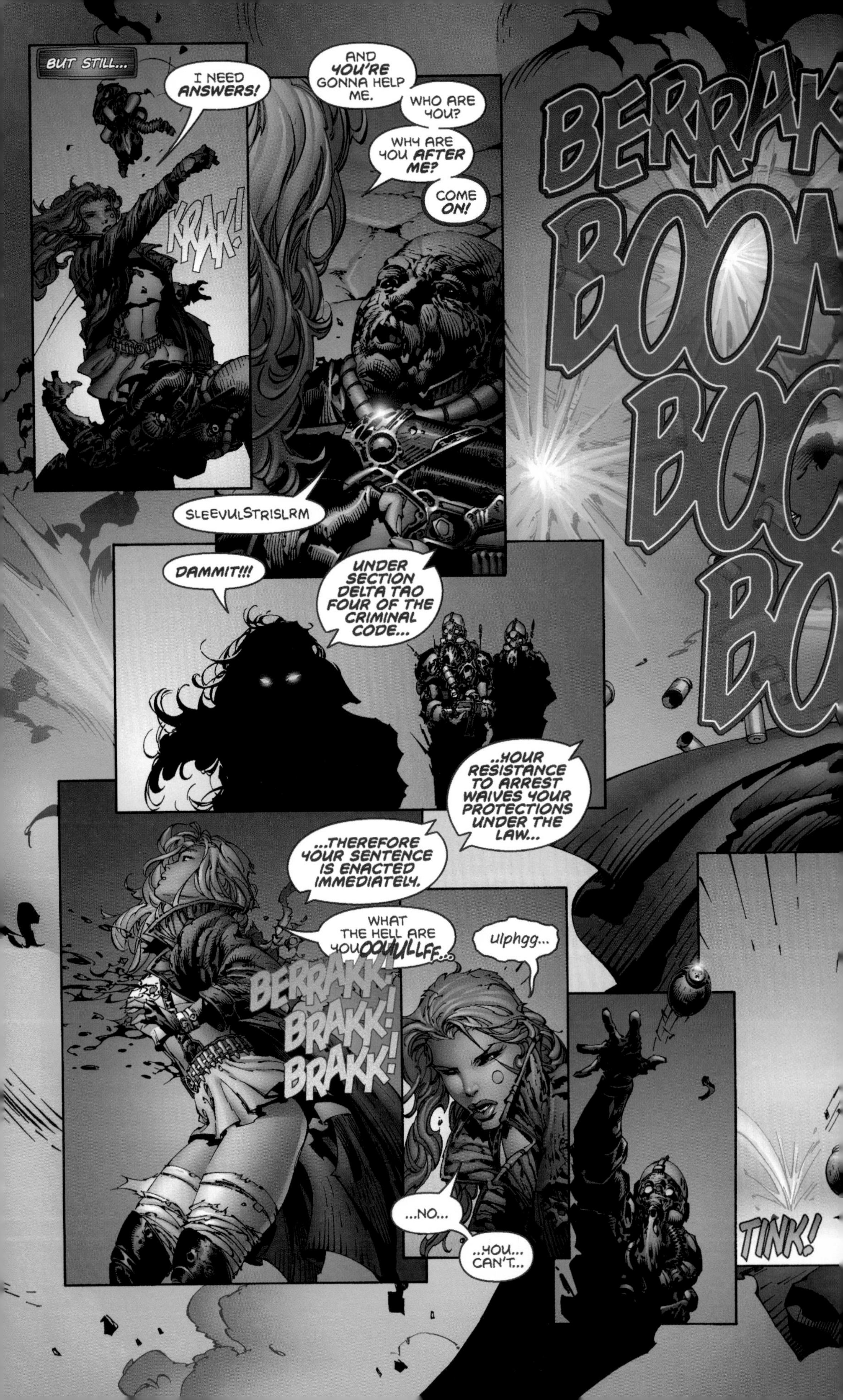

BUT STILL...
I NEED ANSWERS!
KRAK!
AND YOU'RE GONNA HELP ME.
WHO ARE YOU?
WHY ARE YOU AFTER ME?
COME ON!
SLEEVULSTRISLRM
BERRAK
BOOM
BOO
BO
DAMMIT!!!
UNDER SECTION DELTA TAO FOUR OF THE CRIMINAL CODE...
...YOUR RESISTANCE TO ARREST WAIVES YOUR PROTECTIONS UNDER THE LAW...
...THEREFORE YOUR SENTENCE IS ENACTED IMMEDIATELY.
WHAT THE HELL ARE YOUOOUULLFF...
ulphgg...
BERRAKK! BRAKK! BRAKK!
...NO...
...YOU... CAN'T...
TINK!

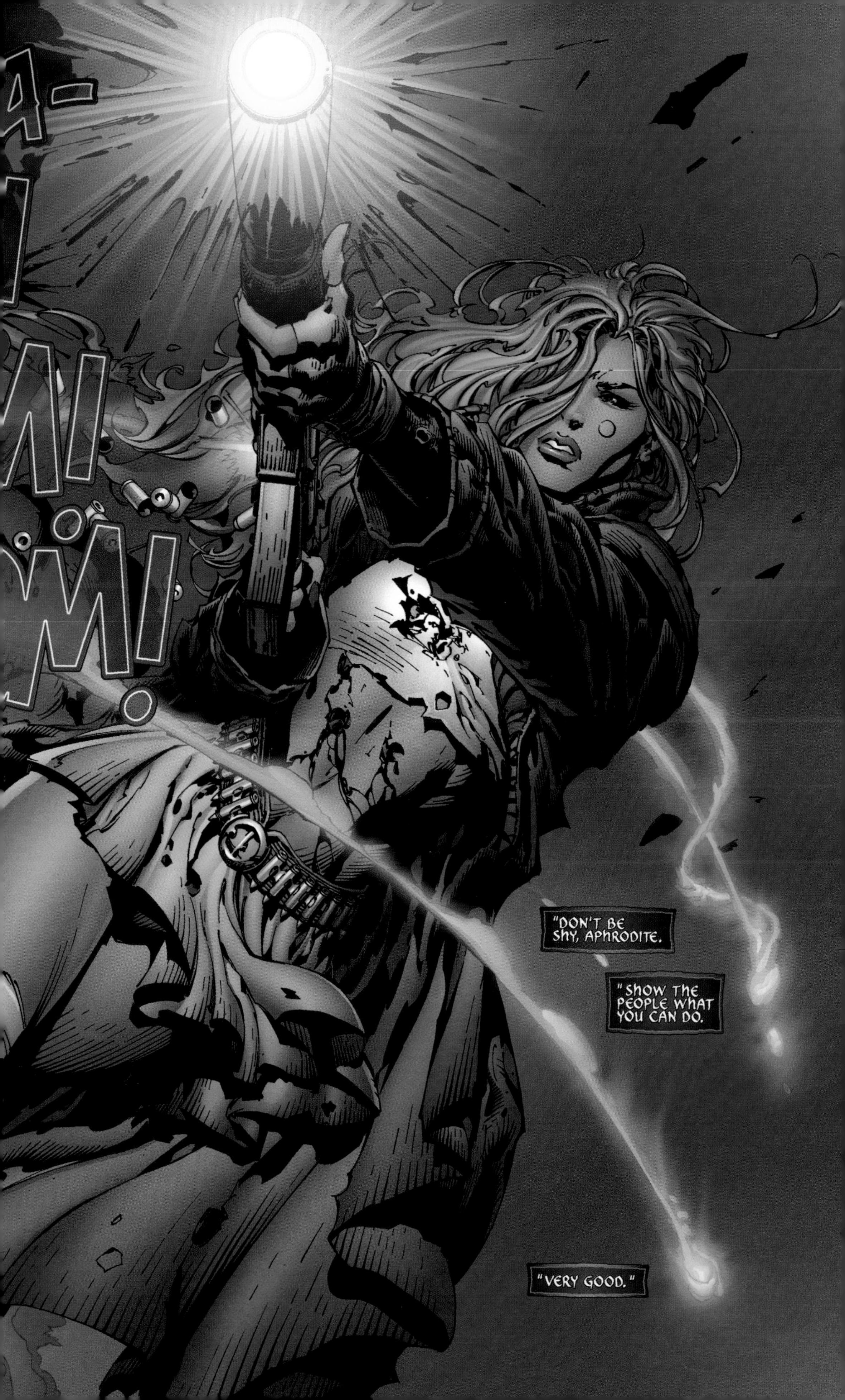
"DON'T BE SHY, APHRODITE.
"SHOW THE PEOPLE WHAT YOU CAN DO.
"VERY GOOD."

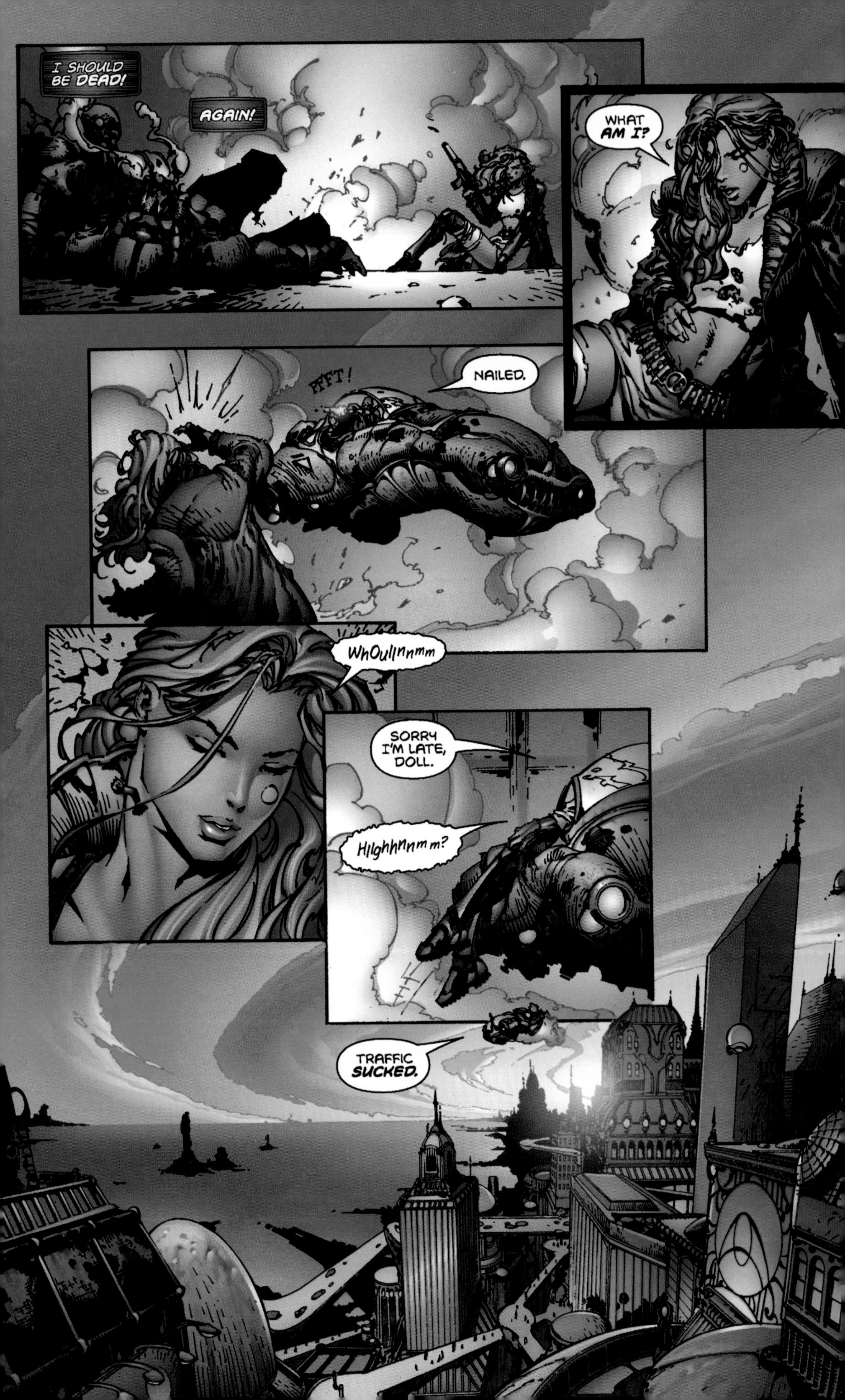
I SHOULD BE DEAD!
AGAIN!
WHAT AM I?
PFFT!
NAILED.
WhOulInnmm
SORRY I'M LATE, DOLL.
HIghhnnmm?
TRAFFIC SUCKED.

Issue #1, Cover C:
Marc Silvestri, Joe Weems V, Steve Firchow

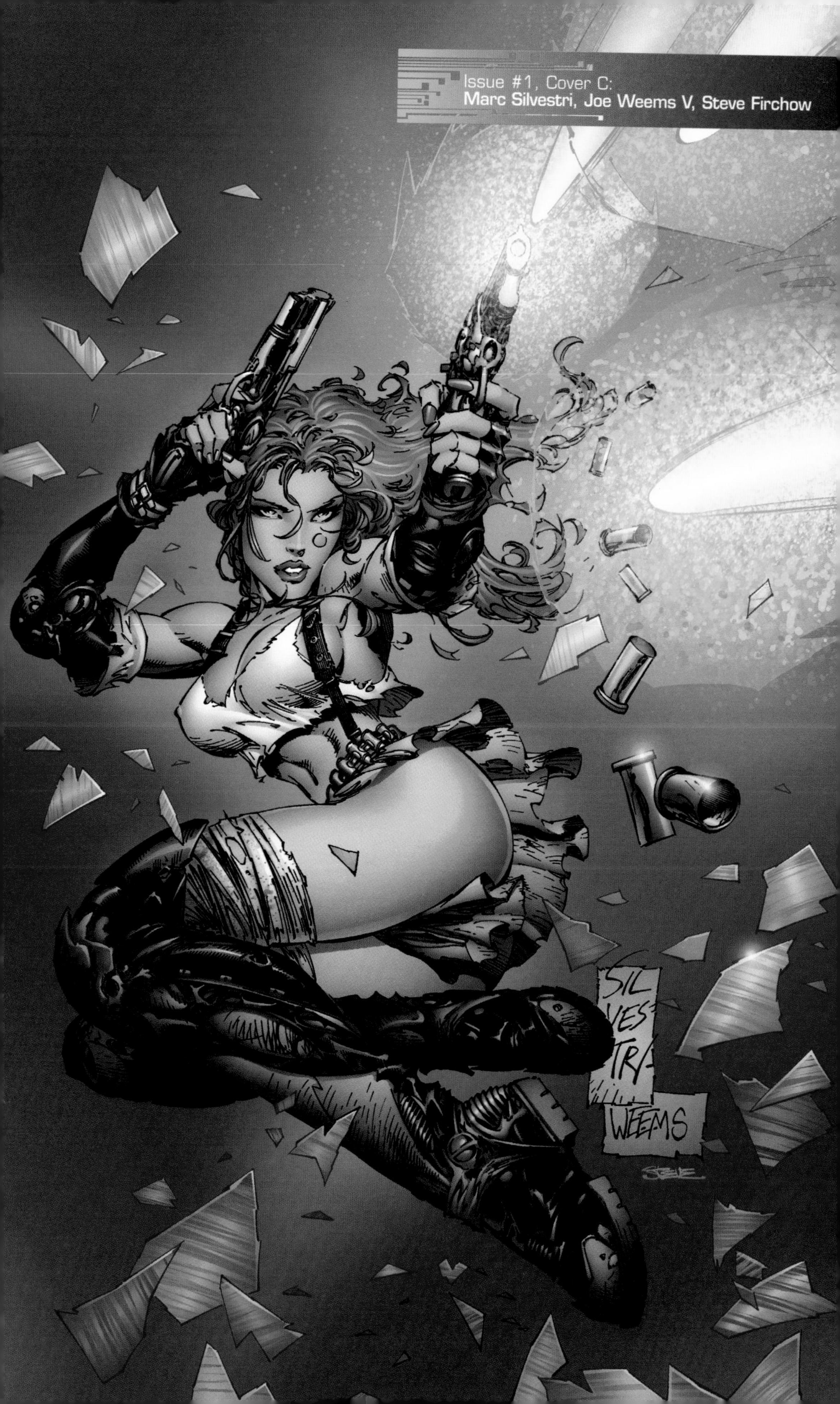
SIL
VES
TRI-
WEEMS
STEVE

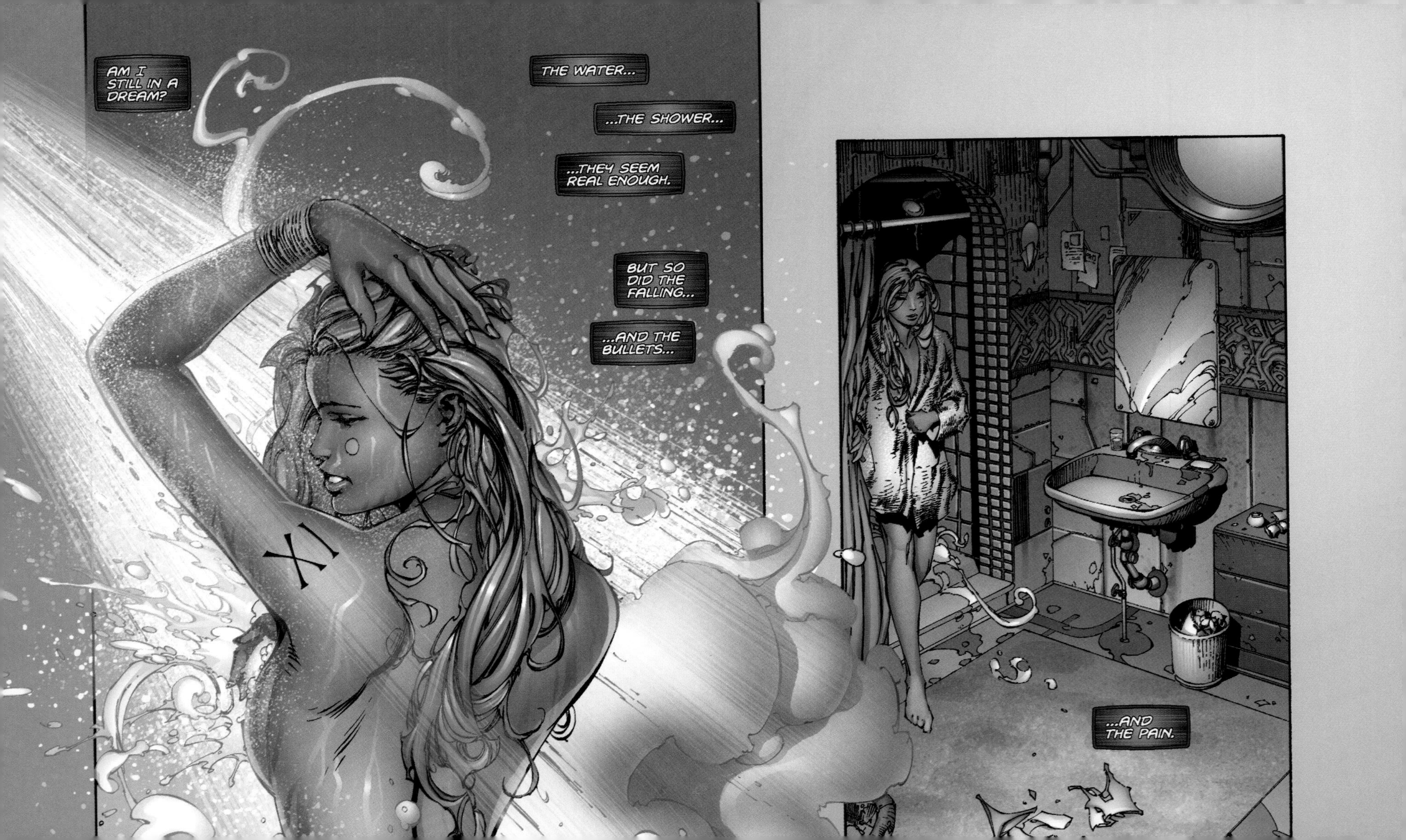
AM I STILL IN A DREAM?
THE WATER...
...THE SHOWER...
...THEY SEEM REAL ENOUGH.
BUT SO DID THE FALLING...
...AND THE BULLETS...
...AND THE PAIN.

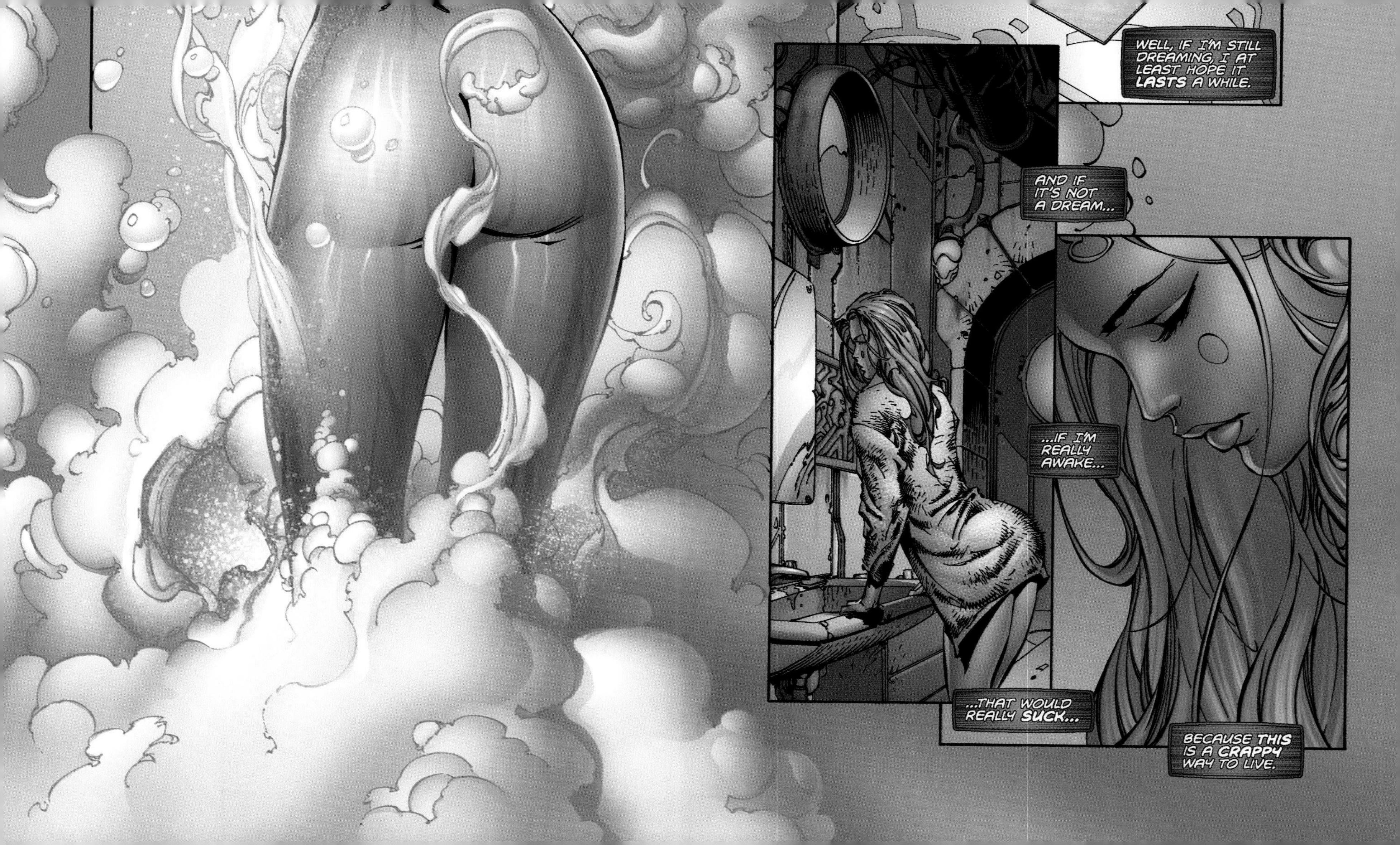
WELL, IF I'M STILL DREAMING, I AT LEAST HOPE IT **LASTS** A WHILE.
AND IF IT'S NOT A DREAM...
...IF I'M REALLY AWAKE...
...THAT WOULD REALLY **SUCK**...
BECAUSE **THIS** IS A **CRAPPY** WAY TO LIVE.

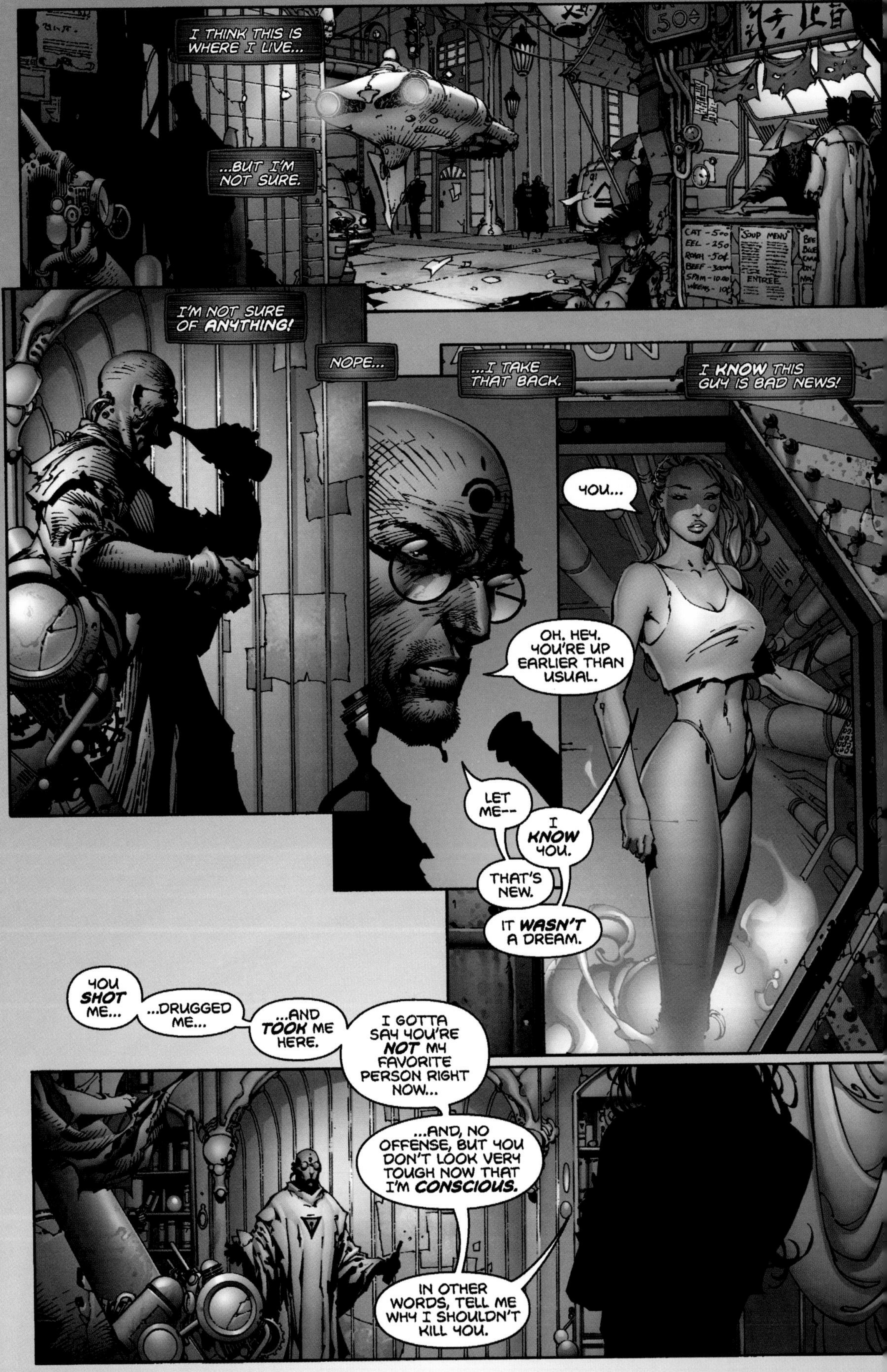

I THINK THIS IS WHERE I LIVE...
...BUT I'M NOT SURE.
I'M NOT SURE OF ANYTHING!
NOPE...
...I TAKE THAT BACK.
I KNOW THIS GUY IS BAD NEWS!
YOU...
OH. HEY. YOU'RE UP EARLIER THAN USUAL.
LET ME--
I KNOW YOU.
THAT'S NEW.
IT WASN'T A DREAM.
YOU SHOT ME...
...DRUGGED ME...
...AND TOOK ME HERE.
I GOTTA SAY YOU'RE NOT MY FAVORITE PERSON RIGHT NOW...
...AND, NO OFFENSE, BUT YOU DON'T LOOK VERY TOUGH NOW THAT I'M CONSCIOUS.
IN OTHER WORDS, TELL ME WHY I SHOULDN'T KILL YOU.

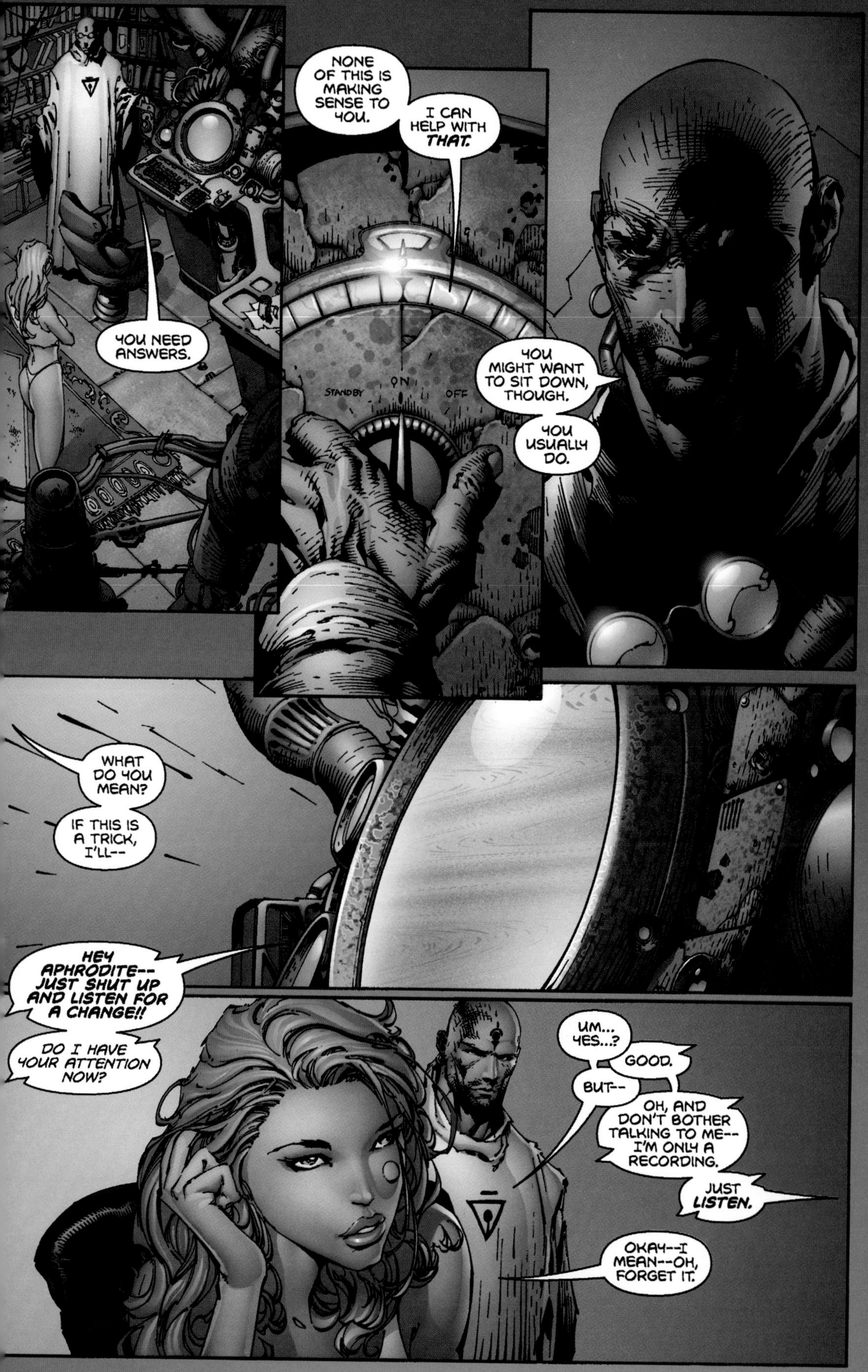
YOU NEED ANSWERS.
NONE OF THIS IS MAKING SENSE TO YOU.
I CAN HELP WITH *THAT.*
STANDBY
ON
OFF
YOU MIGHT WANT TO SIT DOWN, THOUGH.
YOU USUALLY DO.
WHAT DO YOU MEAN?
IF THIS IS A TRICK, I'LL--
HEY APHRODITE-- JUST SHUT UP AND LISTEN FOR A CHANGE!!
DO I HAVE YOUR ATTENTION NOW?
UM... YES...?
GOOD.
BUT--
OH, AND DON'T BOTHER TALKING TO ME-- I'M ONLY A RECORDING.
JUST *LISTEN.*
OKAY--I MEAN--OH, FORGET IT.

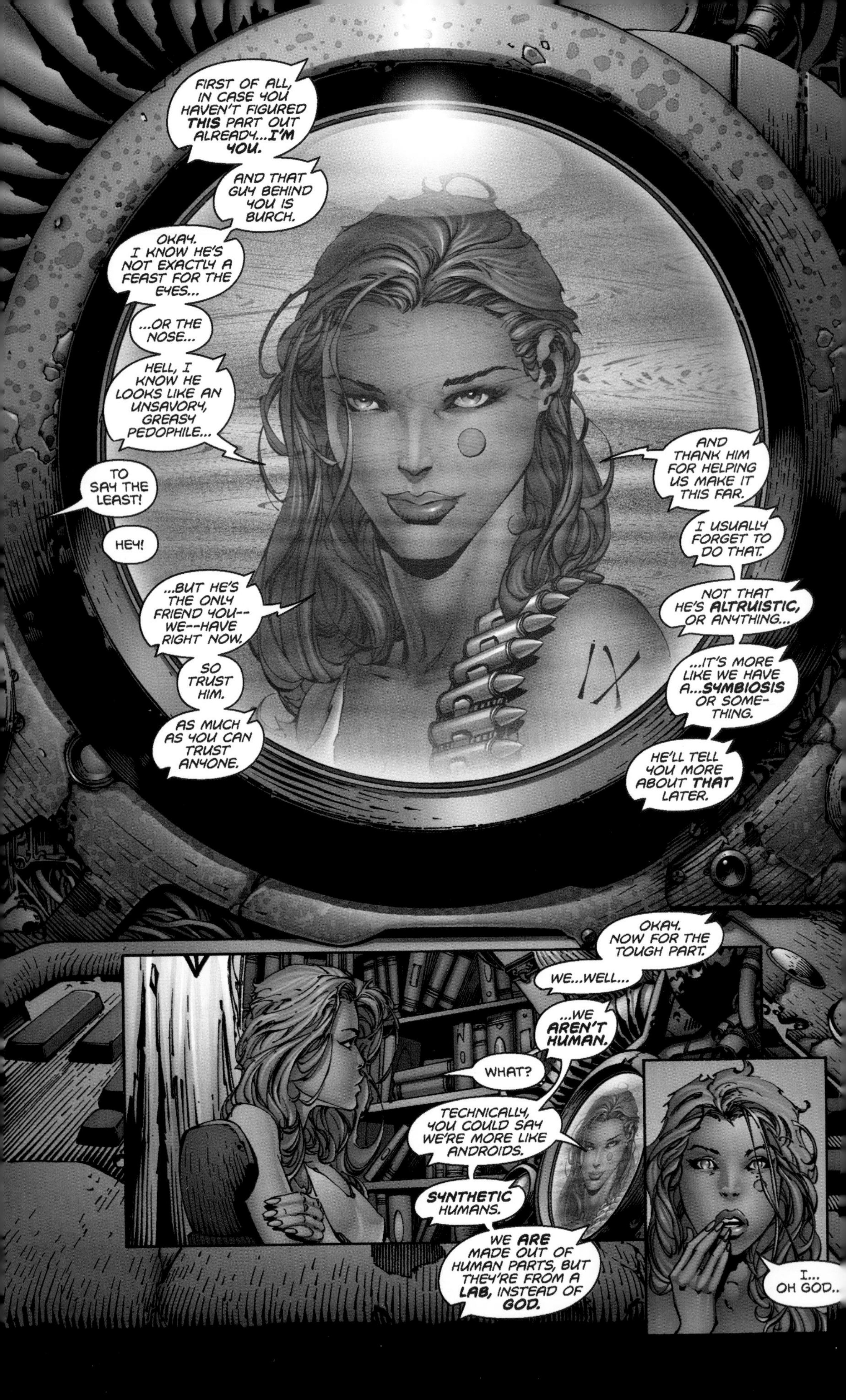

FIRST OF ALL, IN CASE YOU HAVEN'T FIGURED **THIS** PART OUT ALREADY...**I'M YOU.**
AND THAT GUY BEHIND YOU IS BURCH.
OKAY. I KNOW HE'S NOT EXACTLY A FEAST FOR THE EYES...
...OR THE NOSE...
HELL, I KNOW HE LOOKS LIKE AN UNSAVORY, GREASY PEDOPHILE...
TO SAY THE LEAST!
HEY!
...BUT HE'S THE ONLY FRIEND YOU--WE--HAVE RIGHT NOW.
SO TRUST HIM.
AS MUCH AS YOU CAN TRUST ANYONE.
AND THANK HIM FOR HELPING US MAKE IT THIS FAR.
I USUALLY FORGET TO DO THAT.
NOT THAT HE'S **ALTRUISTIC,** OR ANYTHING...
...IT'S MORE LIKE WE HAVE A...**SYMBIOSIS** OR SOME-THING.
HE'LL TELL YOU MORE ABOUT **THAT** LATER.
OKAY. NOW FOR THE TOUGH PART.
WE...WELL...
...WE **AREN'T HUMAN.**
WHAT?
TECHNICALLY, YOU COULD SAY WE'RE MORE LIKE ANDROIDS.
SYNTHETIC HUMANS.
WE **ARE** MADE OUT OF HUMAN PARTS, BUT THEY'RE FROM A **LAB,** INSTEAD OF **GOD.**
I... OH GOD..

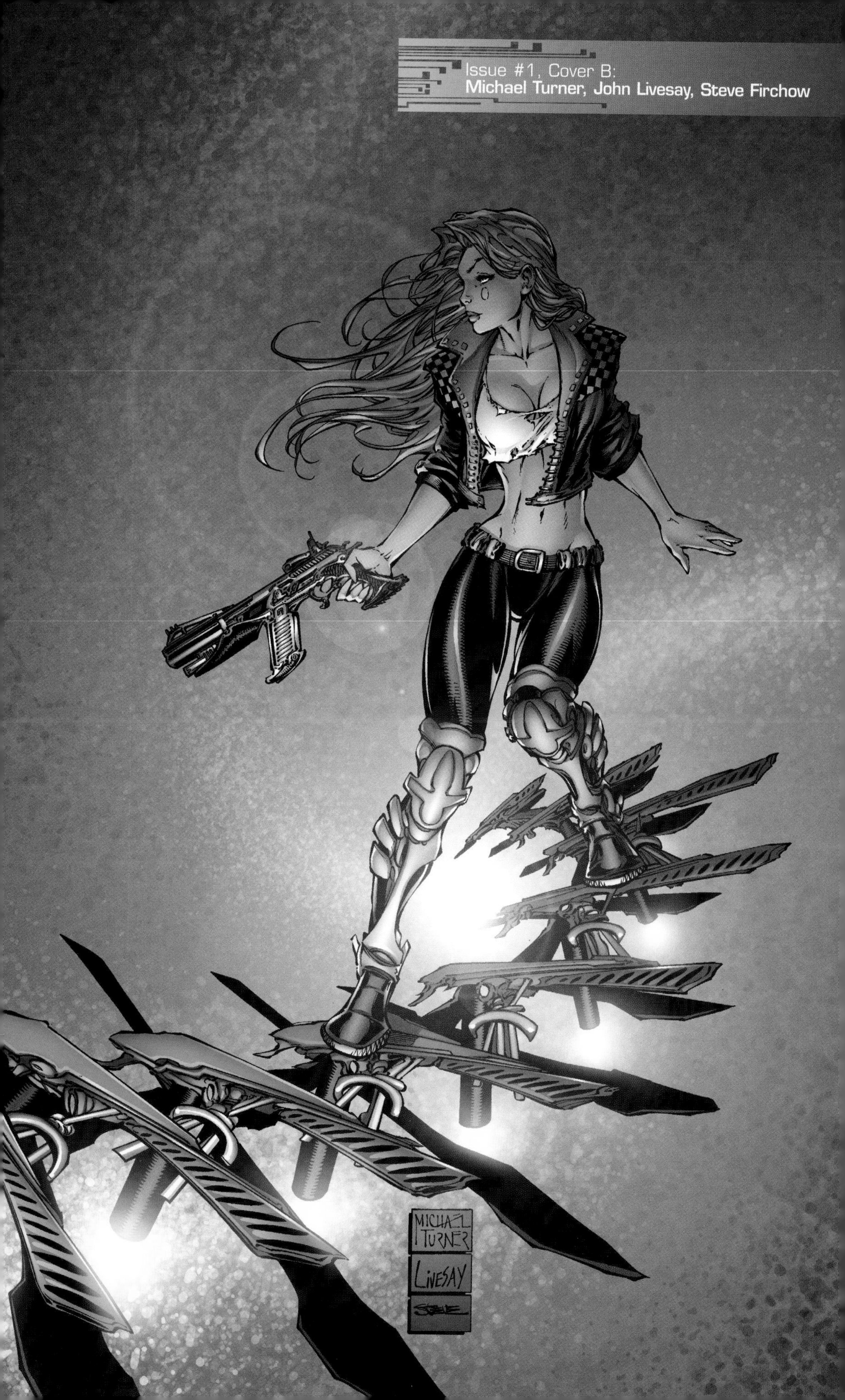

Issue #1, Cover B:
Michael Turner, John Livesay, Steve Firchow

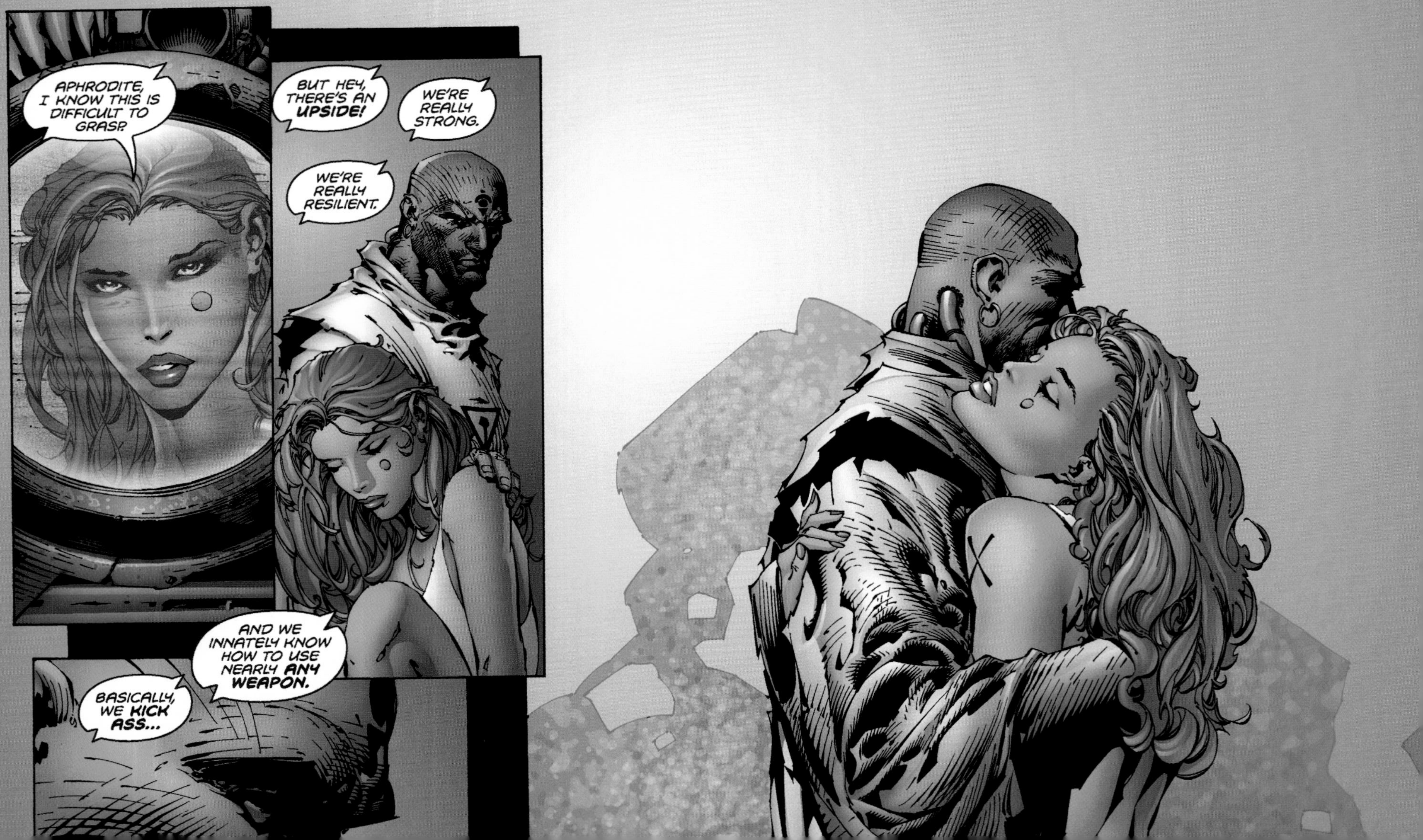
APHRODITE, I KNOW THIS IS DIFFICULT TO GRASP.
BUT HEY, THERE'S AN **UPSIDE!**
WE'RE REALLY STRONG.
WE'RE REALLY RESILIENT.
AND WE INNATELY KNOW HOW TO USE NEARLY **ANY WEAPON.**
BASICALLY, WE **KICK ASS...**

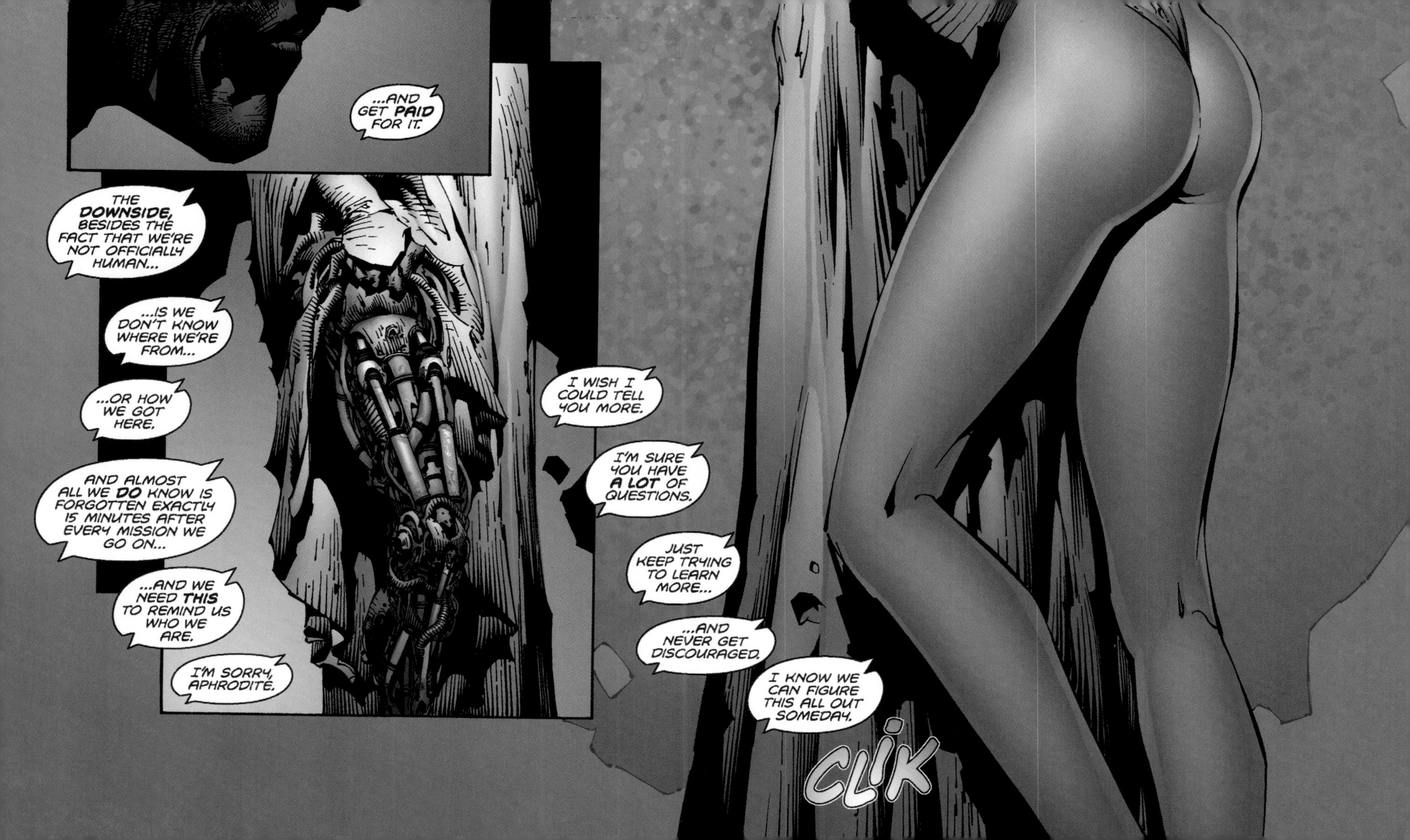
...AND GET PAID FOR IT.
THE DOWNSIDE, BESIDES THE FACT THAT WE'RE NOT OFFICIALLY HUMAN...
...IS WE DON'T KNOW WHERE WE'RE FROM...
...OR HOW WE GOT HERE.
AND ALMOST ALL WE DO KNOW IS FORGOTTEN EXACTLY 15 MINUTES AFTER EVERY MISSION WE GO ON...
...AND WE NEED THIS TO REMIND US WHO WE ARE.
I'M SORRY, APHRODITE.
I WISH I COULD TELL YOU MORE.
I'M SURE YOU HAVE A LOT OF QUESTIONS.
JUST KEEP TRYING TO LEARN MORE...
...AND NEVER GET DISCOURAGED.
I KNOW WE CAN FIGURE THIS ALL OUT SOMEDAY.
CLIK

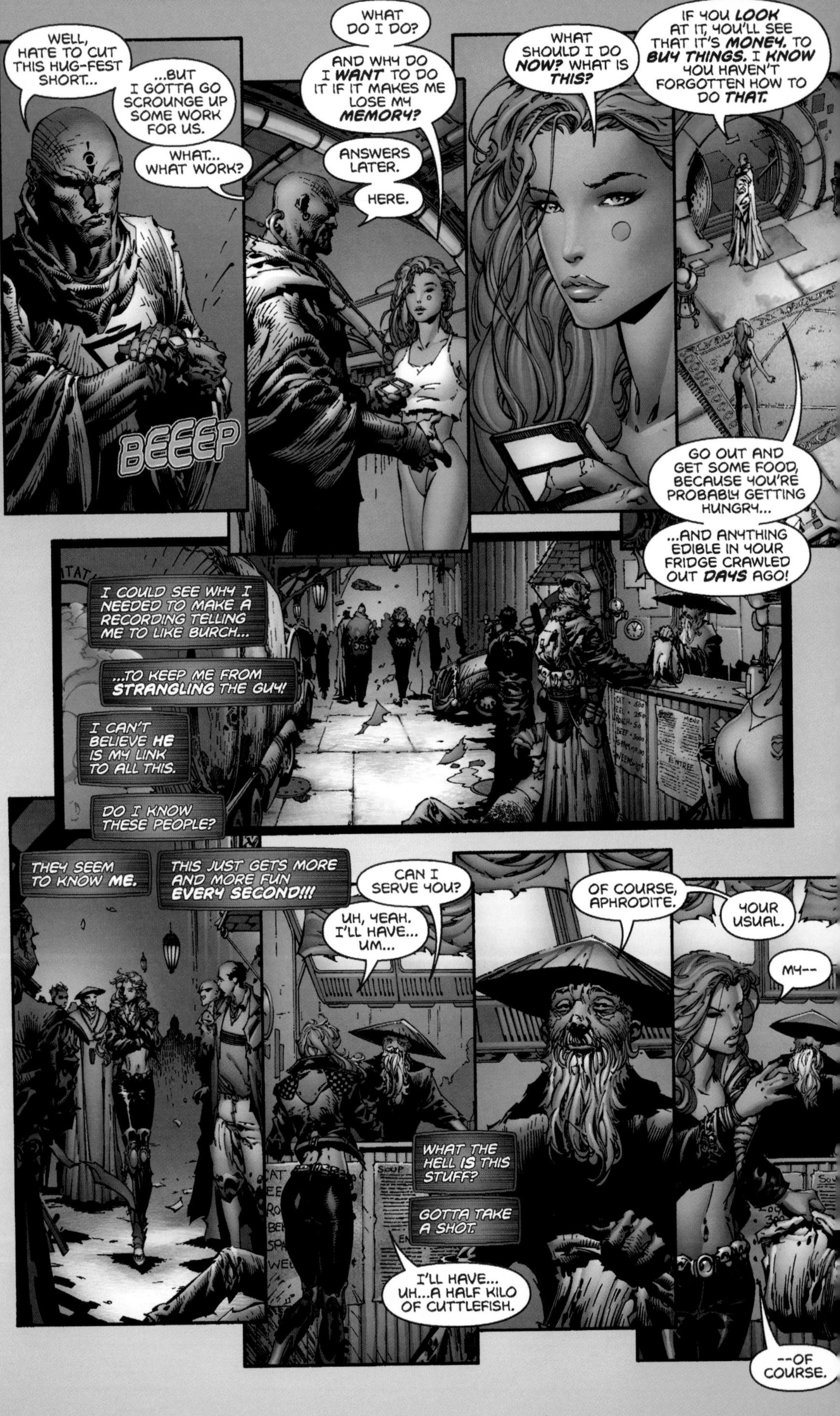
WELL, HATE TO CUT THIS HUG-FEST SHORT...
...BUT I GOTTA GO SCROUNGE UP SOME WORK FOR US.
WHAT... WHAT WORK?
BEEEP
WHAT DO I DO?
AND WHY DO I WANT TO DO IT IF IT MAKES ME LOSE MY MEMORY?
ANSWERS LATER.
HERE.
WHAT SHOULD I DO NOW? WHAT IS THIS?
IF YOU LOOK AT IT, YOU'LL SEE THAT IT'S MONEY. TO BUY THINGS. I KNOW YOU HAVEN'T FORGOTTEN HOW TO DO THAT.
GO OUT AND GET SOME FOOD, BECAUSE YOU'RE PROBABLY GETTING HUNGRY...
...AND ANYTHING EDIBLE IN YOUR FRIDGE CRAWLED OUT DAYS AGO!
I COULD SEE WHY I NEEDED TO MAKE A RECORDING TELLING ME TO LIKE BURCH...
...TO KEEP ME FROM STRANGLING THE GUY!
I CAN'T BELIEVE HE IS MY LINK TO ALL THIS.
DO I KNOW THESE PEOPLE?
THEY SEEM TO KNOW ME.
THIS JUST GETS MORE AND MORE FUN EVERY SECOND!!!
CAN I SERVE YOU?
UH, YEAH. I'LL HAVE... UM...
WHAT THE HELL IS THIS STUFF?
GOTTA TAKE A SHOT.
I'LL HAVE... UH...A HALF KILO OF CUTTLEFISH.
OF COURSE, APHRODITE.
YOUR USUAL.
MY--
--OF COURSE.

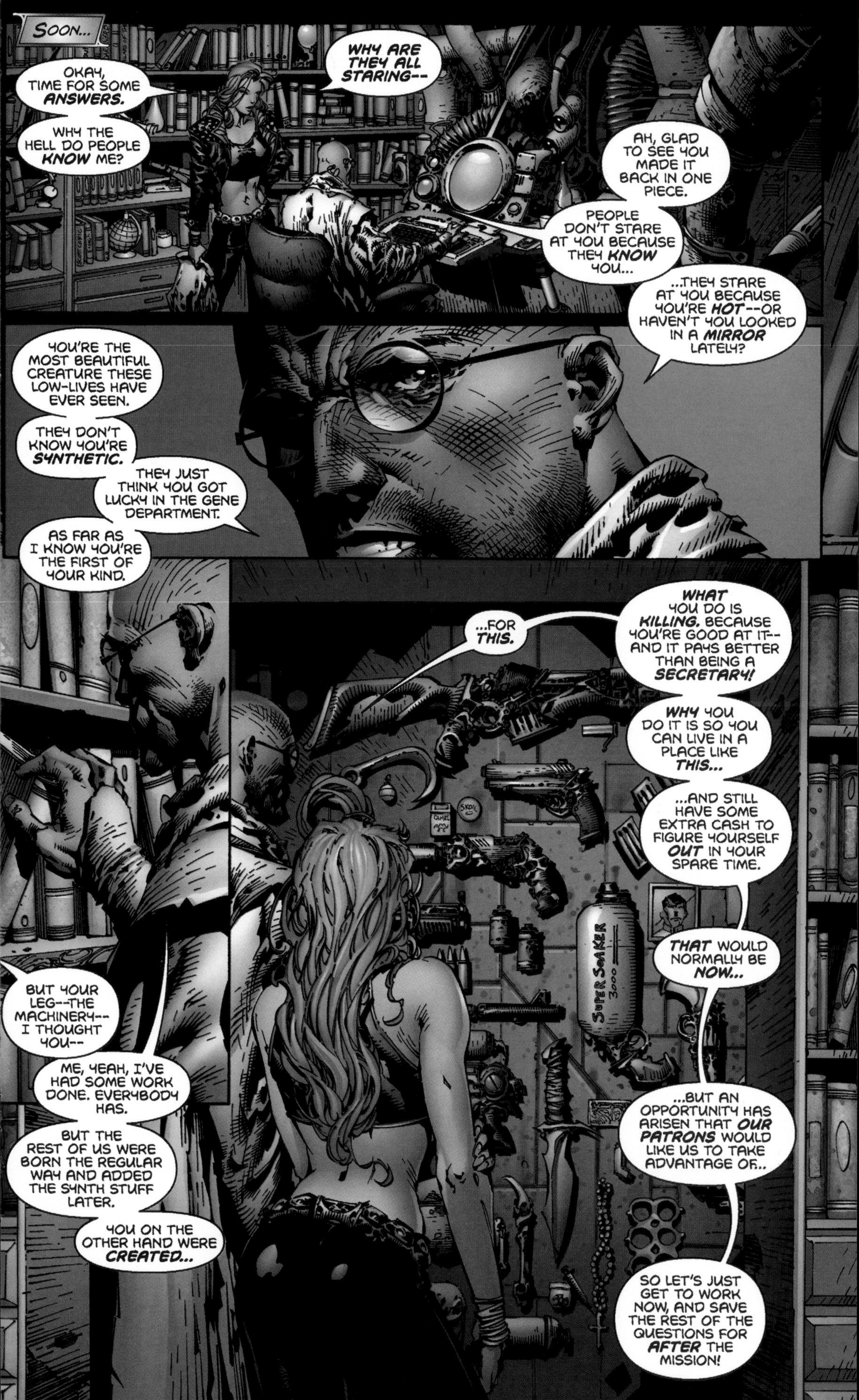
SOON...
OKAY, TIME FOR SOME ANSWERS.
WHY THE HELL DO PEOPLE KNOW ME?
WHY ARE THEY ALL STARING--
AH, GLAD TO SEE YOU MADE IT BACK IN ONE PIECE.
PEOPLE DON'T STARE AT YOU BECAUSE THEY KNOW YOU...
...THEY STARE AT YOU BECAUSE YOU'RE HOT--OR HAVEN'T YOU LOOKED IN A MIRROR LATELY?
YOU'RE THE MOST BEAUTIFUL CREATURE THESE LOW-LIVES HAVE EVER SEEN.
THEY DON'T KNOW YOU'RE SYNTHETIC.
THEY JUST THINK YOU GOT LUCKY IN THE GENE DEPARTMENT.
AS FAR AS I KNOW YOU'RE THE FIRST OF YOUR KIND.
BUT YOUR LEG--THE MACHINERY--I THOUGHT YOU--
ME, YEAH, I'VE HAD SOME WORK DONE. EVERYBODY HAS.
BUT THE REST OF US WERE BORN THE REGULAR WAY AND ADDED THE SYNTH STUFF LATER.
YOU ON THE OTHER HAND WERE CREATED...
...FOR THIS.
WHAT YOU DO IS KILLING. BECAUSE YOU'RE GOOD AT IT--AND IT PAYS BETTER THAN BEING A SECRETARY!
WHY YOU DO IT IS SO YOU CAN LIVE IN A PLACE LIKE THIS...
...AND STILL HAVE SOME EXTRA CASH TO FIGURE YOURSELF OUT IN YOUR SPARE TIME.
THAT WOULD NORMALLY BE NOW...
...BUT AN OPPORTUNITY HAS ARISEN THAT OUR PATRONS WOULD LIKE US TO TAKE ADVANTAGE OF..
SO LET'S JUST GET TO WORK NOW, AND SAVE THE REST OF THE QUESTIONS FOR AFTER THE MISSION!
SUPER SOAKER 3000

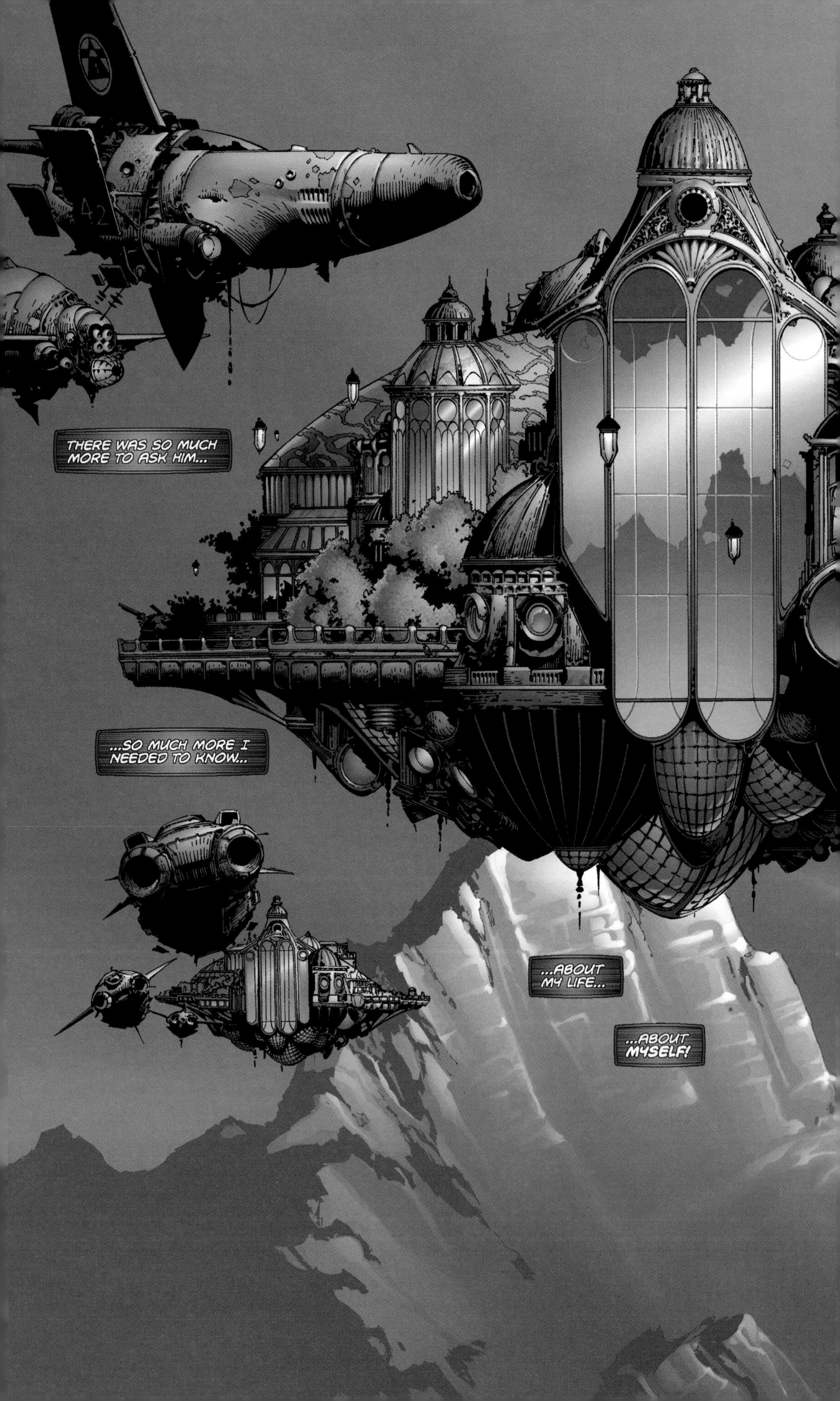
THERE WAS SO MUCH MORE TO ASK HIM...
...SO MUCH MORE I NEEDED TO KNOW...
...ABOUT MY LIFE...
...ABOUT MYSELF!

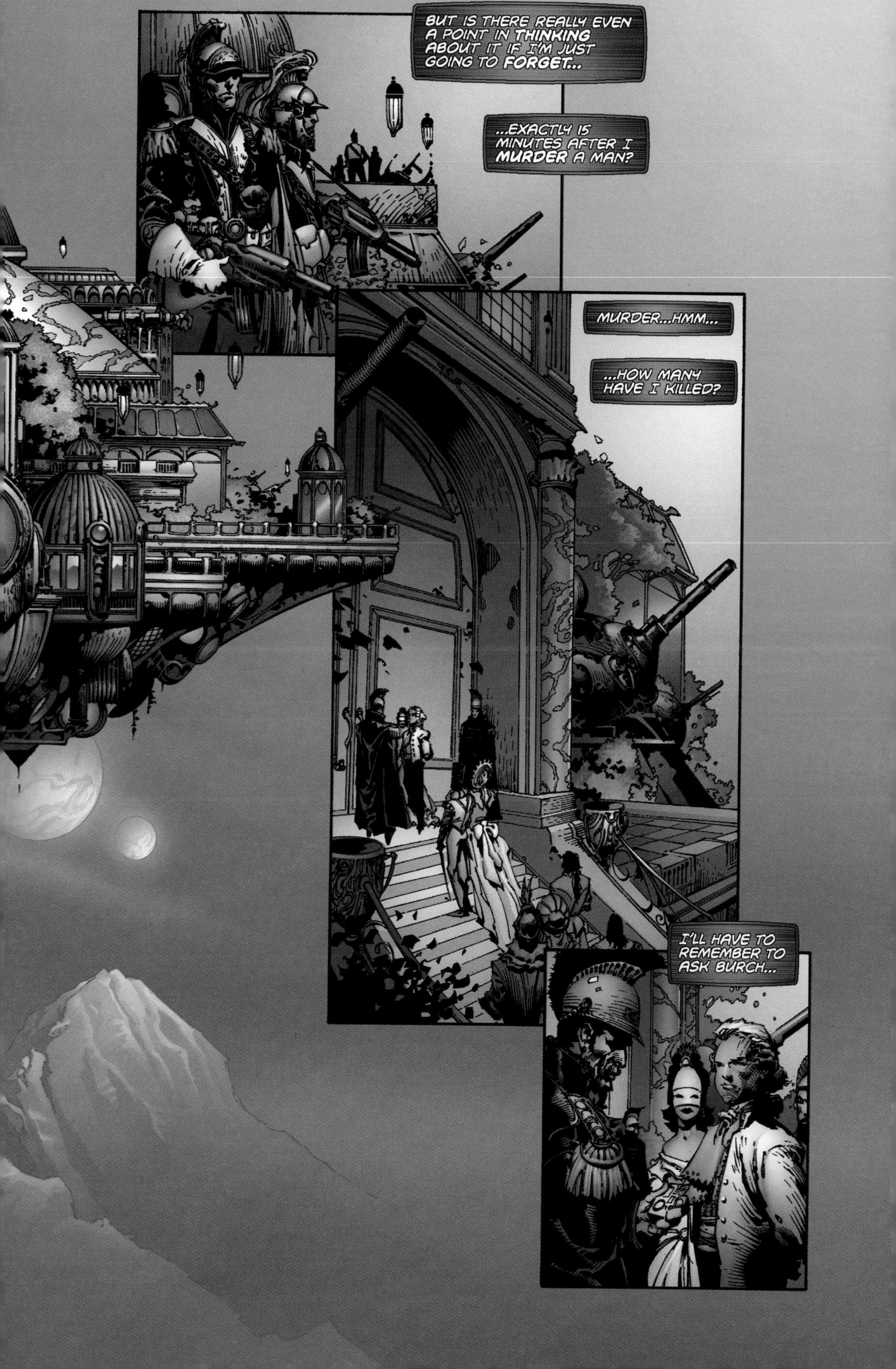
BUT IS THERE REALLY EVEN A POINT IN THINKING ABOUT IT IF I'M JUST GOING TO FORGET...
...EXACTLY 15 MINUTES AFTER I MURDER A MAN?
MURDER...HMM...
...HOW MANY HAVE I KILLED?
I'LL HAVE TO REMEMBER TO ASK BURCH...

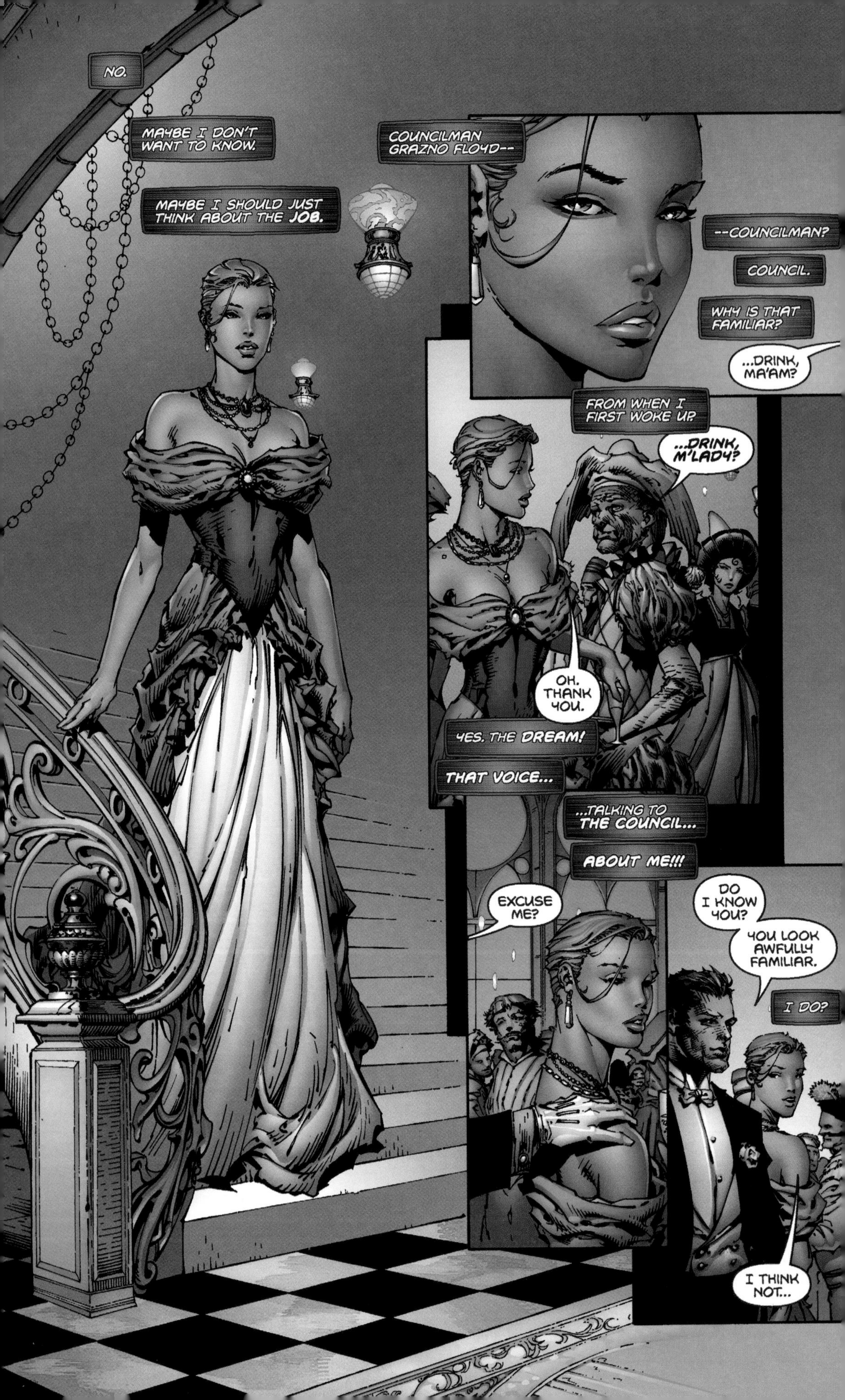
NO.
MAYBE I DON'T WANT TO KNOW.
MAYBE I SHOULD JUST THINK ABOUT THE JOB.
COUNCILMAN GRAZNO FLOYD--
--COUNCILMAN?
COUNCIL.
WHY IS THAT FAMILIAR?
...DRINK, MA'AM?
FROM WHEN I FIRST WOKE UP.
...DRINK, M'LADY?
OH. THANK YOU.
YES. THE DREAM!
THAT VOICE...
...TALKING TO THE COUNCIL...
ABOUT ME!!!
EXCUSE ME?
DO I KNOW YOU?
YOU LOOK AWFULLY FAMILIAR.
I DO?
I THINK NOT...

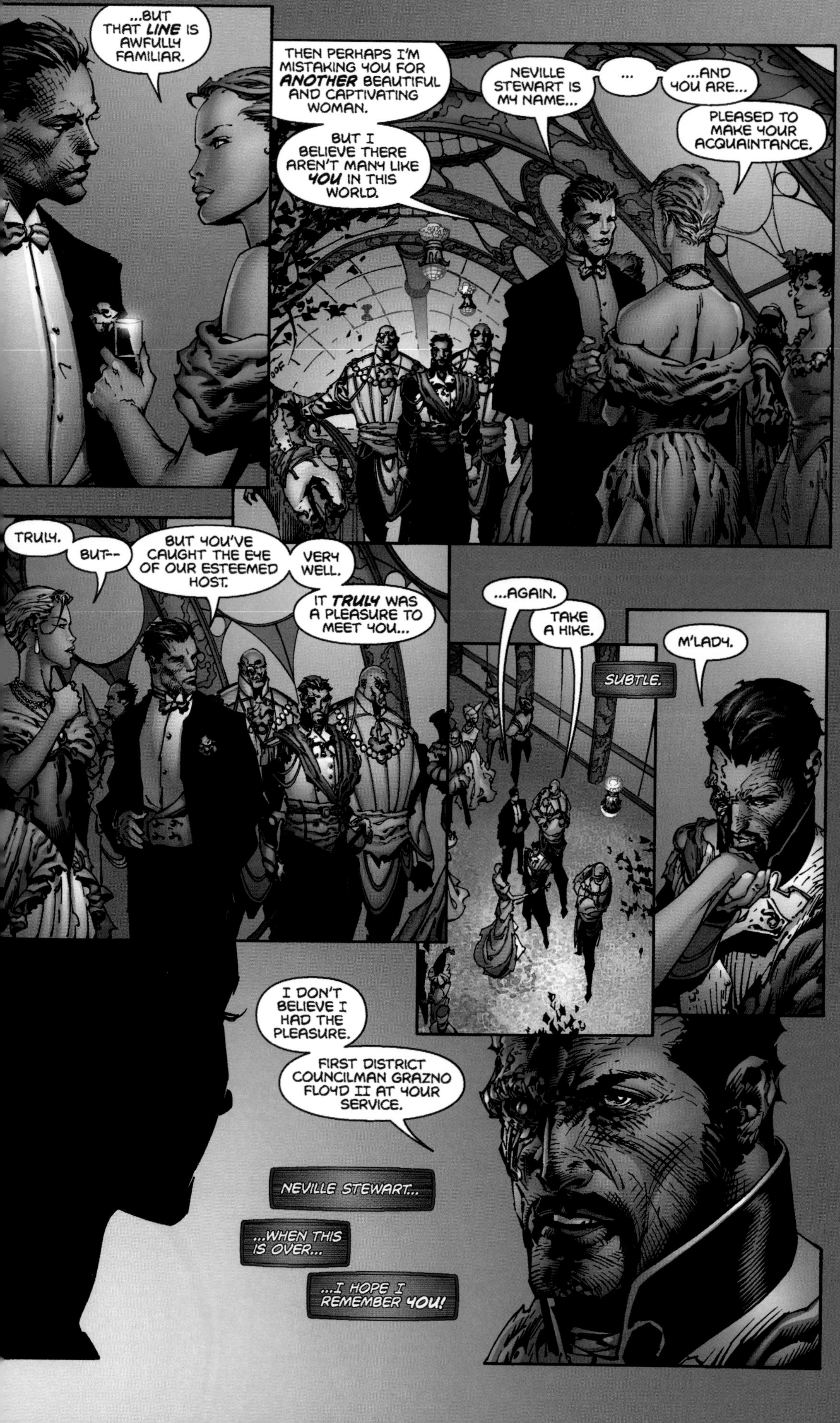

...BUT THAT LINE IS AWFULLY FAMILIAR.
THEN PERHAPS I'M MISTAKING YOU FOR ANOTHER BEAUTIFUL AND CAPTIVATING WOMAN.
BUT I BELIEVE THERE AREN'T MANY LIKE YOU IN THIS WORLD.
NEVILLE STEWART IS MY NAME...
...
...AND YOU ARE...
PLEASED TO MAKE YOUR ACQUAINTANCE.
TRULY.
BUT--
BUT YOU'VE CAUGHT THE EYE OF OUR ESTEEMED HOST.
VERY WELL.
IT TRULY WAS A PLEASURE TO MEET YOU...
...AGAIN.
TAKE A HIKE.
SUBTLE.
M'LADY.
I DON'T BELIEVE I HAD THE PLEASURE.
FIRST DISTRICT COUNCILMAN GRAZNO FLOYD II AT YOUR SERVICE.
NEVILLE STEWART...
...WHEN THIS IS OVER...
...I HOPE I REMEMBER YOU!

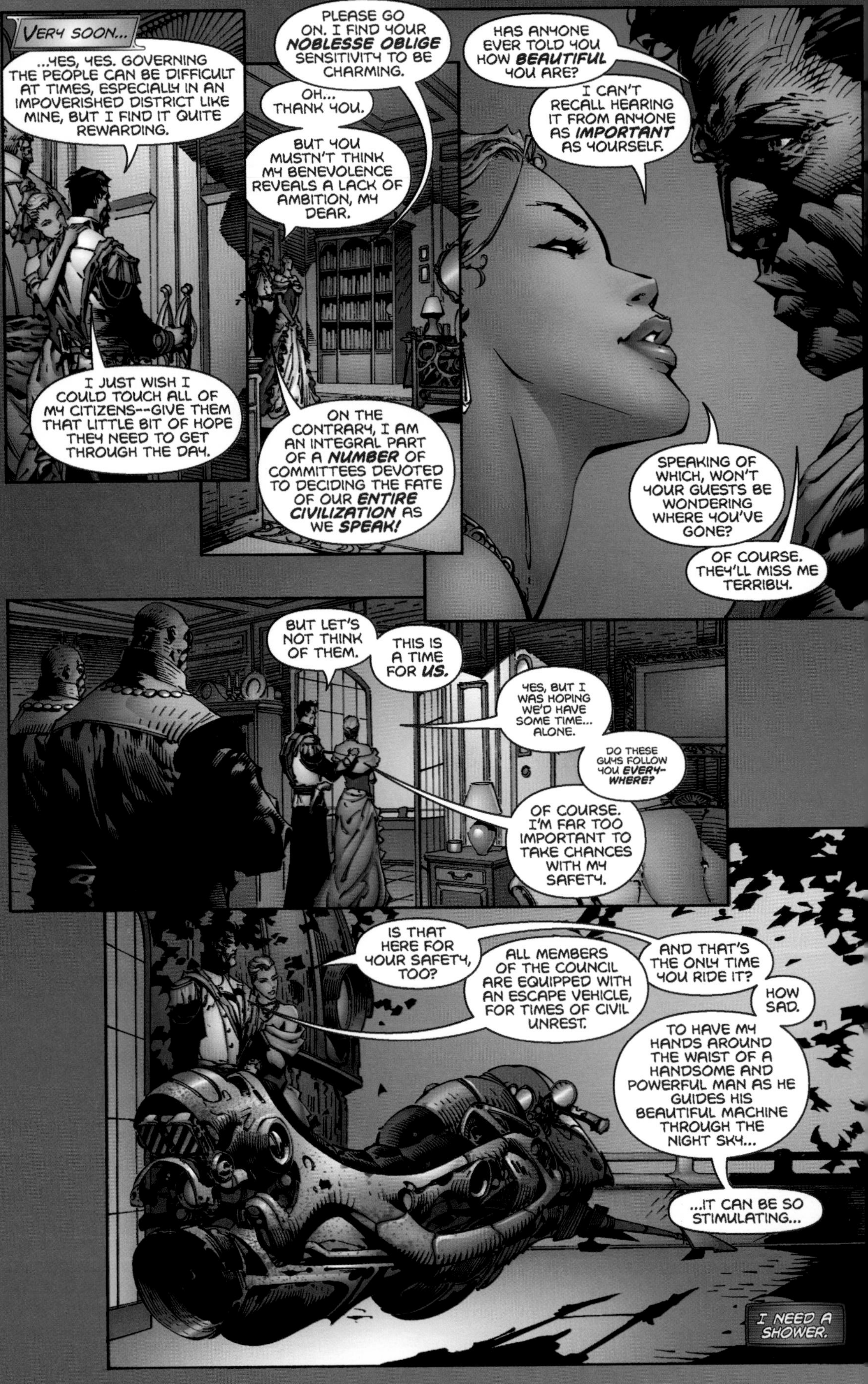
VERY SOON...
...YES, YES. GOVERNING THE PEOPLE CAN BE DIFFICULT AT TIMES, ESPECIALLY IN AN IMPOVERISHED DISTRICT LIKE MINE, BUT I FIND IT QUITE REWARDING.
I JUST WISH I COULD TOUCH ALL OF MY CITIZENS--GIVE THEM THAT LITTLE BIT OF HOPE THEY NEED TO GET THROUGH THE DAY.
PLEASE GO ON. I FIND YOUR NOBLESSE OBLIGE SENSITIVITY TO BE CHARMING.
OH... THANK YOU.
BUT YOU MUSTN'T THINK MY BENEVOLENCE REVEALS A LACK OF AMBITION, MY DEAR.
ON THE CONTRARY, I AM AN INTEGRAL PART OF A NUMBER OF COMMITTEES DEVOTED TO DECIDING THE FATE OF OUR ENTIRE CIVILIZATION AS WE SPEAK!
HAS ANYONE EVER TOLD YOU HOW BEAUTIFUL YOU ARE?
I CAN'T RECALL HEARING IT FROM ANYONE AS IMPORTANT AS YOURSELF.
SPEAKING OF WHICH, WON'T YOUR GUESTS BE WONDERING WHERE YOU'VE GONE?
OF COURSE. THEY'LL MISS ME TERRIBLY.
BUT LET'S NOT THINK OF THEM.
THIS IS A TIME FOR US.
YES, BUT I WAS HOPING WE'D HAVE SOME TIME... ALONE.
DO THESE GUYS FOLLOW YOU EVERY-WHERE?
OF COURSE. I'M FAR TOO IMPORTANT TO TAKE CHANCES WITH MY SAFETY.
IS THAT HERE FOR YOUR SAFETY, TOO?
ALL MEMBERS OF THE COUNCIL ARE EQUIPPED WITH AN ESCAPE VEHICLE, FOR TIMES OF CIVIL UNREST.
AND THAT'S THE ONLY TIME YOU RIDE IT?
HOW SAD.
TO HAVE MY HANDS AROUND THE WAIST OF A HANDSOME AND POWERFUL MAN AS HE GUIDES HIS BEAUTIFUL MACHINE THROUGH THE NIGHT SKY...
...IT CAN BE SO STIMULATING...
I NEED A SHOWER.

Issue #1, Cover D:
Joe Benitez, Victor Llamas, Dan Kemp

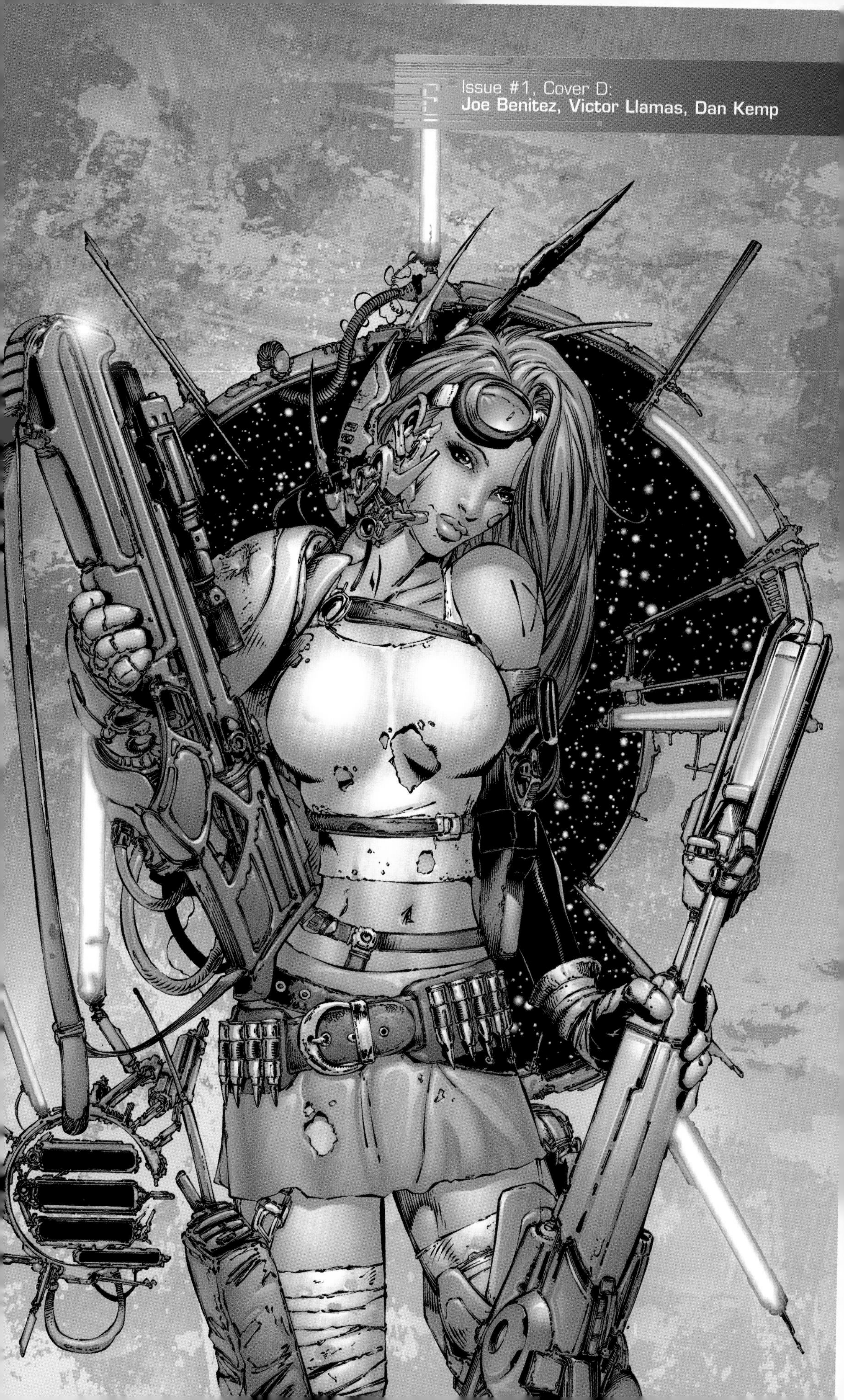

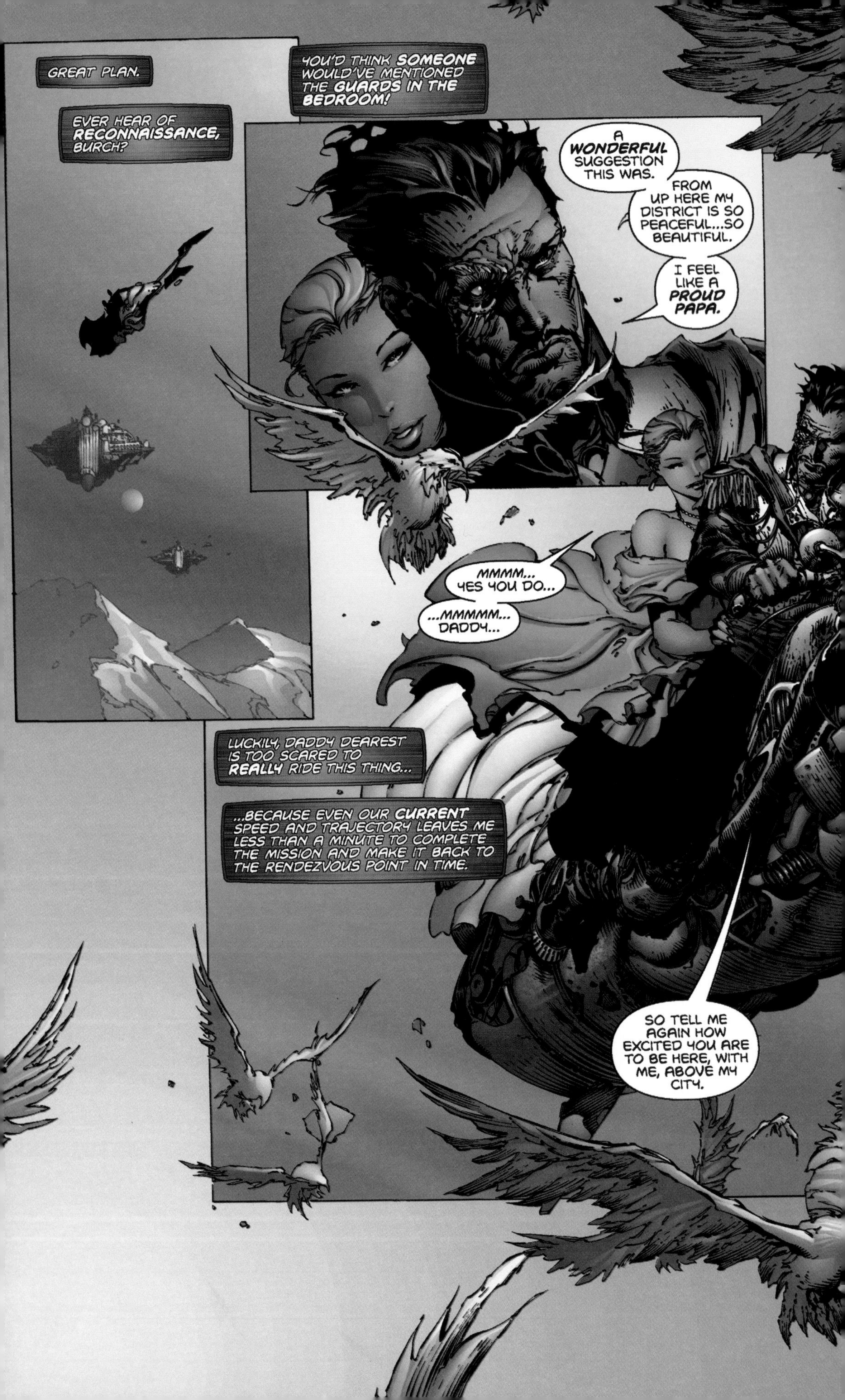
GREAT PLAN.
EVER HEAR OF RECONNAISSANCE, BURCH?
YOU'D THINK SOMEONE WOULD'VE MENTIONED THE GUARDS IN THE BEDROOM!
A WONDERFUL SUGGESTION THIS WAS.
FROM UP HERE MY DISTRICT IS SO PEACEFUL...SO BEAUTIFUL.
I FEEL LIKE A PROUD PAPA.
MMMM... YES YOU DO...
...MMMMM... DADDY...
LUCKILY, DADDY DEAREST IS TOO SCARED TO REALLY RIDE THIS THING...
...BECAUSE EVEN OUR CURRENT SPEED AND TRAJECTORY LEAVES ME LESS THAN A MINUTE TO COMPLETE THE MISSION AND MAKE IT BACK TO THE RENDEZVOUS POINT IN TIME.
SO TELL ME AGAIN HOW EXCITED YOU ARE TO BE HERE, WITH ME, ABOVE MY CITY.

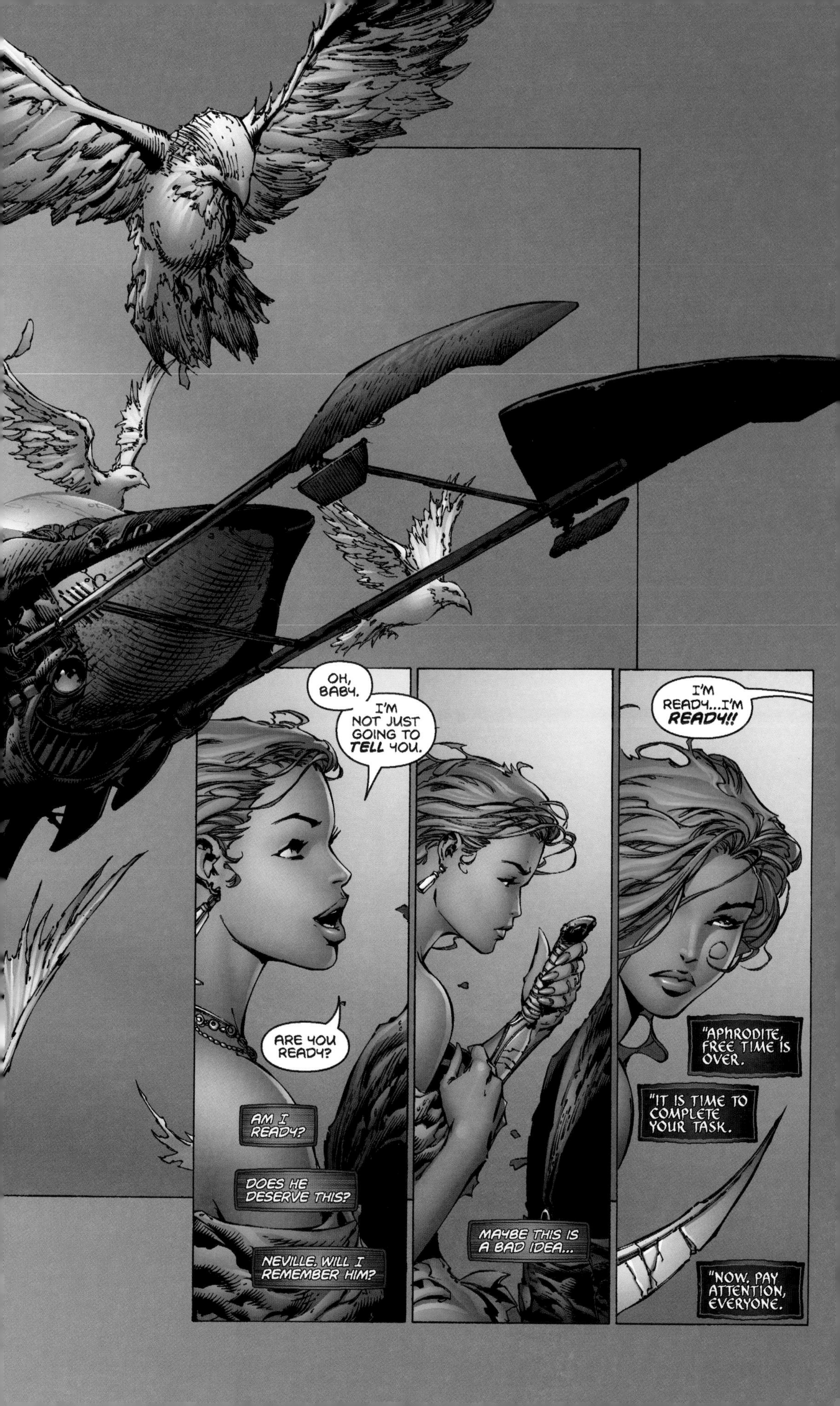

OH, BABY.
I'M NOT JUST GOING TO TELL YOU.
ARE YOU READY?
AM I READY?
DOES HE DESERVE THIS?
NEVILLE. WILL I REMEMBER HIM?
MAYBE THIS IS A BAD IDEA...
I'M READY...I'M READY!!
"APHRODITE, FREE TIME IS OVER.
"IT IS TIME TO COMPLETE YOUR TASK.
"NOW, PAY ATTENTION, EVERYONE.

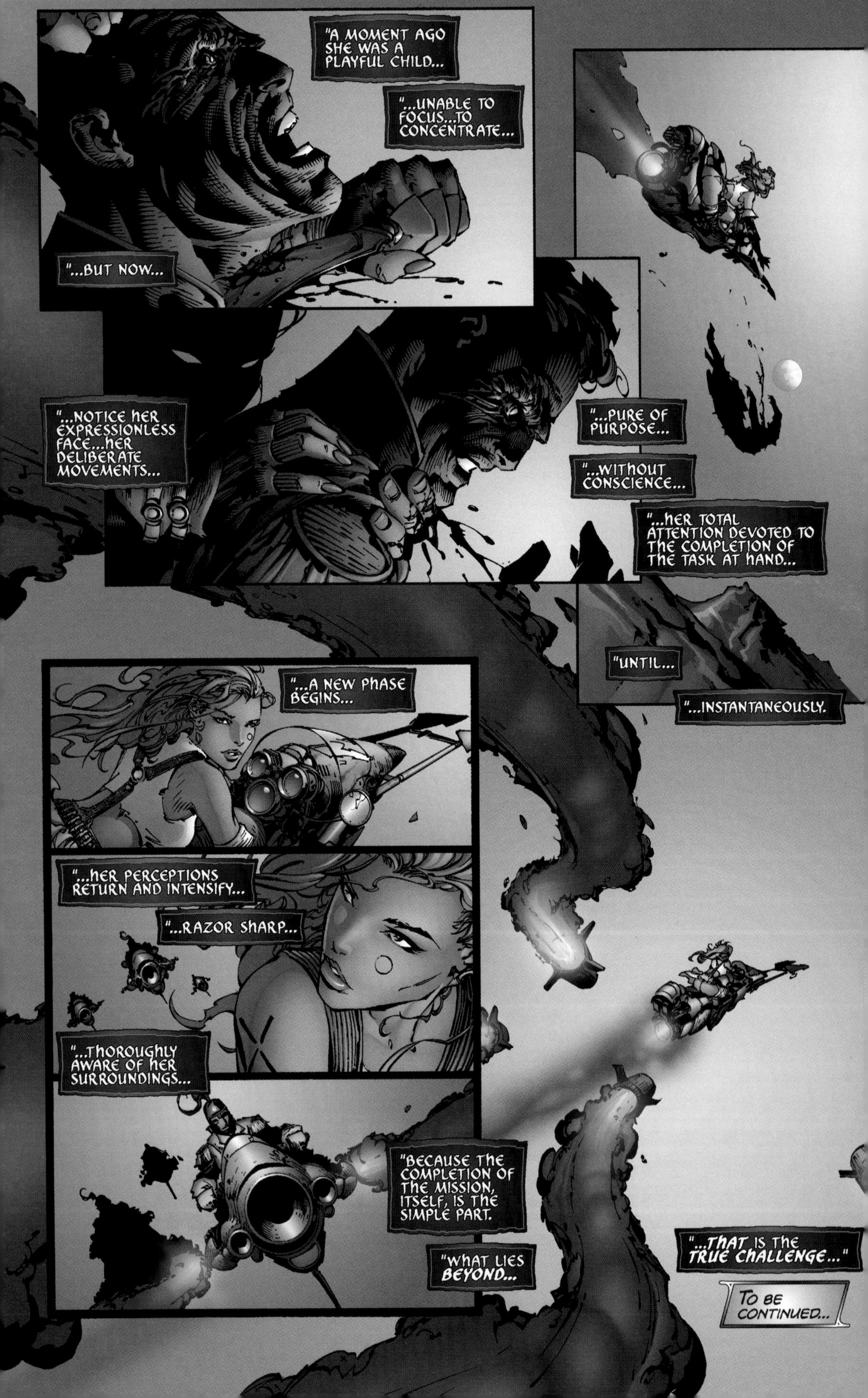
"A MOMENT AGO SHE WAS A PLAYFUL CHILD...
"...UNABLE TO FOCUS...TO CONCENTRATE...
"...BUT NOW...
"...NOTICE HER EXPRESSIONLESS FACE...HER DELIBERATE MOVEMENTS...
"...PURE OF PURPOSE...
"...WITHOUT CONSCIENCE...
"...HER TOTAL ATTENTION DEVOTED TO THE COMPLETION OF THE TASK AT HAND...
"UNTIL...
"...INSTANTANEOUSLY.
"...A NEW PHASE BEGINS...
"...HER PERCEPTIONS RETURN AND INTENSIFY...
"...RAZOR SHARP...
"...THOROUGHLY AWARE OF HER SURROUNDINGS...
"BECAUSE THE COMPLETION OF THE MISSION, ITSELF, IS THE SIMPLE PART.
"WHAT LIES BEYOND...
"...THAT IS THE TRUE CHALLENGE..."
TO BE CONTINUED...

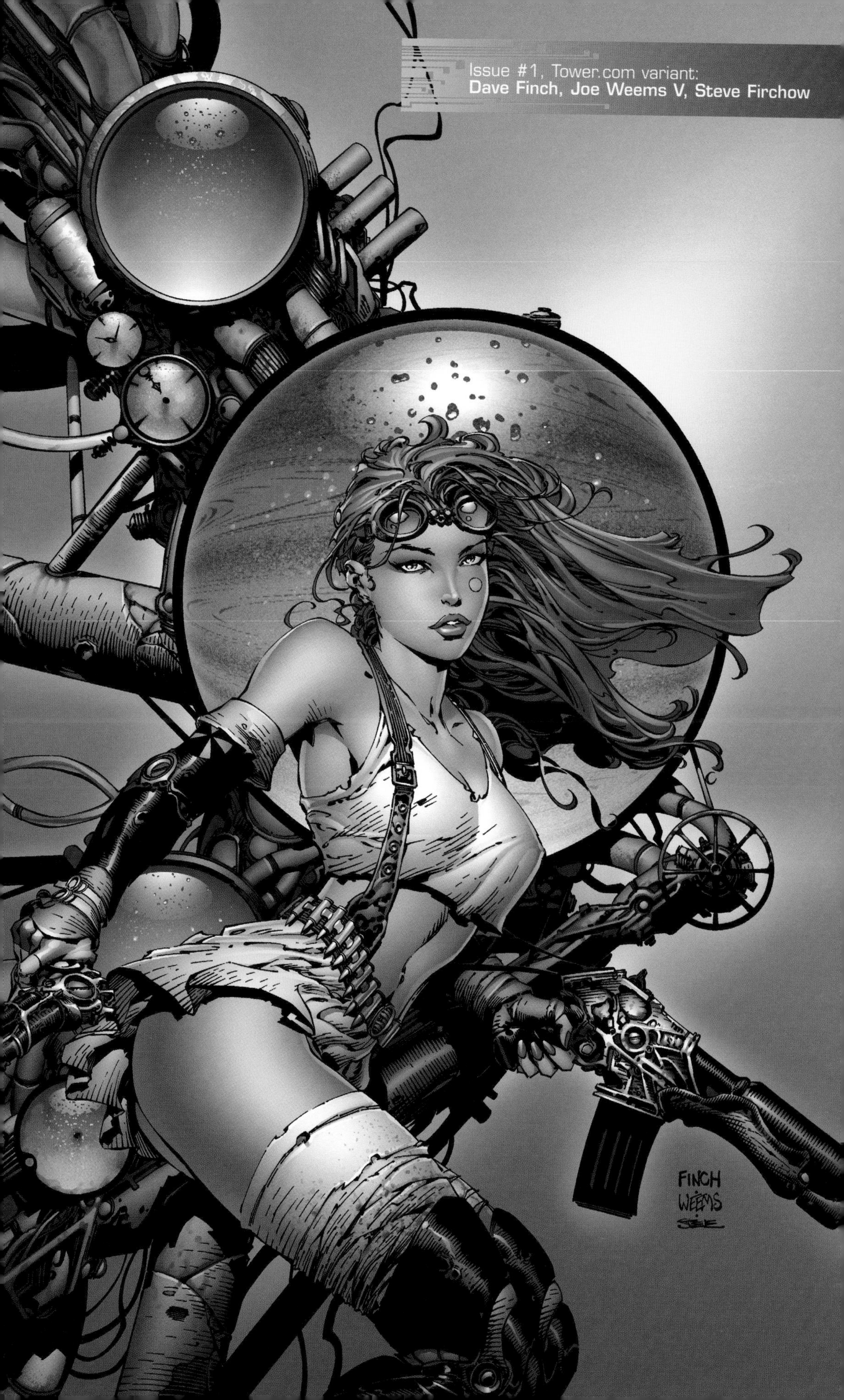
FINCH
WEEMS

Issue #1, Tower.com variant:
Dave Finch, Joe Weems V, Steve Firchow

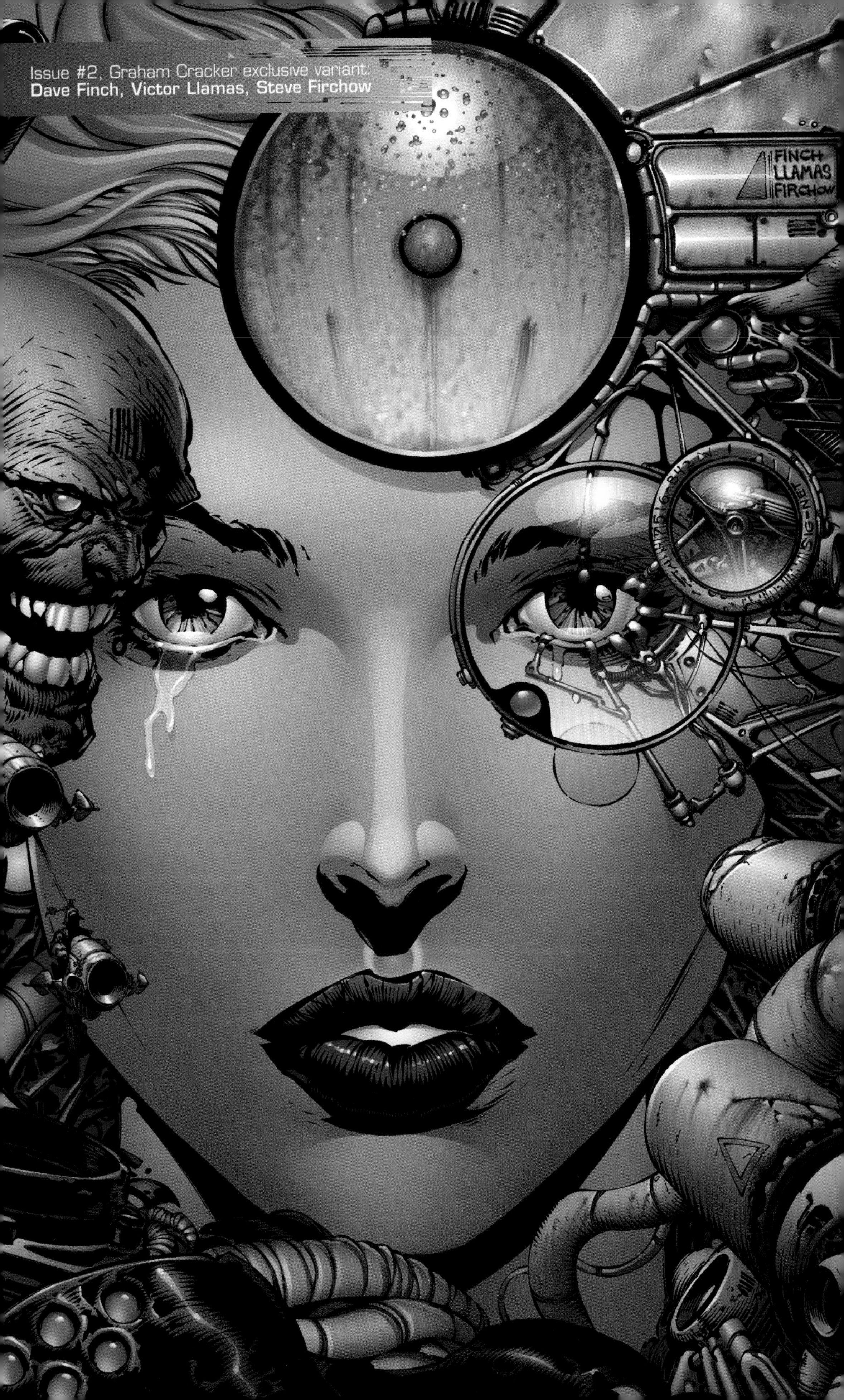
FINCH
LLAMAS
FIRCHOW

Issue #2, Graham Cracker exclusive variant:
Dave Finch, Victor Llamas, Steve Firchow

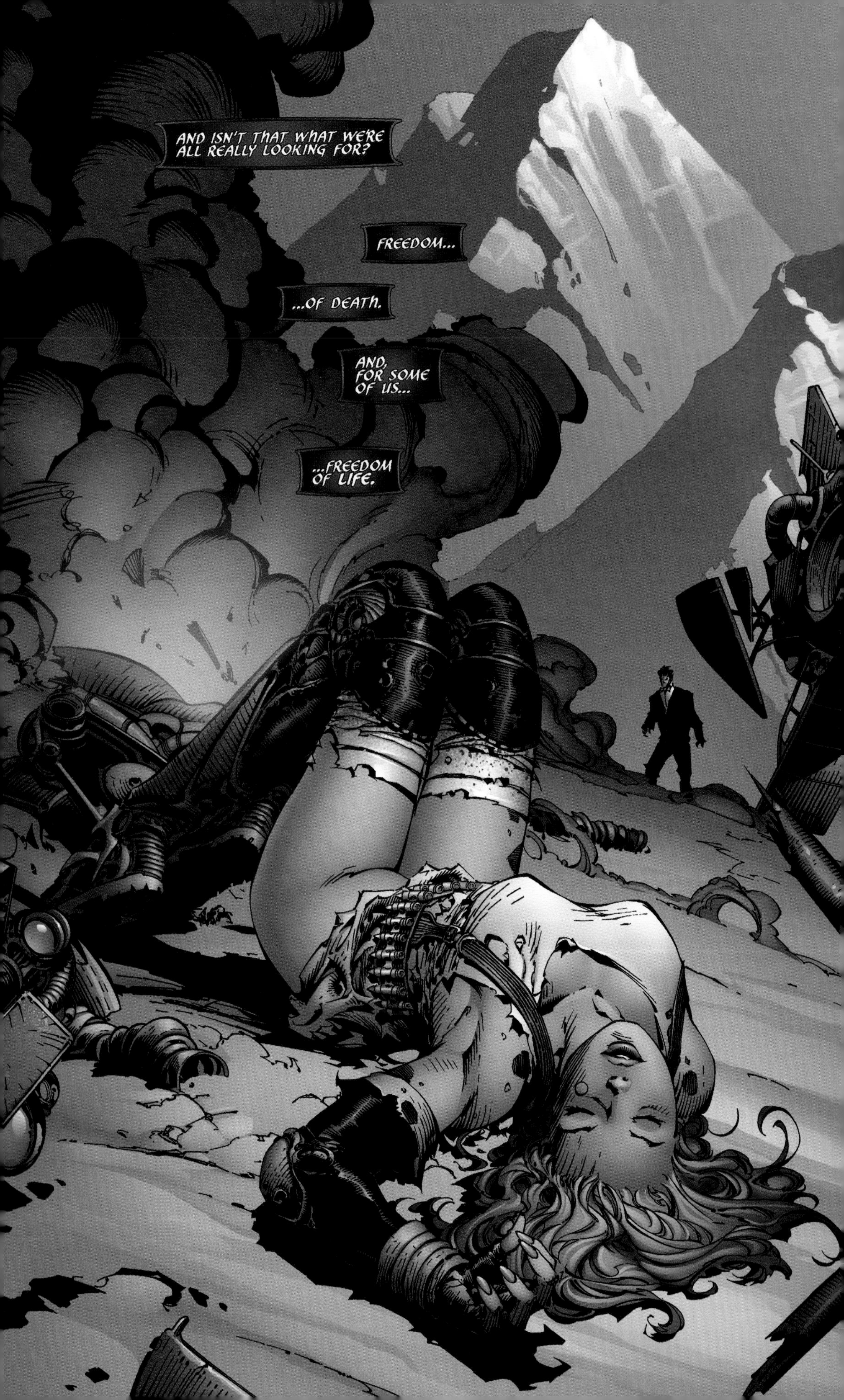
AND ISN'T THAT WHAT WE'RE ALL REALLY LOOKING FOR?
FREEDOM...
...OF DEATH.
AND, FOR SOME OF US...
...FREEDOM OF LIFE.

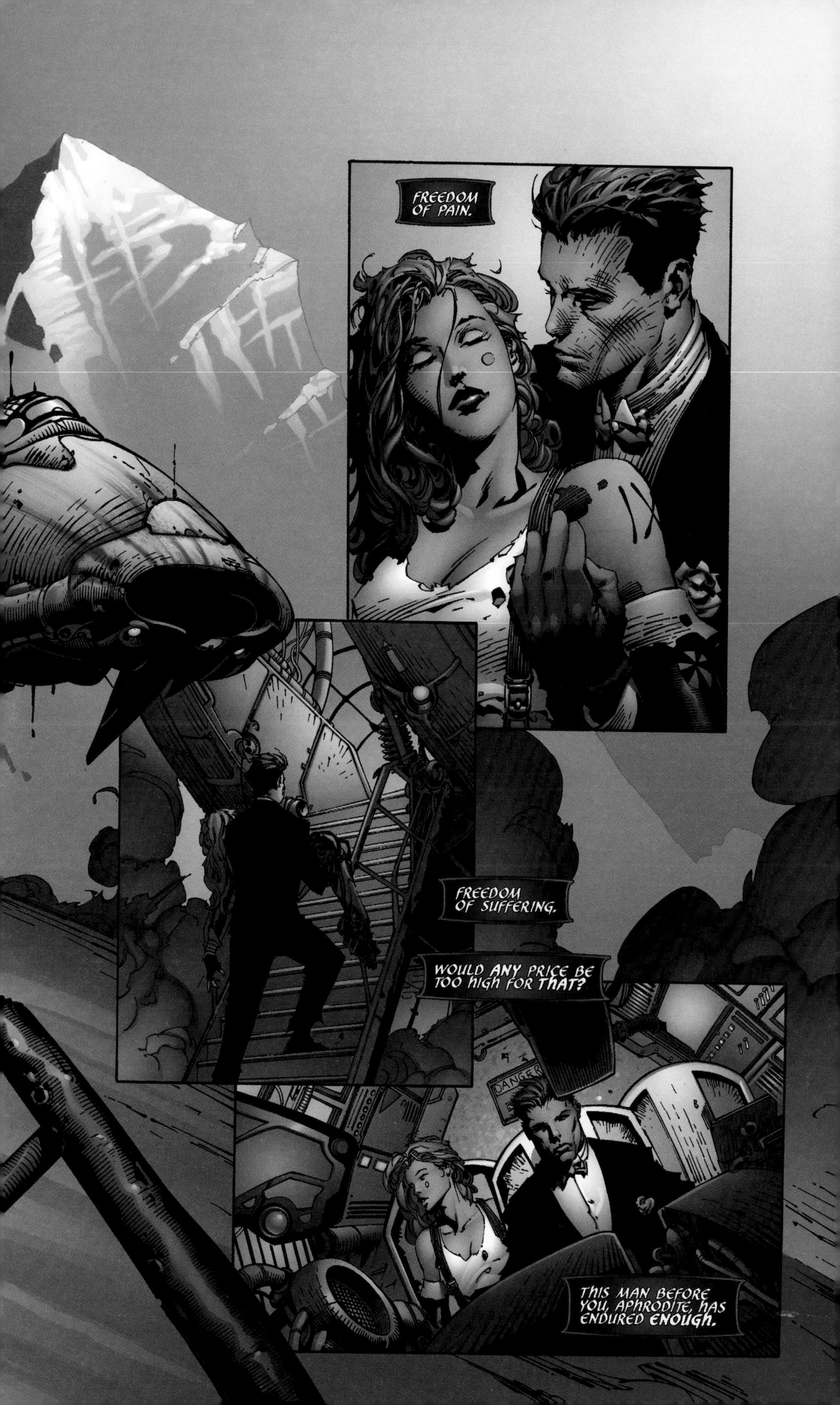
FREEDOM OF PAIN.
FREEDOM OF SUFFERING.
WOULD ANY PRICE BE TOO HIGH FOR THAT?
DANGER
THIS MAN BEFORE YOU, APHRODITE, HAS ENDURED ENOUGH.

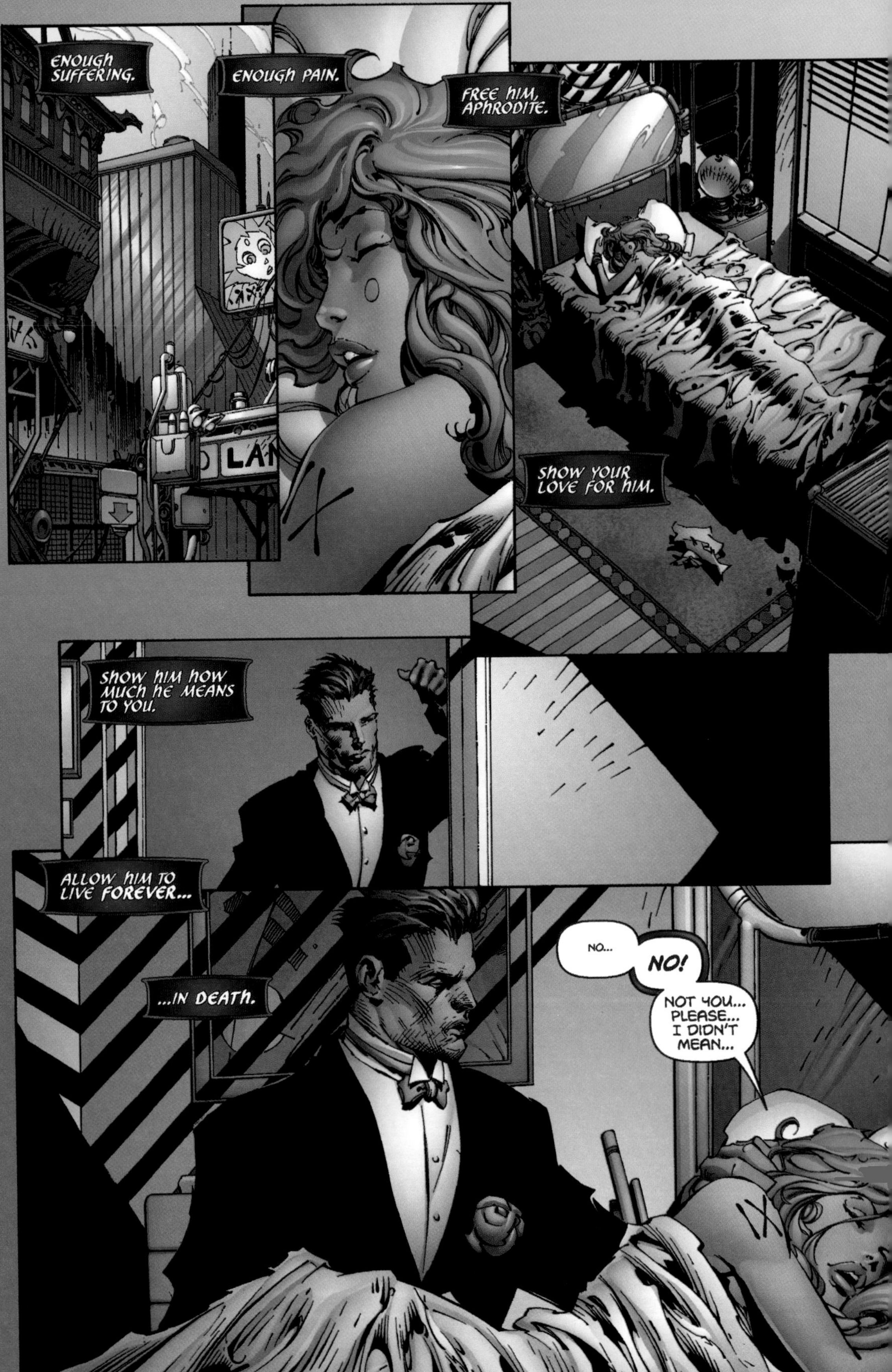
ENOUGH SUFFERING.
ENOUGH PAIN.
FREE HIM, APHRODITE.
SHOW YOUR LOVE FOR HIM.
SHOW HIM HOW MUCH HE MEANS TO YOU.
ALLOW HIM TO LIVE FOREVER...
...IN DEATH.
NO...
NO!
NOT YOU... PLEASE... I DIDN'T MEAN...

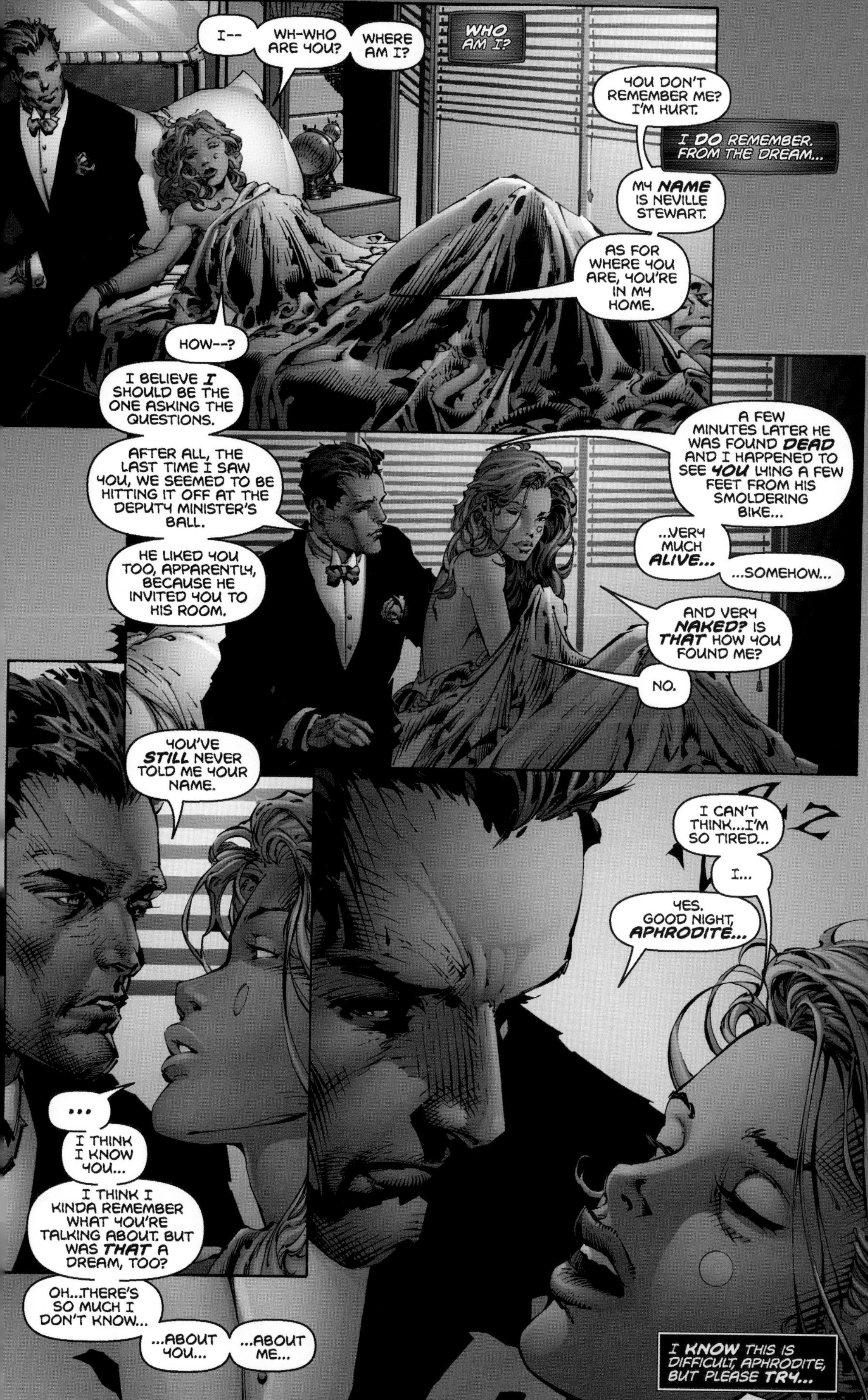
I--
WH-WHO ARE YOU?
WHERE AM I?
WHO AM I?
YOU DON'T REMEMBER ME? I'M HURT.
I DO REMEMBER. FROM THE DREAM...
MY NAME IS NEVILLE STEWART.
AS FOR WHERE YOU ARE, YOU'RE IN MY HOME.
HOW--?
I BELIEVE I SHOULD BE THE ONE ASKING THE QUESTIONS.
AFTER ALL, THE LAST TIME I SAW YOU, WE SEEMED TO BE HITTING IT OFF AT THE DEPUTY MINISTER'S BALL.
HE LIKED YOU TOO, APPARENTLY, BECAUSE HE INVITED YOU TO HIS ROOM.
A FEW MINUTES LATER HE WAS FOUND DEAD AND I HAPPENED TO SEE YOU LYING A FEW FEET FROM HIS SMOLDERING BIKE...
...VERY MUCH ALIVE...
...SOMEHOW...
AND VERY NAKED? IS THAT HOW YOU FOUND ME?
NO.
YOU'VE STILL NEVER TOLD ME YOUR NAME.
...
I THINK I KNOW YOU...
I THINK I KINDA REMEMBER WHAT YOU'RE TALKING ABOUT. BUT WAS THAT A DREAM, TOO?
OH...THERE'S SO MUCH I DON'T KNOW...
...ABOUT YOU...
...ABOUT ME...
I CAN'T THINK...I'M SO TIRED...
I...
YES. GOOD NIGHT, APHRODITE...
I KNOW THIS IS DIFFICULT, APHRODITE, BUT PLEASE TRY...

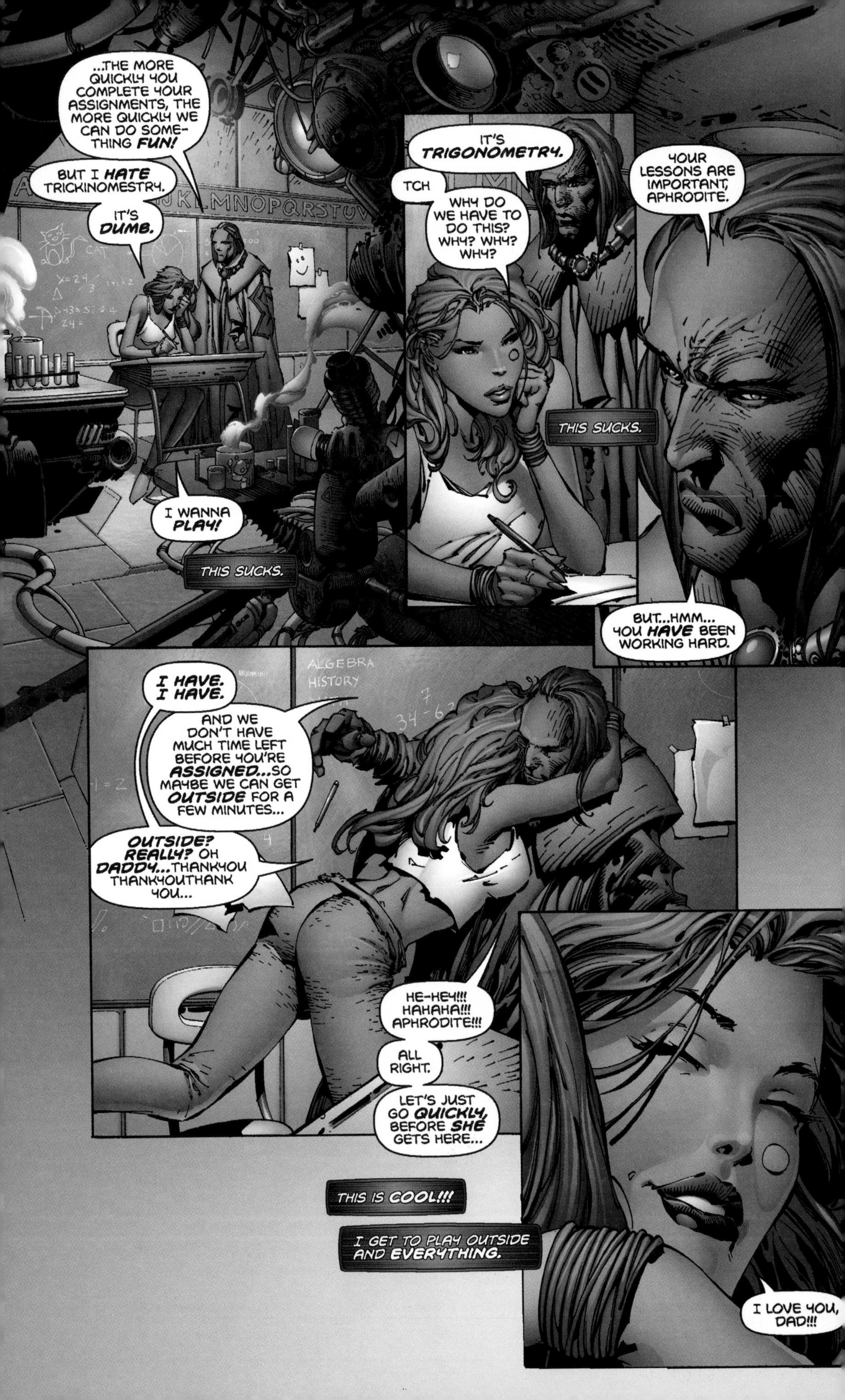
...THE MORE QUICKLY YOU COMPLETE YOUR ASSIGNMENTS, THE MORE QUICKLY WE CAN DO SOME-THING FUN!
BUT I HATE TRICKINOMESTRY.
IT'S DUMB.
I WANNA PLAY!
THIS SUCKS.
IT'S TRIGONOMETRY.
TCH
WHY DO WE HAVE TO DO THIS? WHY? WHY? WHY?
THIS SUCKS.
YOUR LESSONS ARE IMPORTANT, APHRODITE.
BUT...HMM... YOU HAVE BEEN WORKING HARD.
I HAVE. I HAVE.
AND WE DON'T HAVE MUCH TIME LEFT BEFORE YOU'RE ASSIGNED...SO MAYBE WE CAN GET OUTSIDE FOR A FEW MINUTES...
OUTSIDE? REALLY? OH DADDY...THANKYOU THANKYOUTHANK YOU...
HE-HEY!!! HAHAHA!!! APHRODITE!!!
ALL RIGHT.
LET'S JUST GO QUICKLY, BEFORE SHE GETS HERE...
THIS IS COOL!!!
I GET TO PLAY OUTSIDE AND EVERYTHING.
I LOVE YOU, DAD!!!

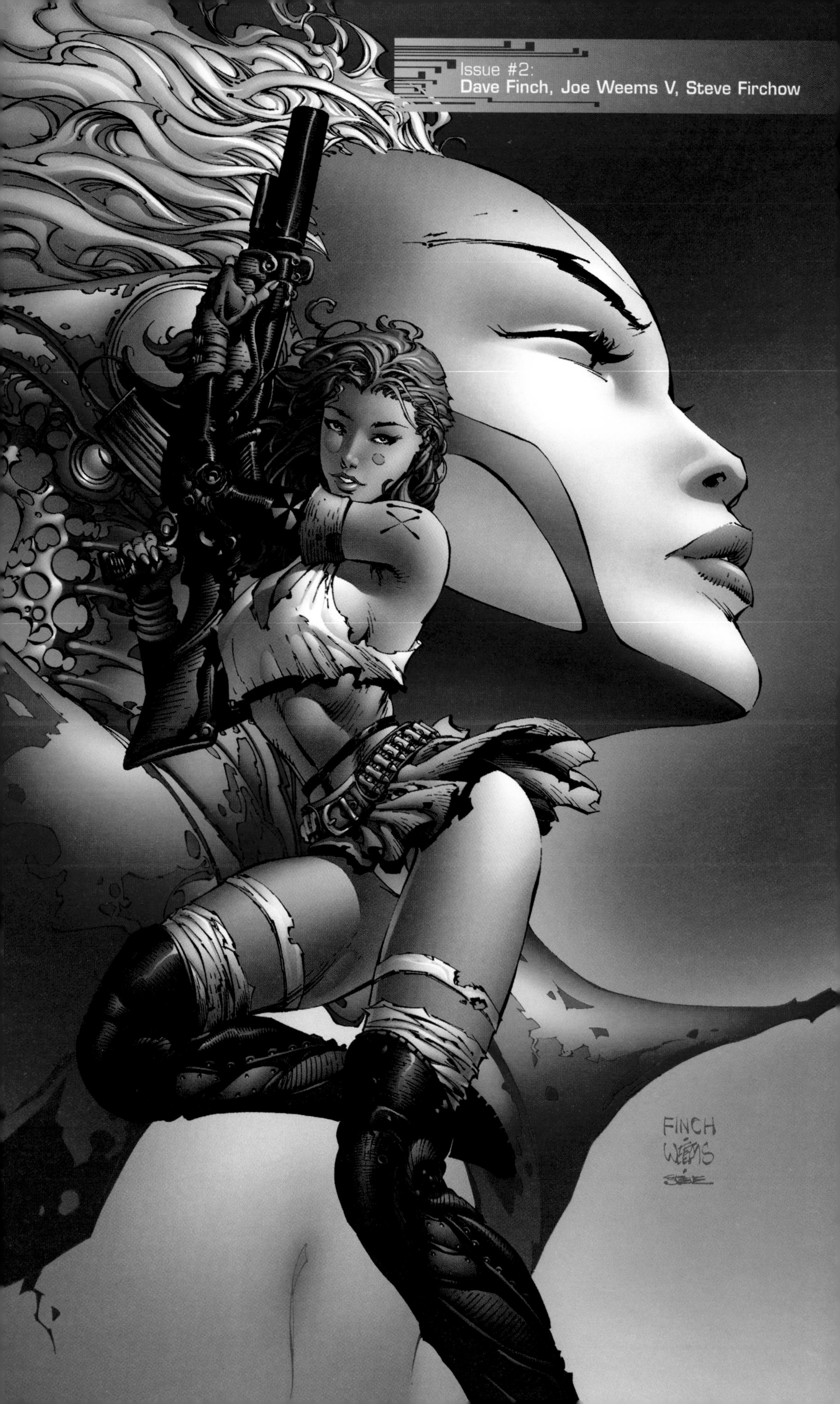
Issue #2:
Dave Finch, Joe Weems V, Steve Firchow

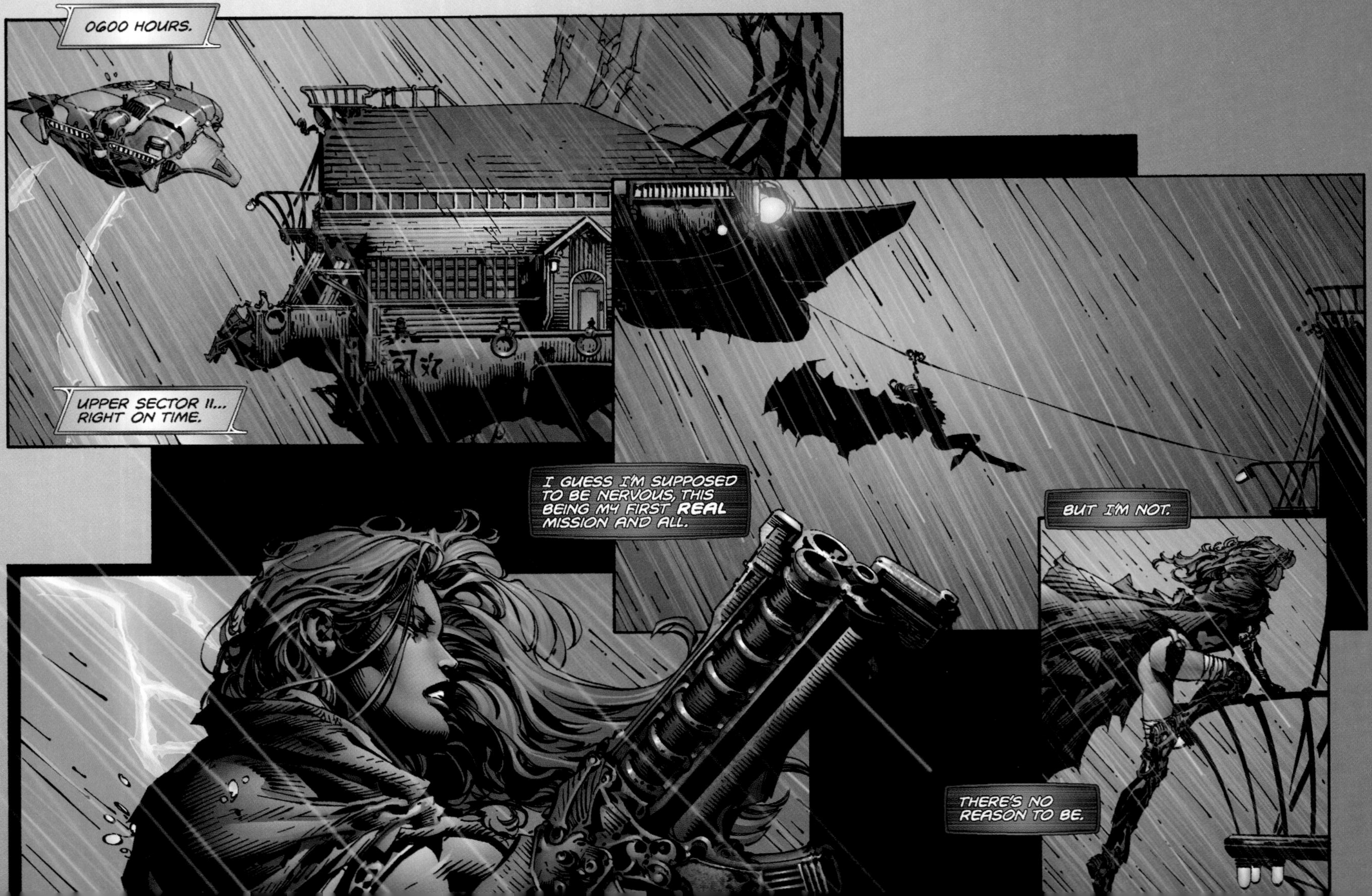
0600 HOURS.
UPPER SECTOR 11... RIGHT ON TIME.
I GUESS I'M SUPPOSED TO BE NERVOUS, THIS BEING MY FIRST **REAL** MISSION AND ALL.
BUT I'M NOT.
THERE'S NO REASON TO BE.

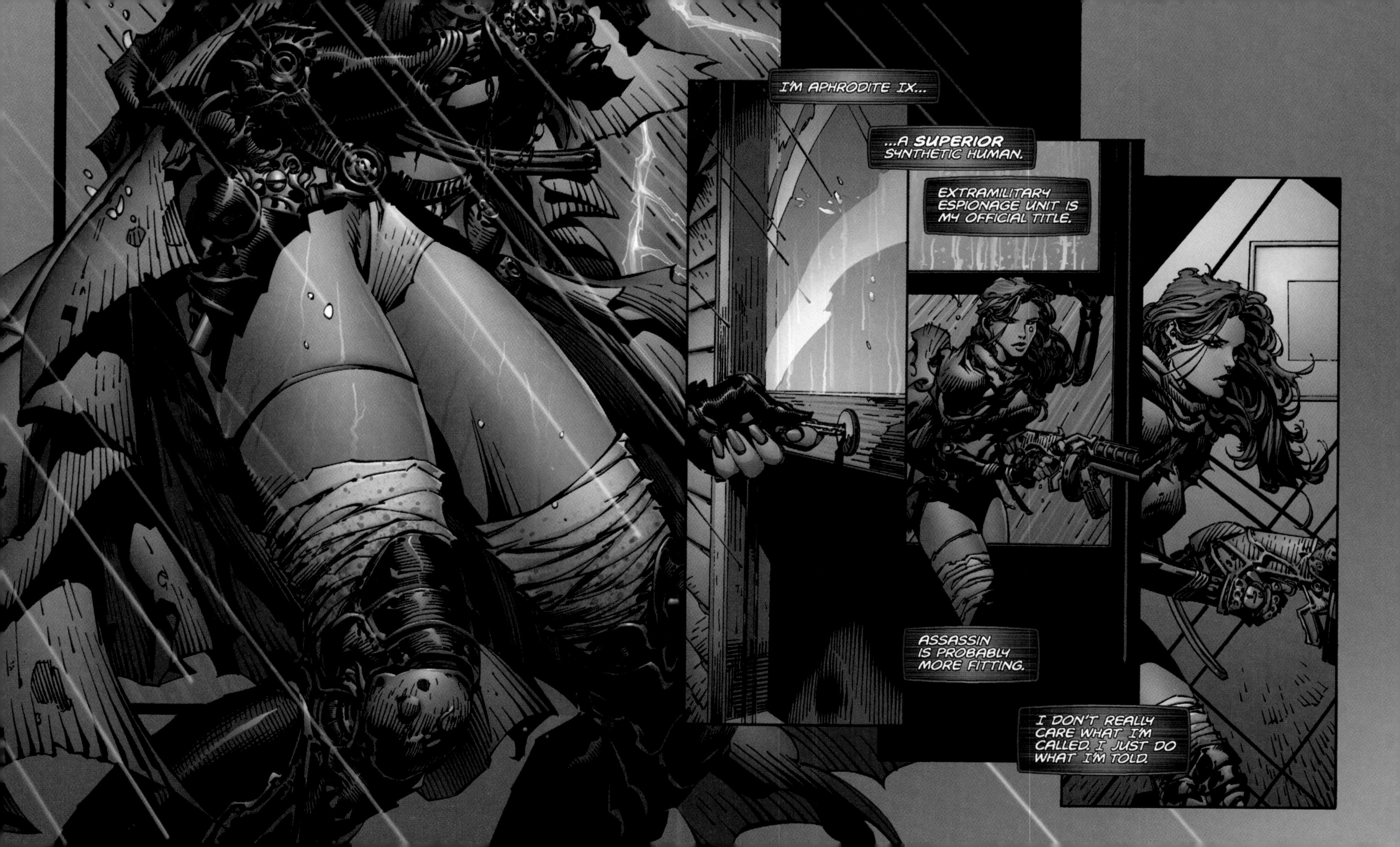
I'M APHRODITE IX...
...A SUPERIOR SYNTHETIC HUMAN.
EXTRAMILITARY ESPIONAGE UNIT IS MY OFFICIAL TITLE.
ASSASSIN IS PROBABLY MORE FITTING.
I DON'T REALLY CARE WHAT I'M CALLED. I JUST DO WHAT I'M TOLD.

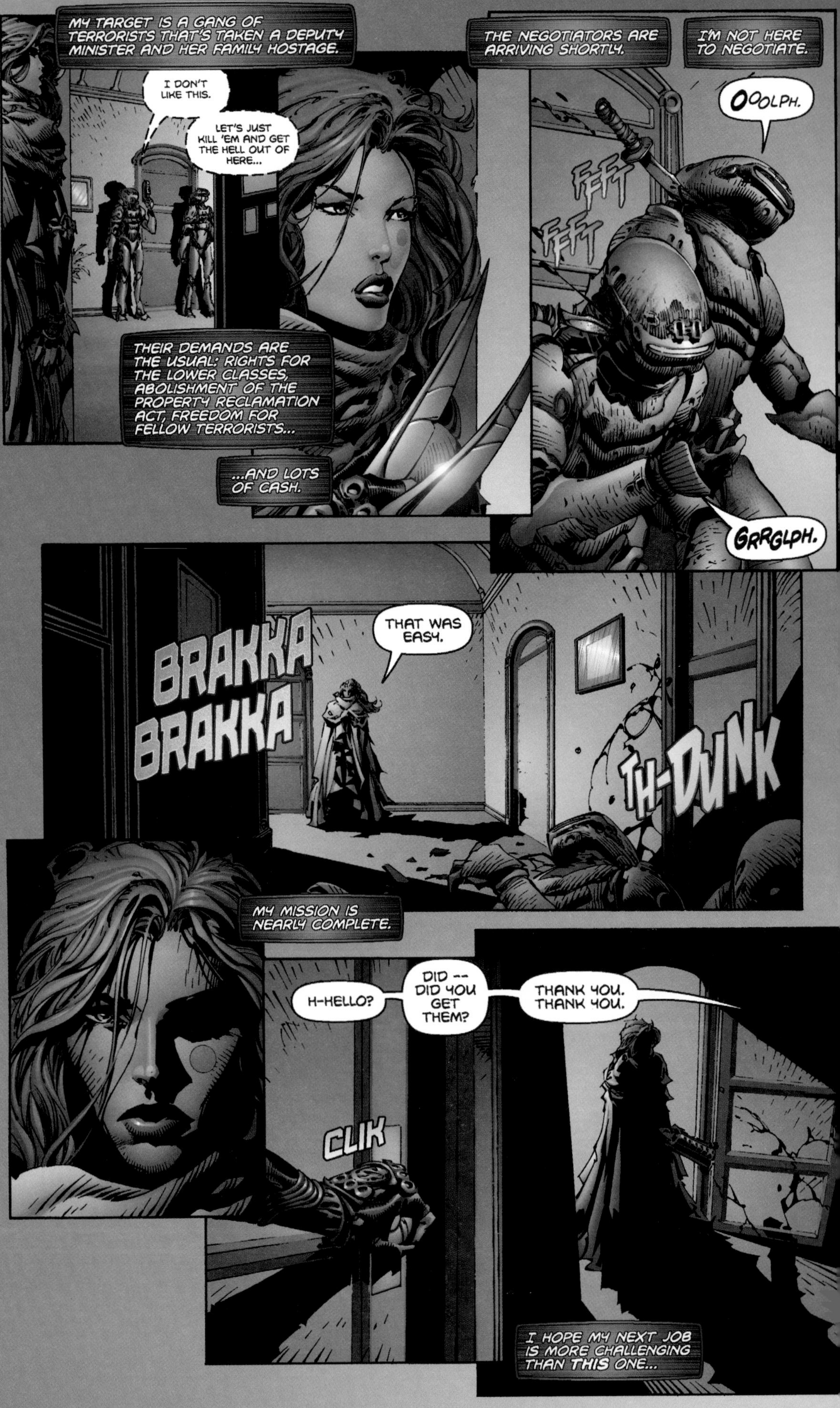
MY TARGET IS A GANG OF TERRORISTS THAT'S TAKEN A DEPUTY MINISTER AND HER FAMILY HOSTAGE.
I DON'T LIKE THIS.
LET'S JUST KILL 'EM AND GET THE HELL OUT OF HERE...
THEIR DEMANDS ARE THE USUAL: RIGHTS FOR THE LOWER CLASSES, ABOLISHMENT OF THE PROPERTY RECLAMATION ACT, FREEDOM FOR FELLOW TERRORISTS...
...AND LOTS OF CASH.
THE NEGOTIATORS ARE ARRIVING SHORTLY.
I'M NOT HERE TO NEGOTIATE.
OOOLPH.
FFFT
FFFT
GRRGLPH.
BRAKKA
BRAKKA
THAT WAS EASY.
TH-DUNK
MY MISSION IS NEARLY COMPLETE.
H-HELLO?
DID -- DID YOU GET THEM?
THANK YOU. THANK YOU.
CLIK
I HOPE MY NEXT JOB IS MORE CHALLENGING THAN THIS ONE...

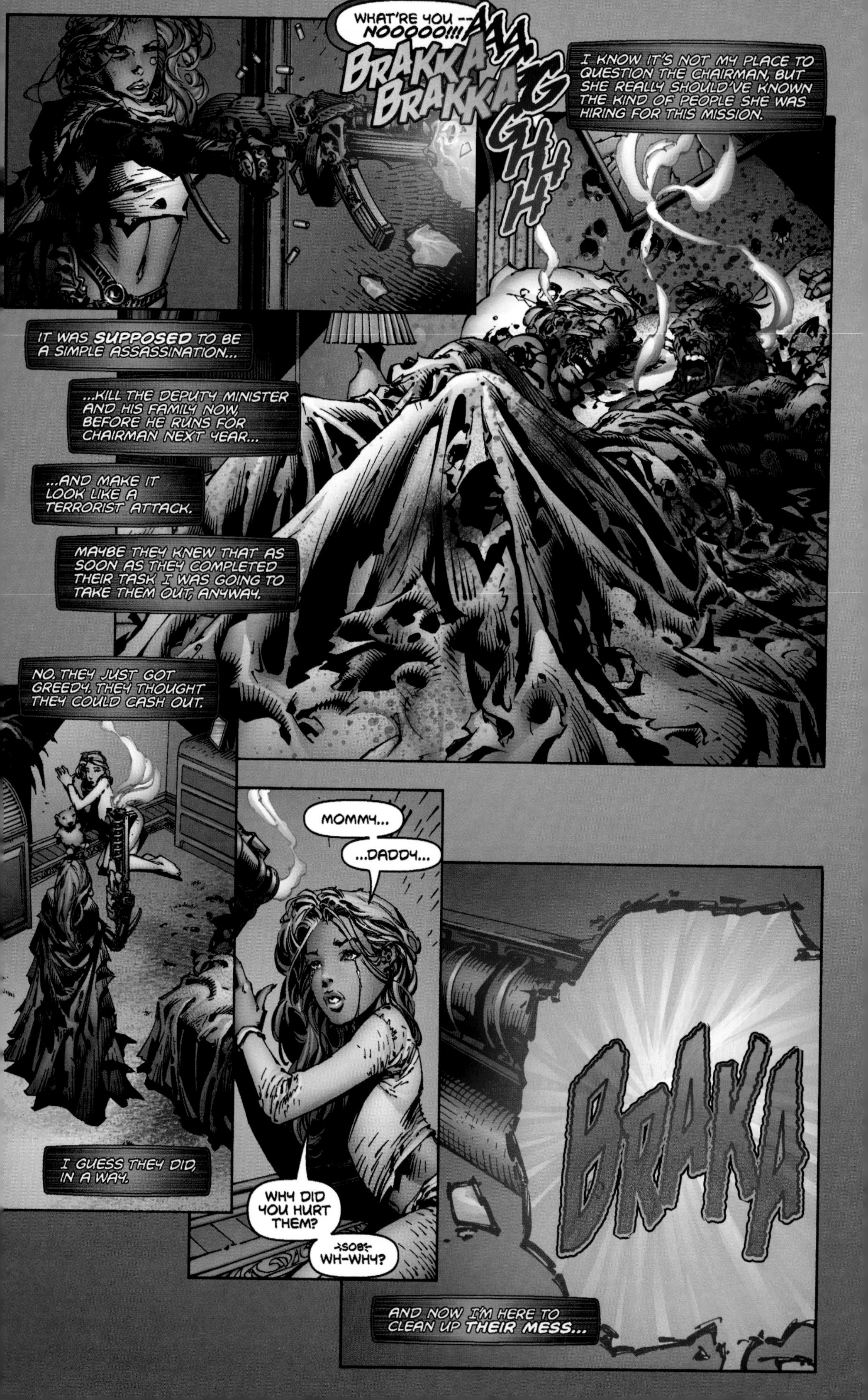
WHAT'RE YOU -- NOOOOO!!!
BRAKKA BRAKKA
AAAGHHH
I KNOW IT'S NOT MY PLACE TO QUESTION THE CHAIRMAN, BUT SHE REALLY SHOULD'VE KNOWN THE KIND OF PEOPLE SHE WAS HIRING FOR THIS MISSION.
IT WAS SUPPOSED TO BE A SIMPLE ASSASSINATION...
...KILL THE DEPUTY MINISTER AND HIS FAMILY NOW, BEFORE HE RUNS FOR CHAIRMAN NEXT YEAR...
...AND MAKE IT LOOK LIKE A TERRORIST ATTACK.
MAYBE THEY KNEW THAT AS SOON AS THEY COMPLETED THEIR TASK I WAS GOING TO TAKE THEM OUT, ANYWAY.
NO. THEY JUST GOT GREEDY. THEY THOUGHT THEY COULD CASH OUT.
I GUESS THEY DID, IN A WAY.
MOMMY...
...DADDY...
WHY DID YOU HURT THEM?
SOB
WH-WHY?
BRAKA
AND NOW I'M HERE TO CLEAN UP THEIR MESS...

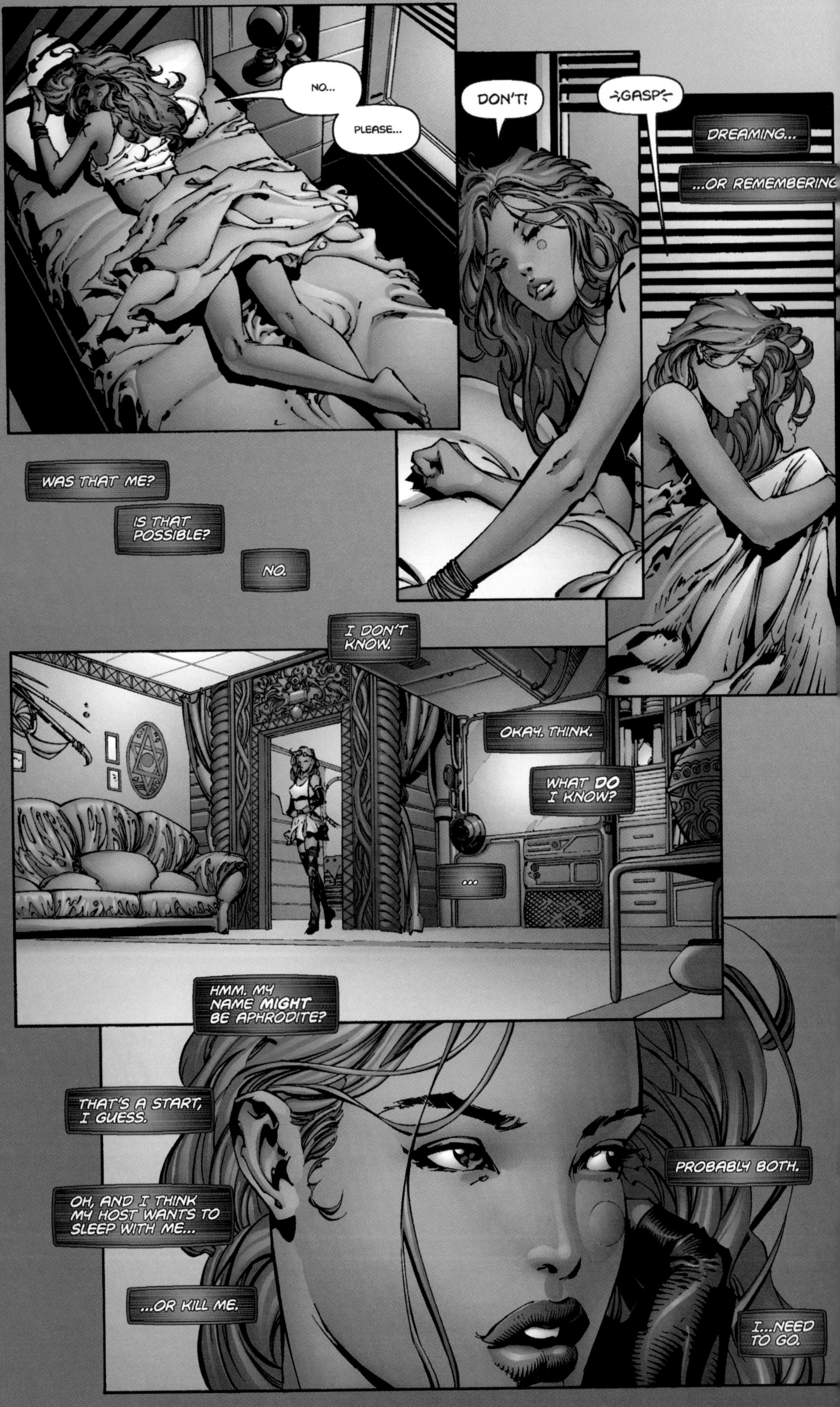
NO...
PLEASE...
DON'T!
GASP
DREAMING...
...OR REMEMBERING
WAS THAT ME?
IS THAT POSSIBLE?
NO.
I DON'T KNOW.
OKAY. THINK.
WHAT DO I KNOW?
...
HMM. MY NAME MIGHT BE APHRODITE?
THAT'S A START, I GUESS.
OH, AND I THINK MY HOST WANTS TO SLEEP WITH ME...
...OR KILL ME.
PROBABLY BOTH.
I...NEED TO GO.

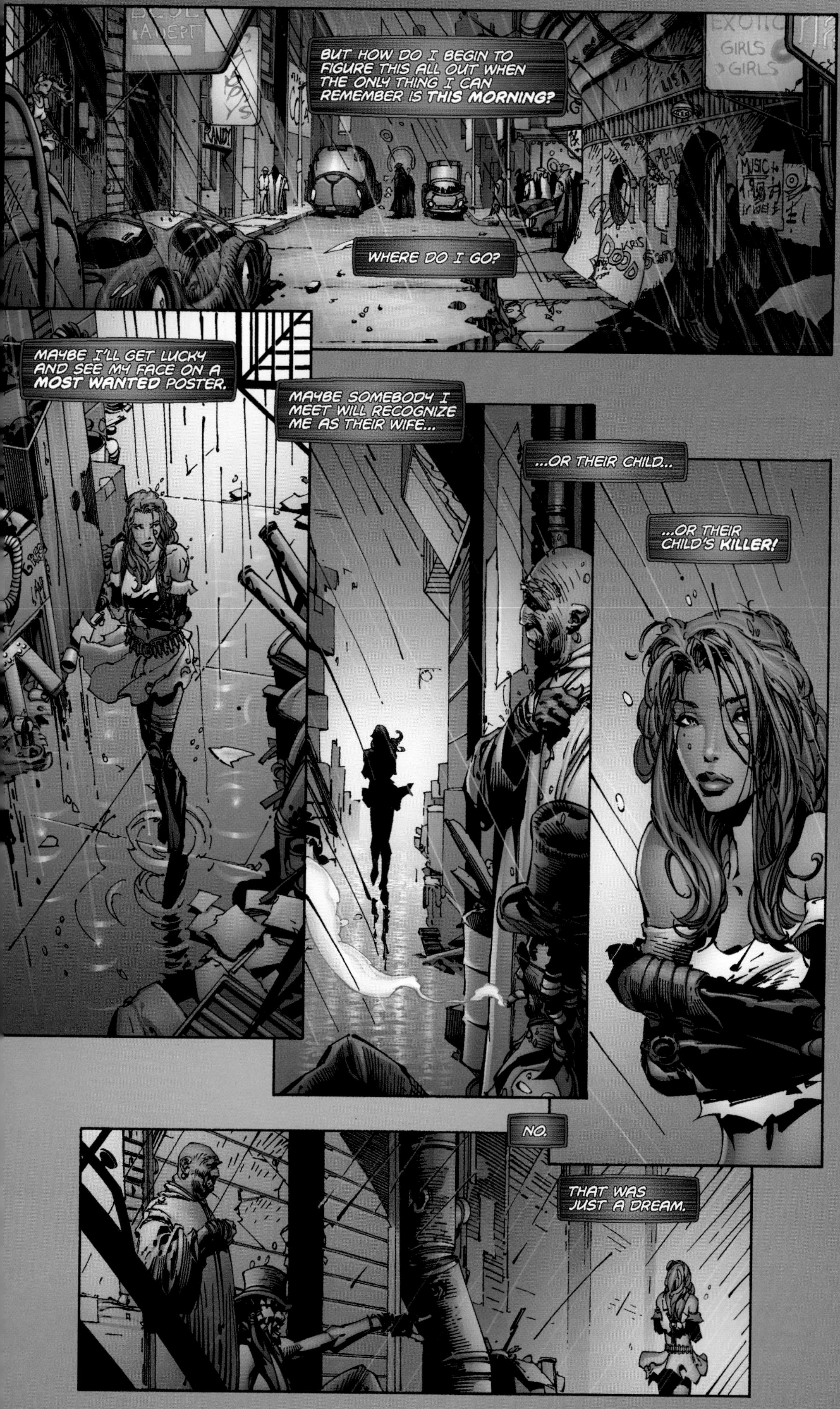
BUT HOW DO I BEGIN TO FIGURE THIS ALL OUT WHEN THE ONLY THING I CAN REMEMBER IS THIS MORNING?
WHERE DO I GO?
EXOTIC GIRLS GIRLS
RANDY
MUSIC
MAYBE I'LL GET LUCKY AND SEE MY FACE ON A MOST WANTED POSTER.
MAYBE SOMEBODY I MEET WILL RECOGNIZE ME AS THEIR WIFE...
...OR THEIR CHILD...
...OR THEIR CHILD'S KILLER!
NO.
THAT WAS JUST A DREAM.

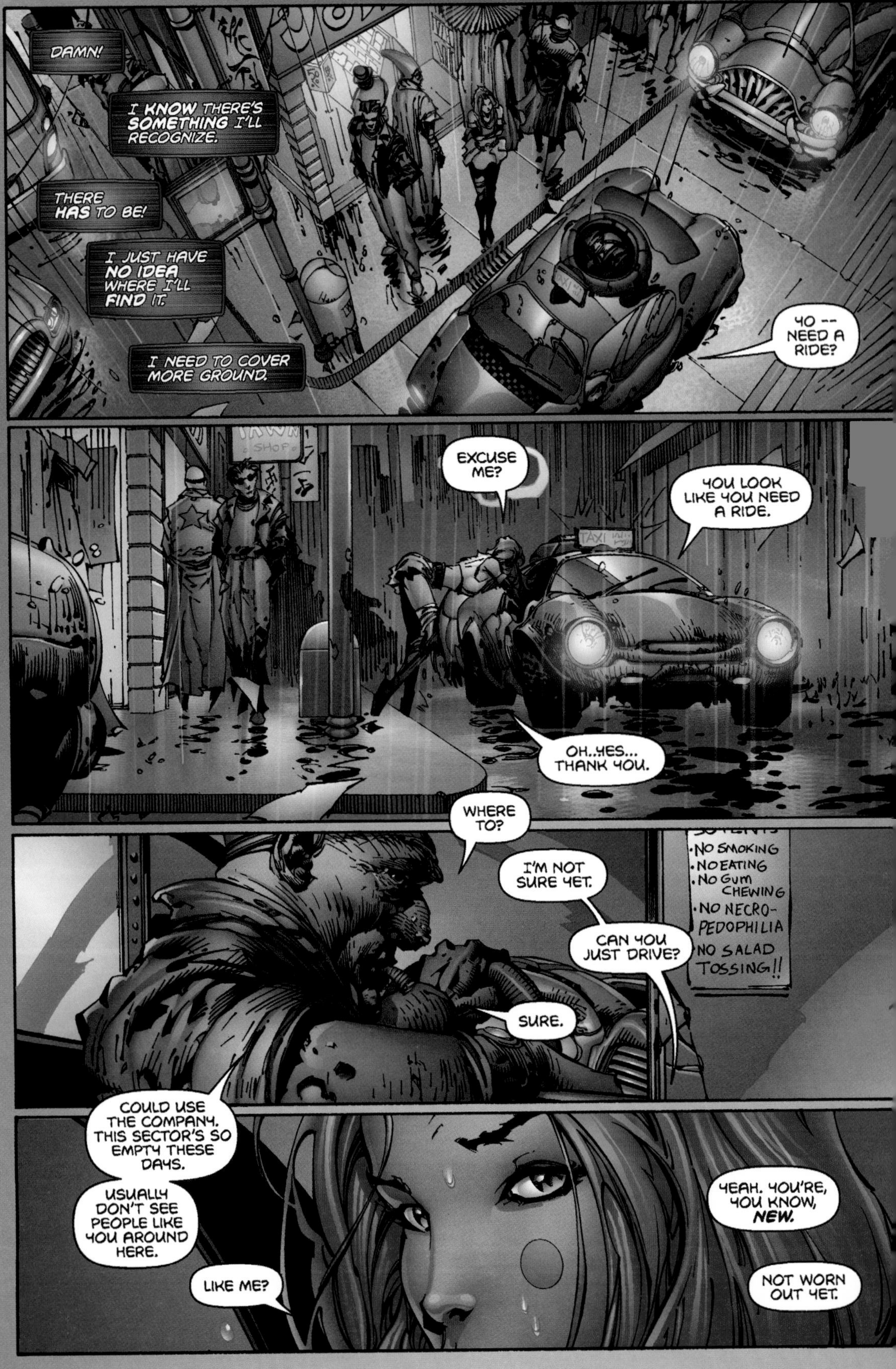
DAMN!
I KNOW THERE'S SOMETHING I'LL RECOGNIZE.
THERE HAS TO BE!
I JUST HAVE NO IDEA WHERE I'LL FIND IT.
I NEED TO COVER MORE GROUND.
YO -- NEED A RIDE?
EXCUSE ME?
YOU LOOK LIKE YOU NEED A RIDE.
OH...YES... THANK YOU.
WHERE TO?
I'M NOT SURE YET.
CAN YOU JUST DRIVE?
SURE.
•NO SMOKING
•NO EATING
•NO GUM CHEWING
•NO NECRO-PEDOPHILIA
NO SALAD TOSSING!!
COULD USE THE COMPANY. THIS SECTOR'S SO EMPTY THESE DAYS.
USUALLY DON'T SEE PEOPLE LIKE YOU AROUND HERE.
LIKE ME?
YEAH. YOU'RE, YOU KNOW, NEW.
NOT WORN OUT YET.

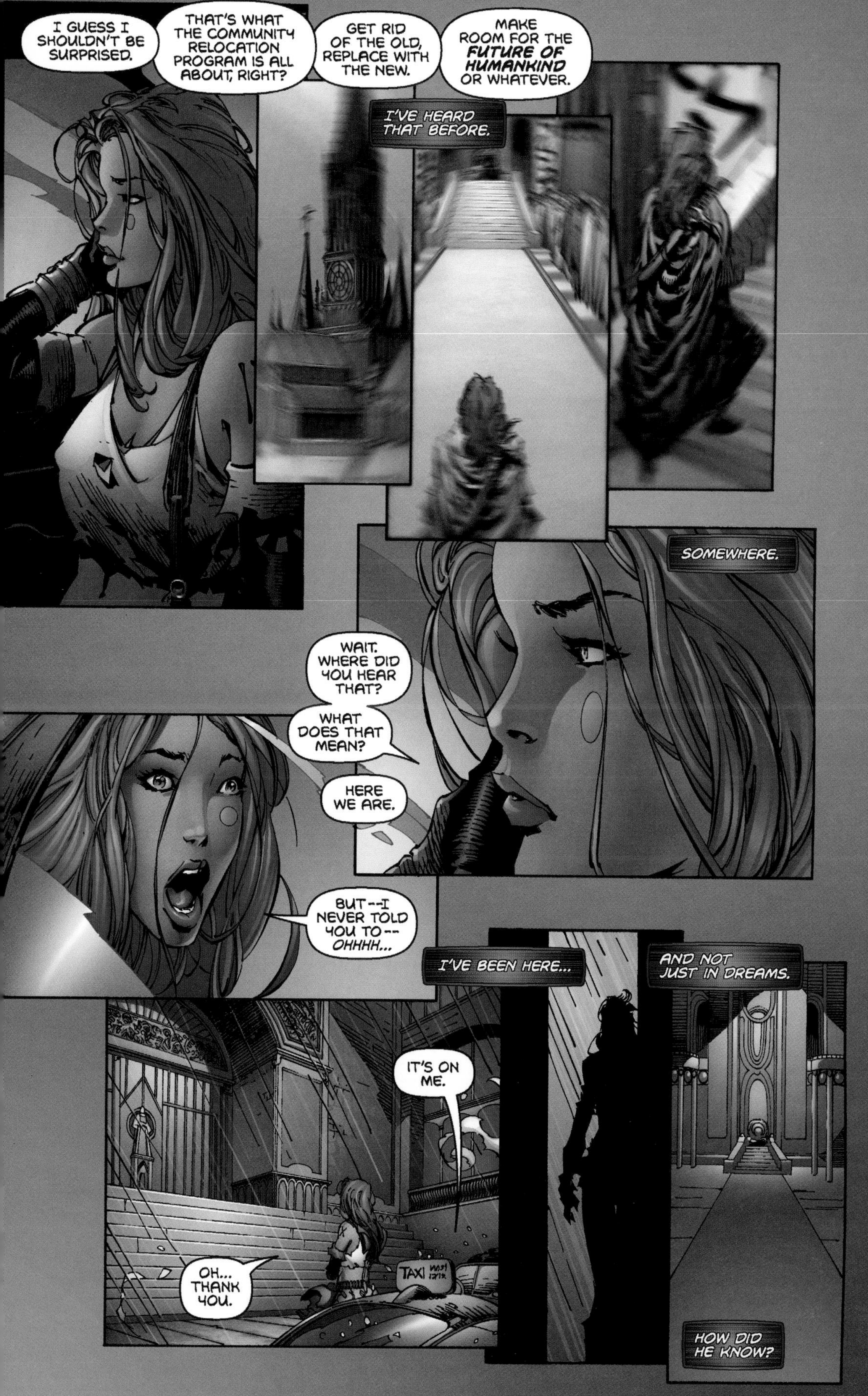
I GUESS I SHOULDN'T BE SURPRISED.
THAT'S WHAT THE COMMUNITY RELOCATION PROGRAM IS ALL ABOUT, RIGHT?
GET RID OF THE OLD, REPLACE WITH THE NEW.
MAKE ROOM FOR THE FUTURE OF HUMANKIND OR WHATEVER.
I'VE HEARD THAT BEFORE.
SOMEWHERE.
WAIT. WHERE DID YOU HEAR THAT?
WHAT DOES THAT MEAN?
HERE WE ARE.
BUT--I NEVER TOLD YOU TO-- OHHHH...
I'VE BEEN HERE...
AND NOT JUST IN DREAMS.
IT'S ON ME.
OH... THANK YOU.
TAXI
HOW DID HE KNOW?

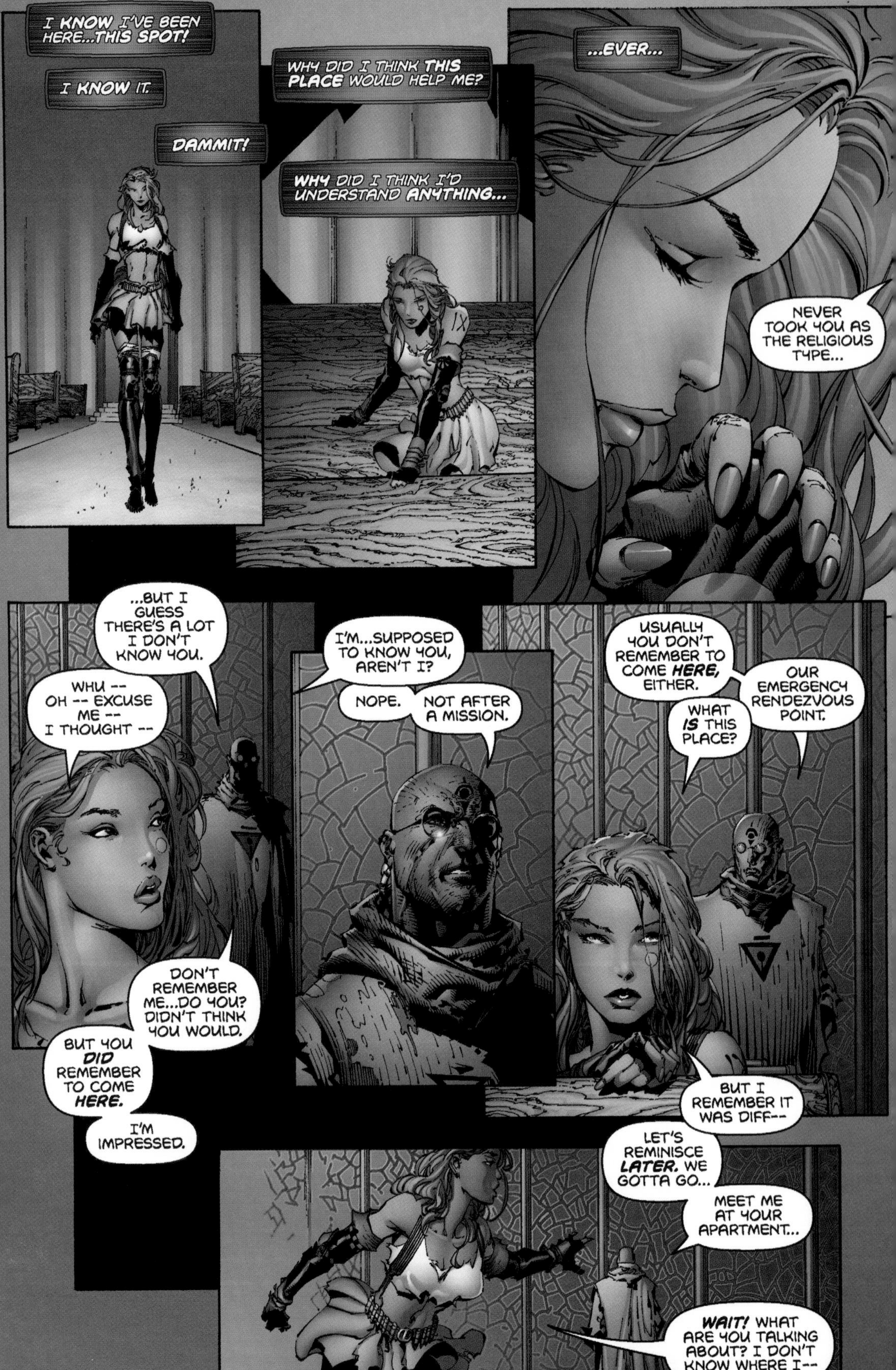

I KNOW I'VE BEEN HERE...THIS SPOT!
I KNOW IT.
DAMMIT!
WHY DID I THINK THIS PLACE WOULD HELP ME?
WHY DID I THINK I'D UNDERSTAND ANYTHING...
...EVER...
NEVER TOOK YOU AS THE RELIGIOUS TYPE...
...BUT I GUESS THERE'S A LOT I DON'T KNOW YOU.
WHU -- OH -- EXCUSE ME -- I THOUGHT --
DON'T REMEMBER ME...DO YOU? DIDN'T THINK YOU WOULD.
BUT YOU DID REMEMBER TO COME HERE.
I'M IMPRESSED.
I'M...SUPPOSED TO KNOW YOU, AREN'T I?
NOPE.
NOT AFTER A MISSION.
USUALLY YOU DON'T REMEMBER TO COME HERE, EITHER.
WHAT IS THIS PLACE?
OUR EMERGENCY RENDEZVOUS POINT.
BUT I REMEMBER IT WAS DIFF--
LET'S REMINISCE LATER. WE GOTTA GO...
MEET ME AT YOUR APARTMENT...
WAIT! WHAT ARE YOU TALKING ABOUT? I DON'T KNOW WHERE I--

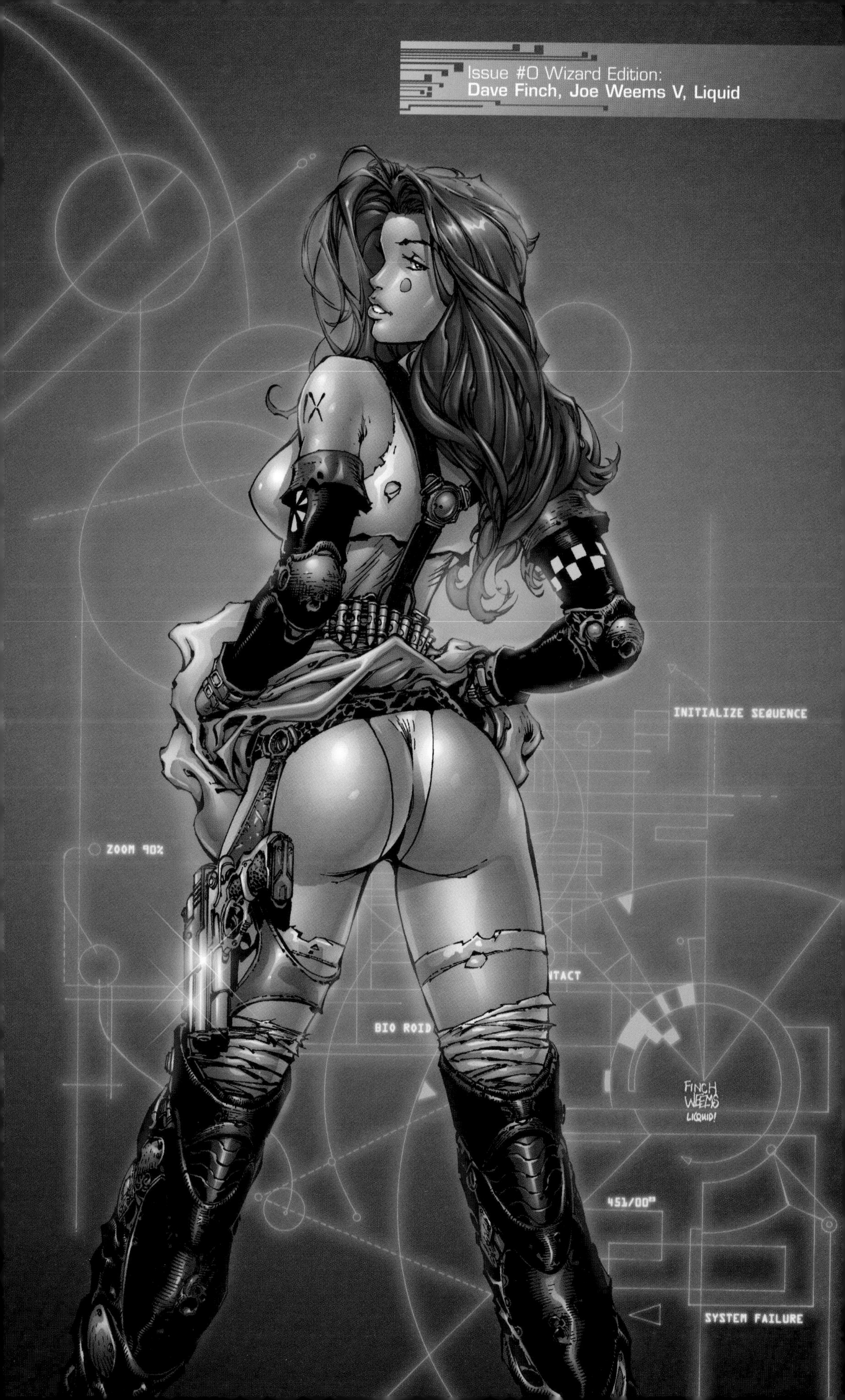
INITIALIZE SEQUENCE
ZOOM 90%
NTACT
BIO ROID
FINCH WEEMS LIQUID!
451/00"
SYSTEM FAILURE
Issue #0 Wizard Edition:
Dave Finch, Joe Weems V, Liquid

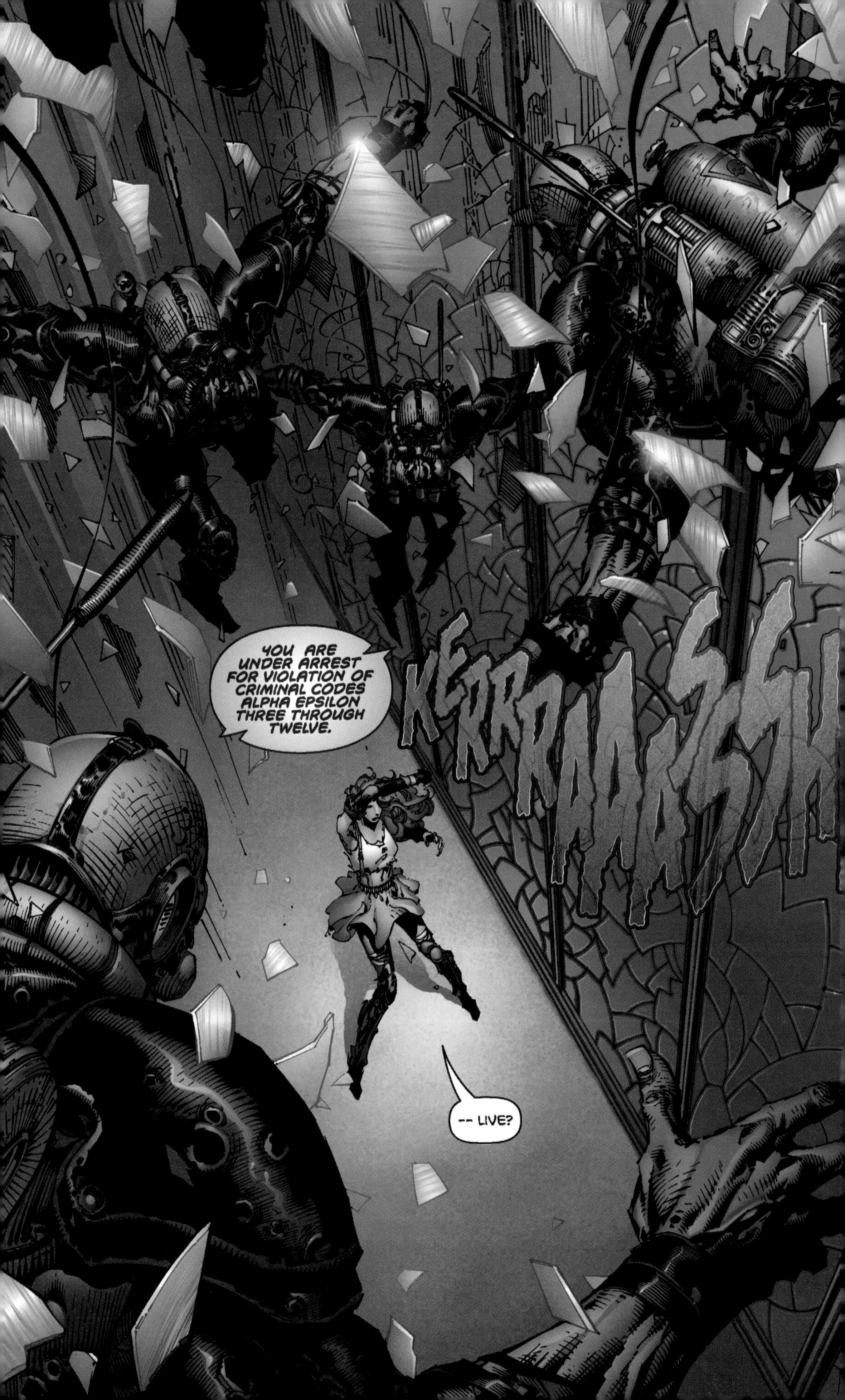
YOU ARE UNDER ARREST FOR VIOLATION OF CRIMINAL CODES ALPHA EPSILON THREE THROUGH TWELVE.
KERRRAAASSH
-- LIVE?

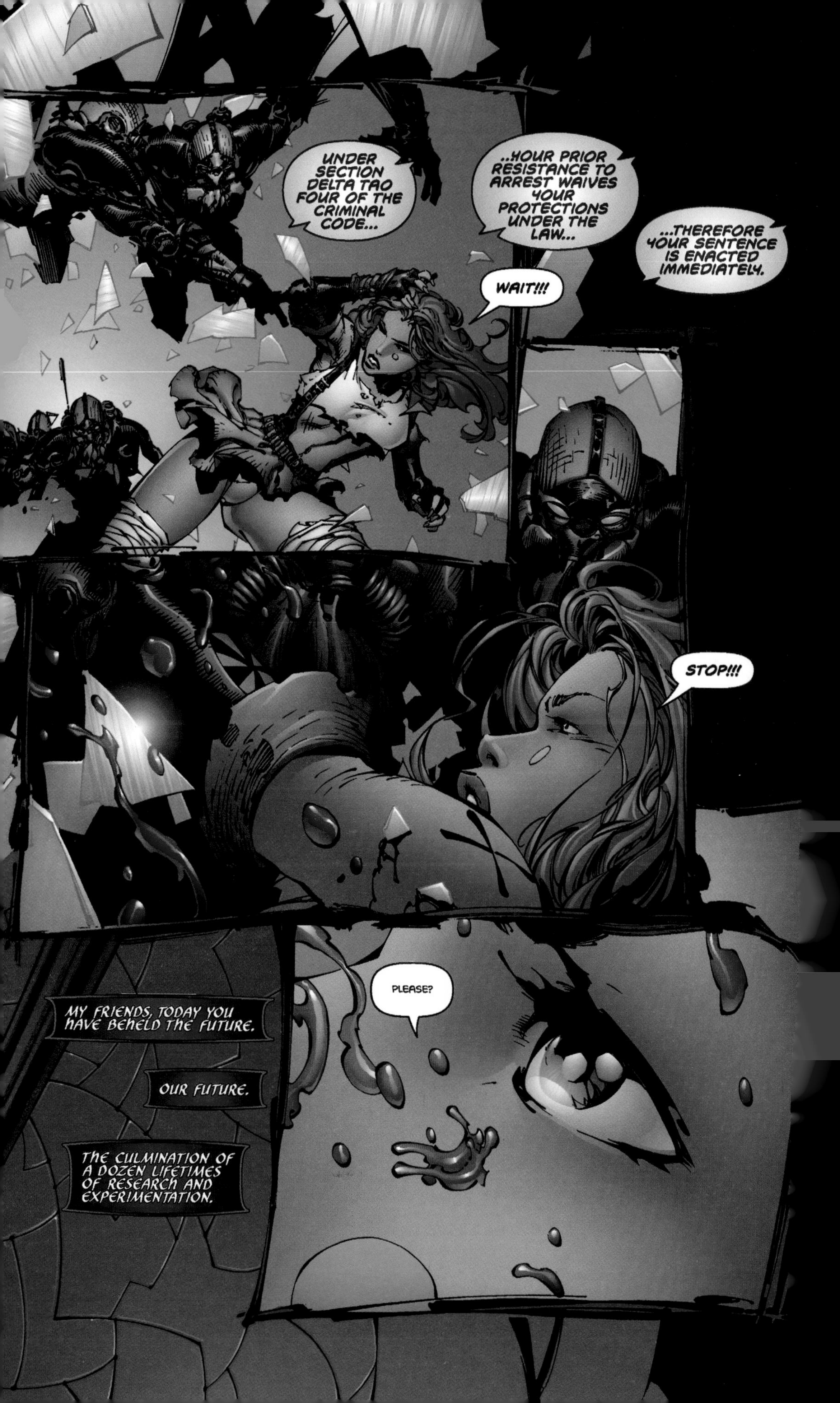
UNDER SECTION DELTA TAO FOUR OF THE CRIMINAL CODE...
..YOUR PRIOR RESISTANCE TO ARREST WAIVES YOUR PROTECTIONS UNDER THE LAW...
...THEREFORE YOUR SENTENCE IS ENACTED IMMEDIATELY.
WAIT!!!
STOP!!!
PLEASE?
MY FRIENDS, TODAY YOU HAVE BEHELD THE FUTURE.
OUR FUTURE.
THE CULMINATION OF A DOZEN LIFETIMES OF RESEARCH AND EXPERIMENTATION.

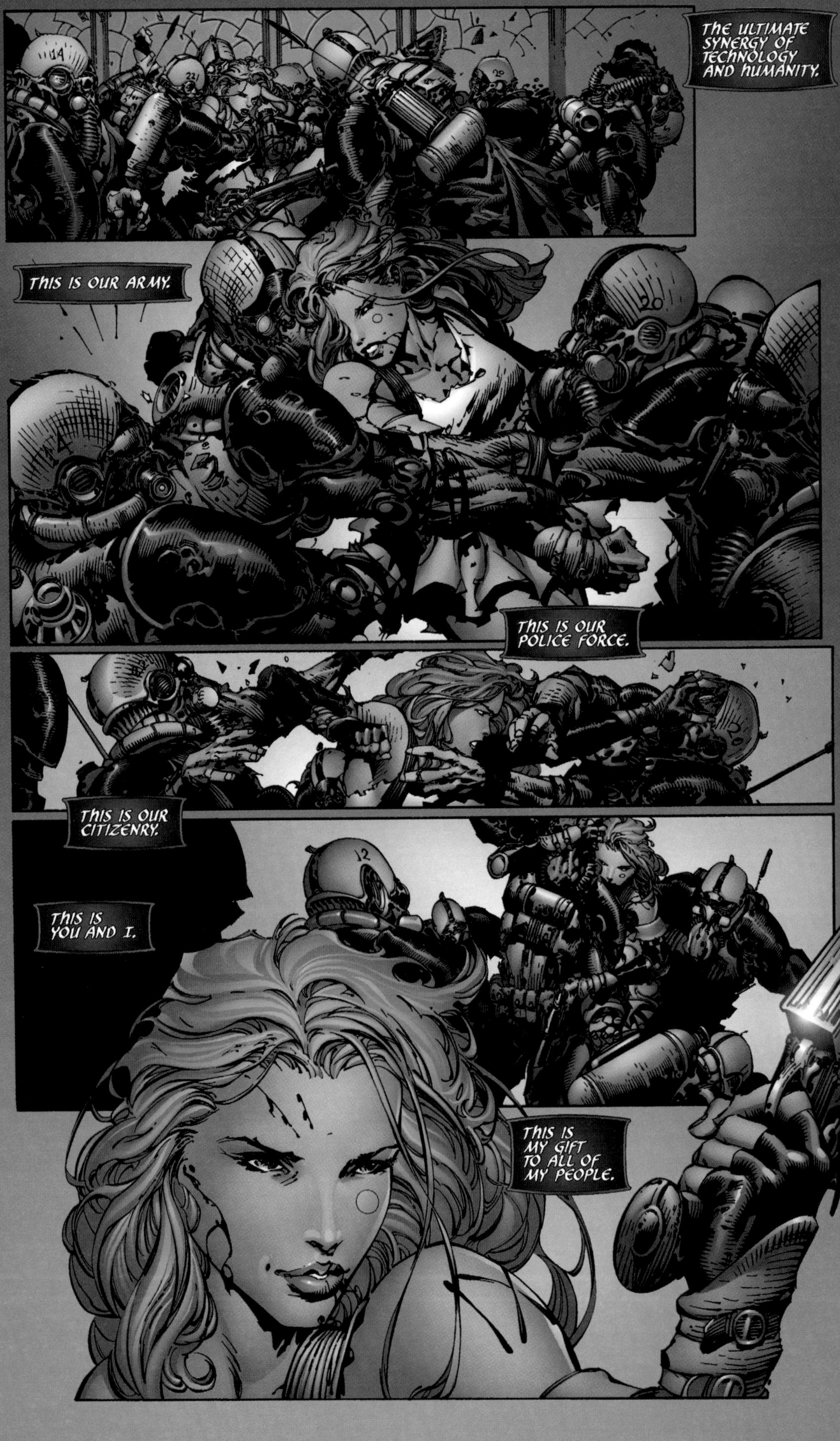
THE ULTIMATE SYNERGY OF TECHNOLOGY AND HUMANITY.
THIS IS OUR ARMY.
THIS IS OUR POLICE FORCE.
THIS IS OUR CITIZENRY.
THIS IS YOU AND I.
THIS IS MY GIFT TO ALL OF MY PEOPLE.

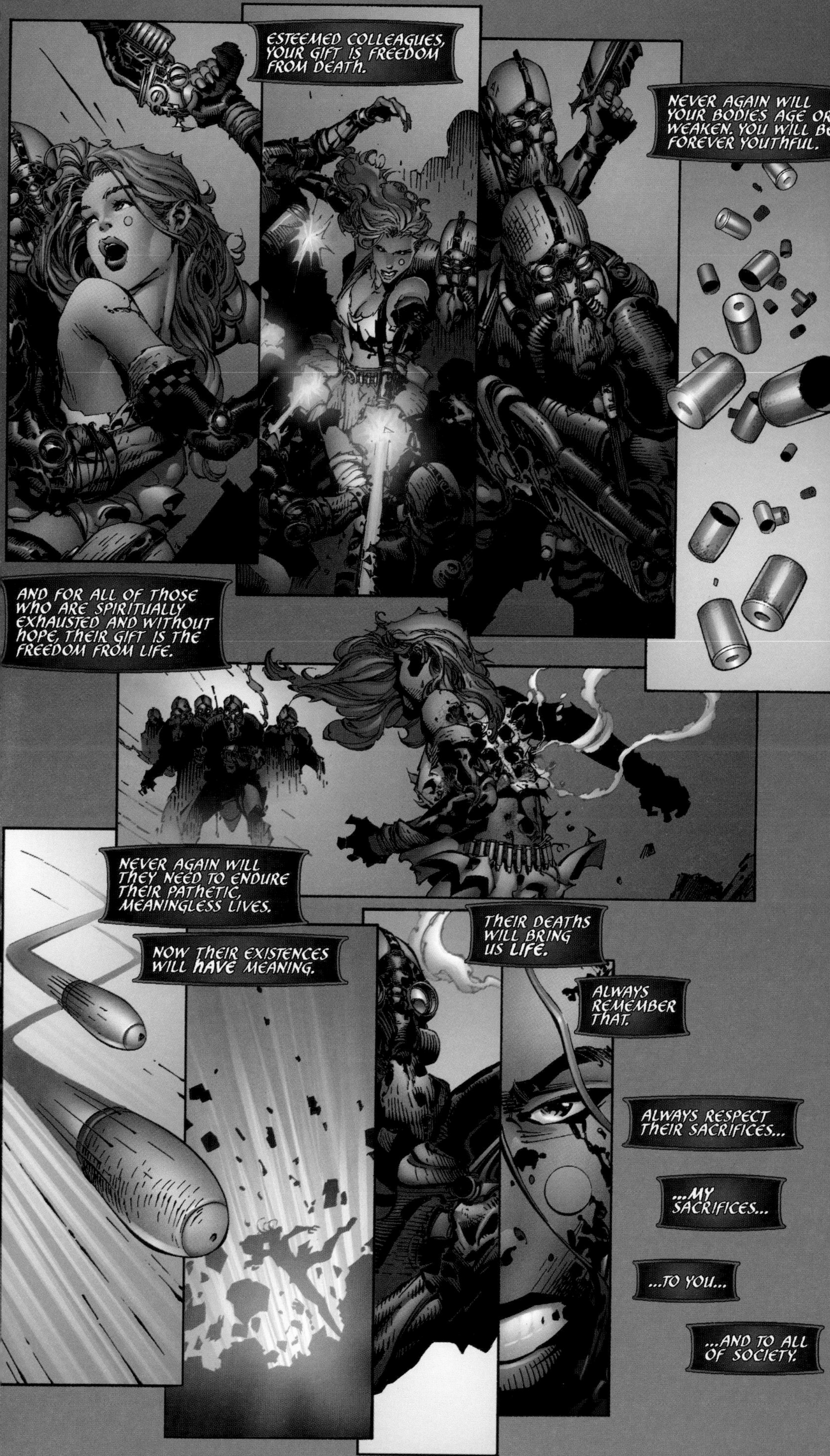
ESTEEMED COLLEAGUES, YOUR GIFT IS FREEDOM FROM DEATH.
NEVER AGAIN WILL YOUR BODIES AGE OR WEAKEN. YOU WILL BE FOREVER YOUTHFUL.
AND FOR ALL OF THOSE WHO ARE SPIRITUALLY EXHAUSTED AND WITHOUT HOPE, THEIR GIFT IS THE FREEDOM FROM LIFE.
NEVER AGAIN WILL THEY NEED TO ENDURE THEIR PATHETIC, MEANINGLESS LIVES.
NOW THEIR EXISTENCES WILL HAVE MEANING.
THEIR DEATHS WILL BRING US LIFE.
ALWAYS REMEMBER THAT.
ALWAYS RESPECT THEIR SACRIFICES...
...MY SACRIFICES...
...TO YOU...
...AND TO ALL OF SOCIETY.

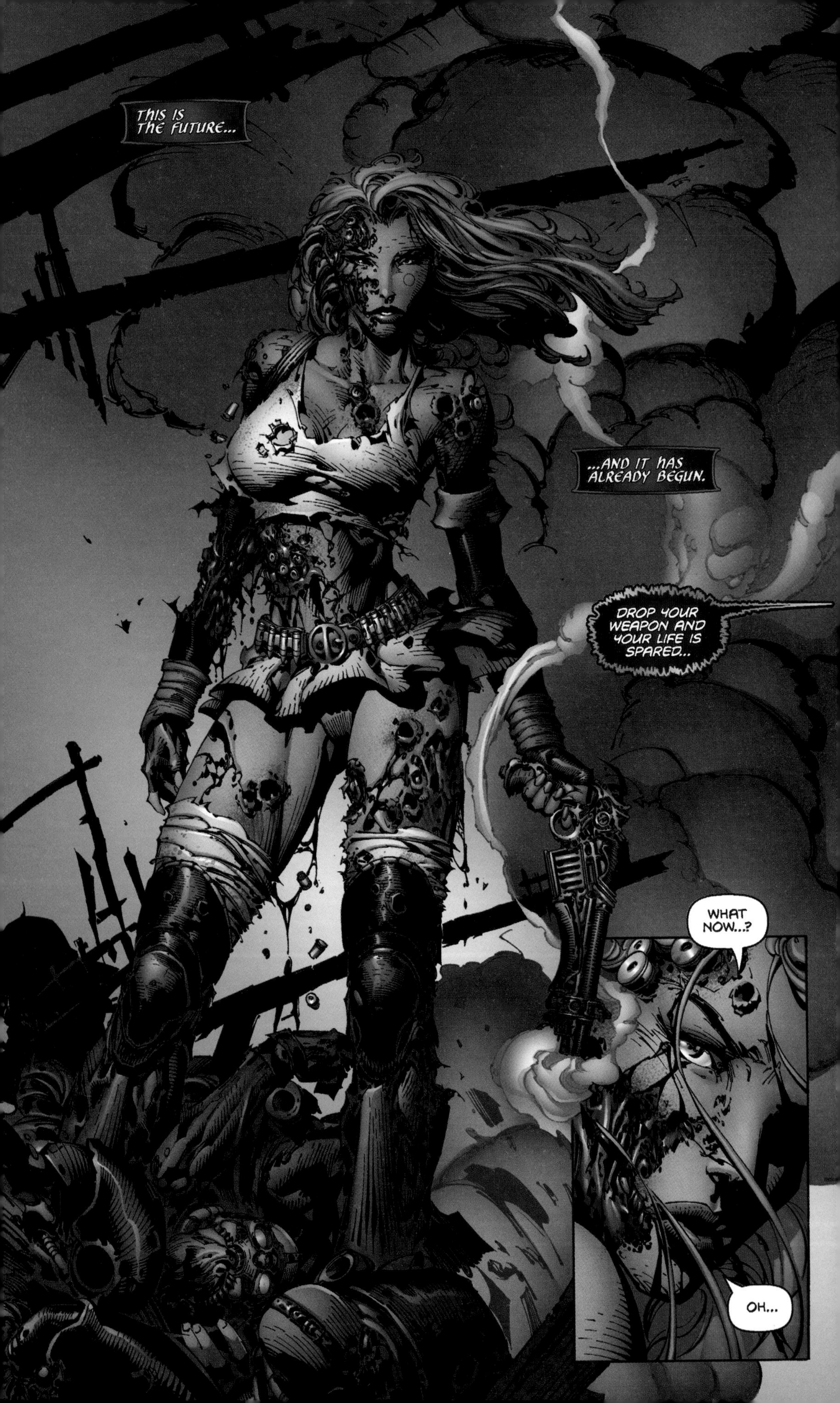
THIS IS THE FUTURE...
...AND IT HAS ALREADY BEGUN.
DROP YOUR WEAPON AND YOUR LIFE IS SPARED...
WHAT NOW...?
OH...

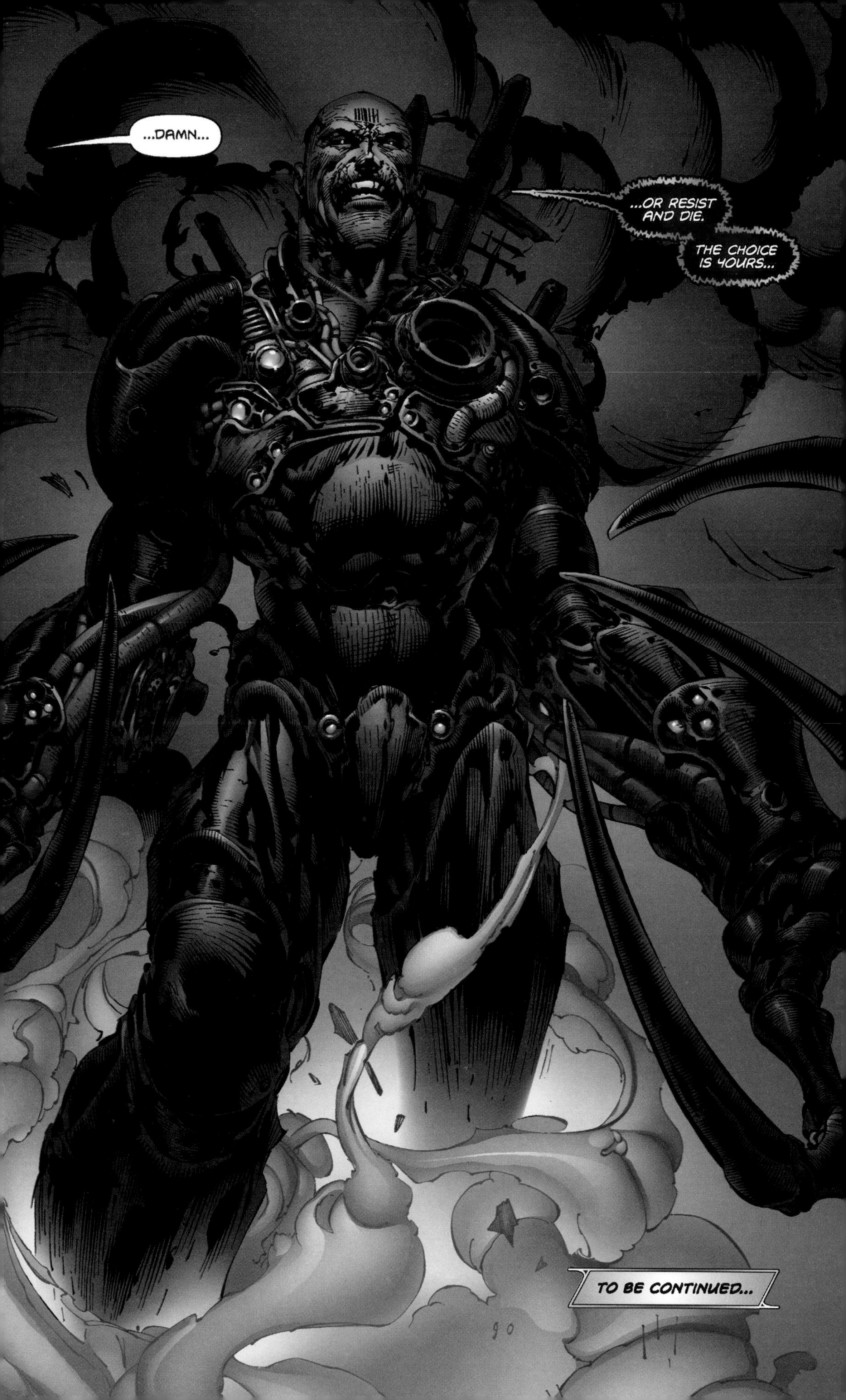
...DAMN...
...OR RESIST AND DIE.
THE CHOICE IS YOURS...
TO BE CONTINUED...

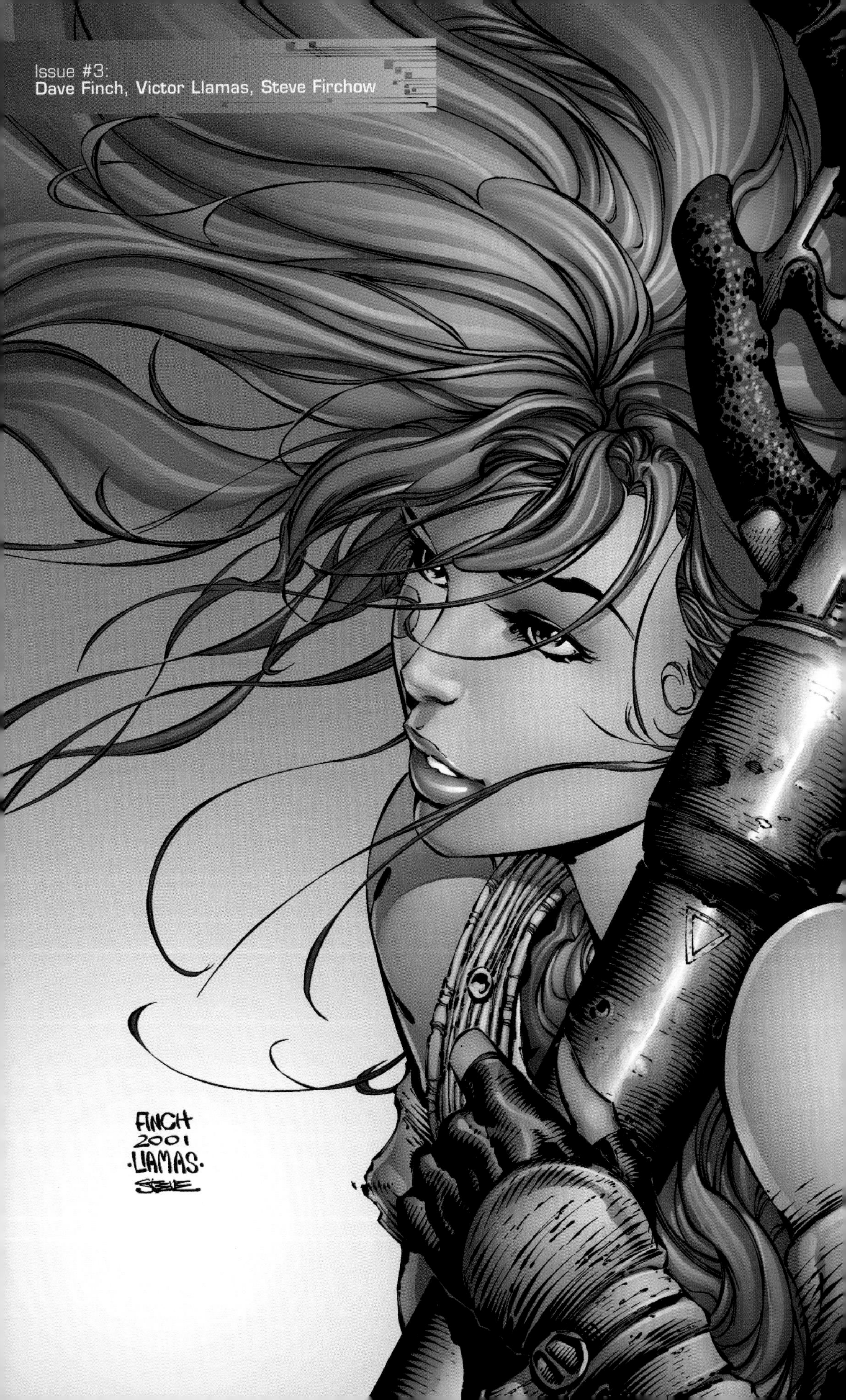
FINCH
2001
·LLAMAS·
STEVE

Issue #3:
Dave Finch, Victor Llamas, Steve Firchow

DONOVAN BLAINE. STRANGLED.

WHY--

QUIET.

COUNCILMAN GABOR OSVATH. CHOKED ON OWN VOMIT. PRESUMED SUICIDE.

WAIT-- I--

SHH. YOU'LL GET YOUR CHANCE TO TALK.

UNDERSECRETARY OF HUMAN DEVELOPMENT KENDALL STOOPS. IMPALED.

DEPUTY CHIEF MARCHRESE CHAVEZ. DROWNED.

SYLVIE DOMISCU. SHOT IN THE HEAD.

HORACE MACK. BLED TO DEATH FROM MULTIPLE STAB WOUNDS.

ANTOINE ECHOLS. MULTIPLE IMPACTS ON HIS HEAD FROM A BLUNT OBJECT.

ARCHMINISTER GASTON EDWARDS. BURNED TO DEATH.

CHAIRMAN'S ADMINISTRATIVE ADVISOR ON GENETIC AFFAIRS BERTRAM CHUN. POISONED.

TROY HUDSON. DECAPITATED.

COUNCILMAN ELECT FERDINAND NESBY. ELECTROCUTED.

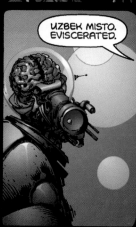

UZBEK MISTO. EVISCERATED.

SECRETARY OF SYSTEM ANALYSIS ALONZO BANNISTER. CRUSHED BY HIS OWN VEHICLE.

MALIK LOPRESTI. PERFORATED LUNGS.

LIEUTENANT GENERAL SYLVESTER WISTROM. ARTIFICIALLY GENERATED CARDIAC ARREST.

VANESSA HALLOWELL. DISSOLVED BY CAUSTIC SUBSTANCE.

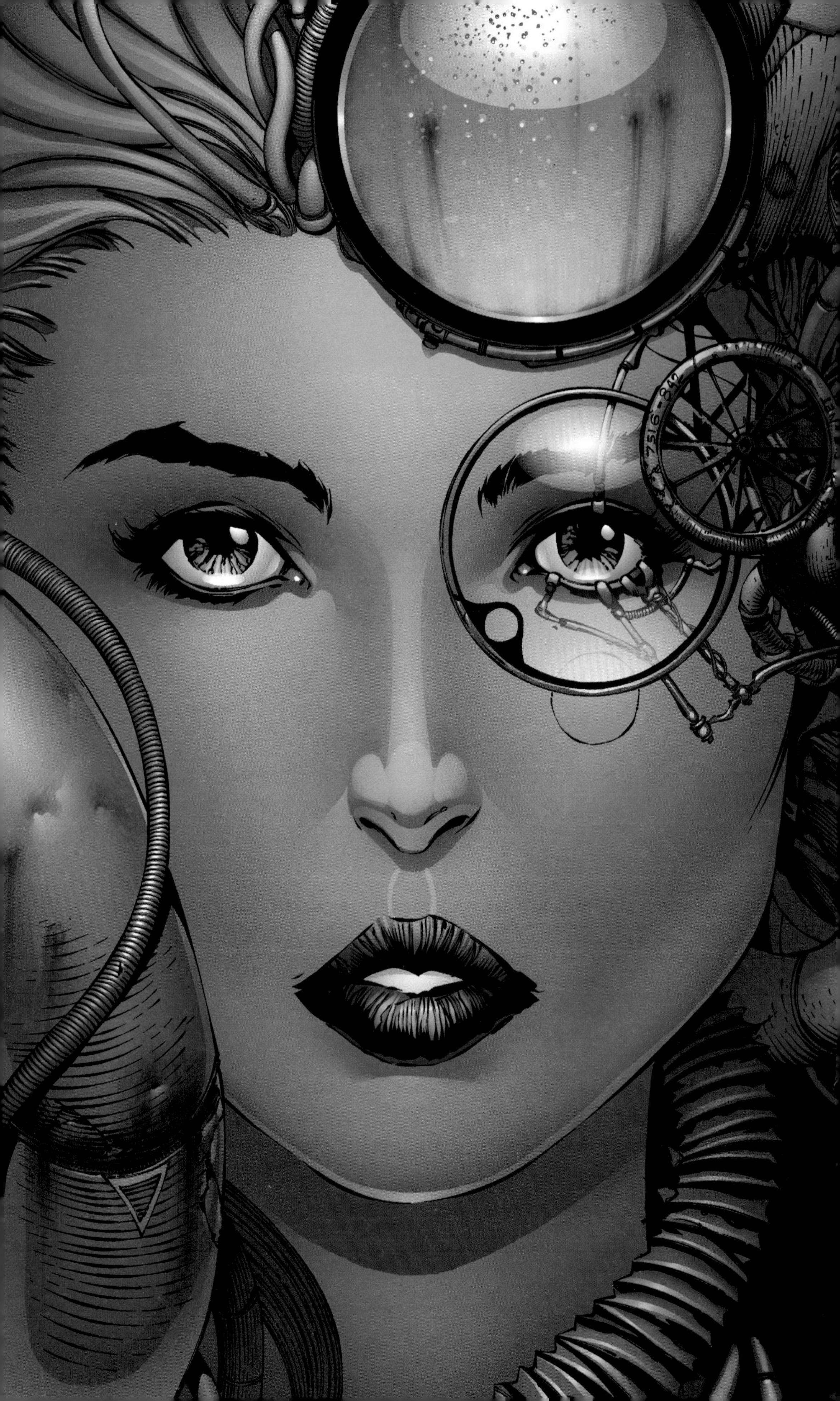
7516-842

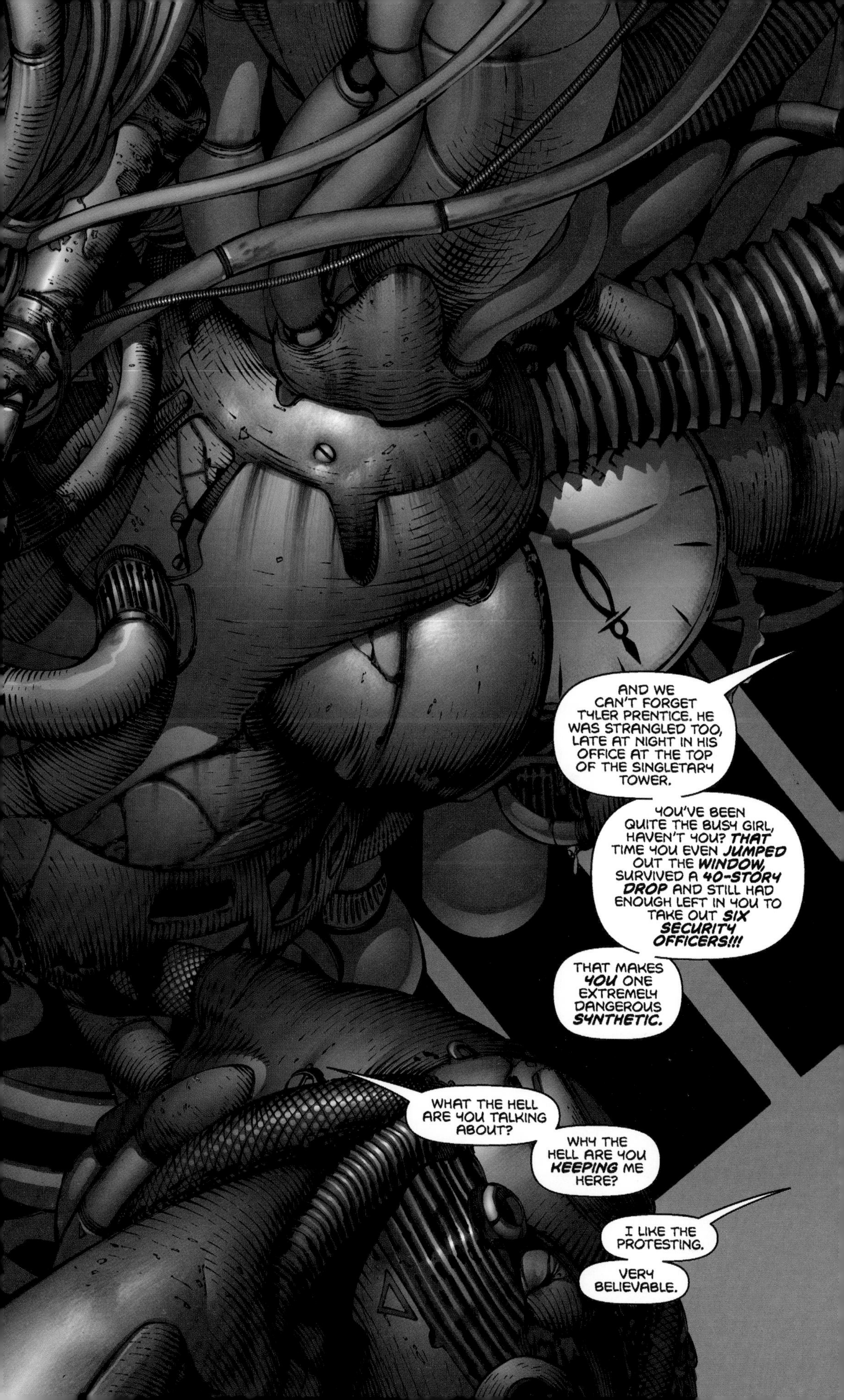
AND WE CAN'T FORGET TYLER PRENTICE. HE WAS STRANGLED TOO, LATE AT NIGHT IN HIS OFFICE AT THE TOP OF THE SINGLETARY TOWER.
YOU'VE BEEN QUITE THE BUSY GIRL, HAVEN'T YOU? THAT TIME YOU EVEN JUMPED OUT THE WINDOW, SURVIVED A 40-STORY DROP AND STILL HAD ENOUGH LEFT IN YOU TO TAKE OUT SIX SECURITY OFFICERS!!!
THAT MAKES YOU ONE EXTREMELY DANGEROUS SYNTHETIC.
WHAT THE HELL ARE YOU TALKING ABOUT?
WHY THE HELL ARE YOU KEEPING ME HERE?
I LIKE THE PROTESTING.
VERY BELIEVABLE.

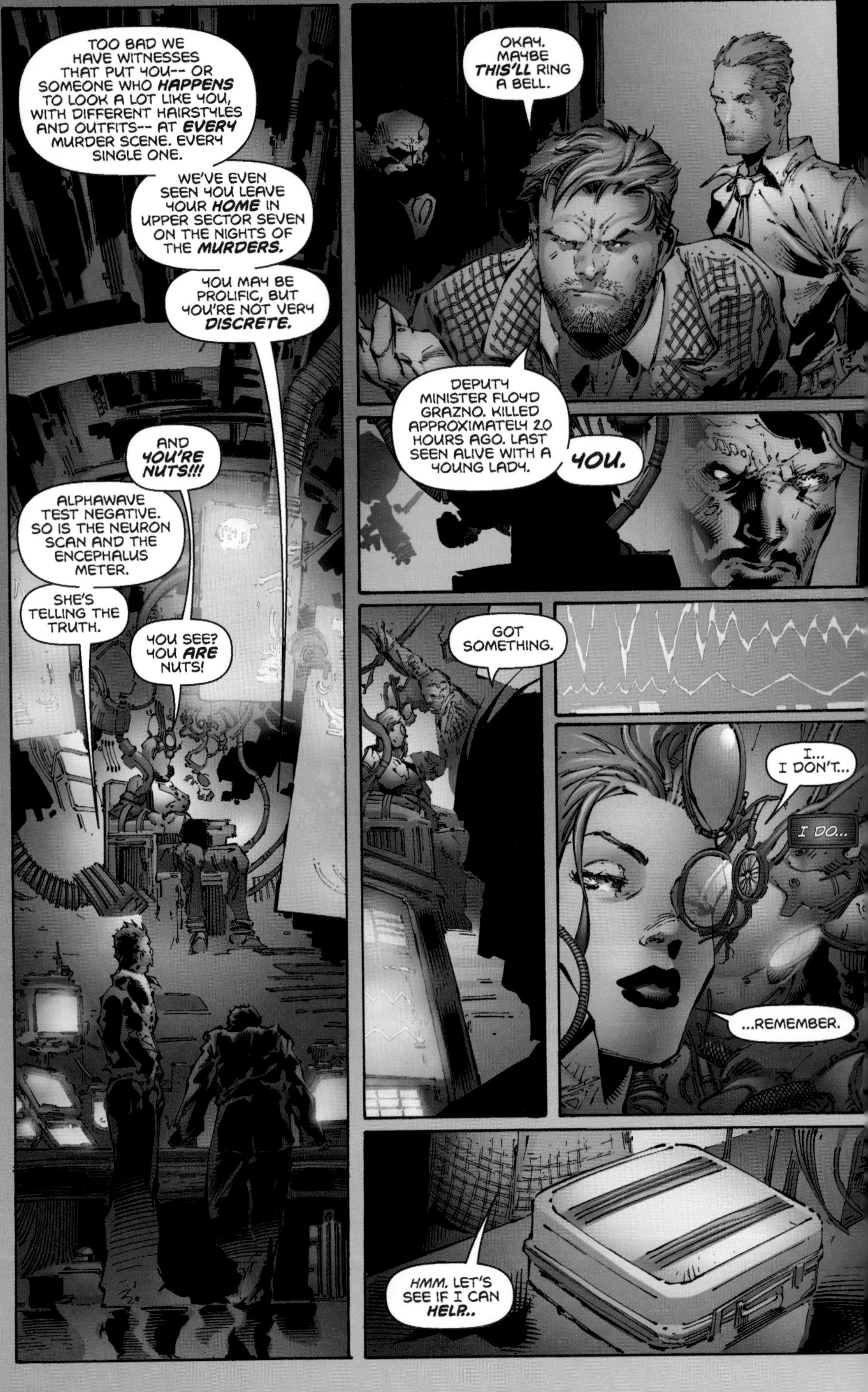
TOO BAD WE HAVE WITNESSES THAT PUT YOU-- OR SOMEONE WHO HAPPENS TO LOOK A LOT LIKE YOU, WITH DIFFERENT HAIRSTYLES AND OUTFITS-- AT EVERY MURDER SCENE. EVERY SINGLE ONE.
WE'VE EVEN SEEN YOU LEAVE YOUR HOME IN UPPER SECTOR SEVEN ON THE NIGHTS OF THE MURDERS.
YOU MAY BE PROLIFIC, BUT YOU'RE NOT VERY DISCRETE.
AND YOU'RE NUTS!!!
ALPHAWAVE TEST NEGATIVE. SO IS THE NEURON SCAN AND THE ENCEPHALUS METER.
SHE'S TELLING THE TRUTH.
YOU SEE? YOU ARE NUTS!
OKAY. MAYBE THIS'LL RING A BELL.
DEPUTY MINISTER FLOYD GRAZNO. KILLED APPROXIMATELY 20 HOURS AGO. LAST SEEN ALIVE WITH A YOUNG LADY.
YOU.
GOT SOMETHING.
I... I DON'T...
I DO...
...REMEMBER.
HMM. LET'S SEE IF I CAN HELP..

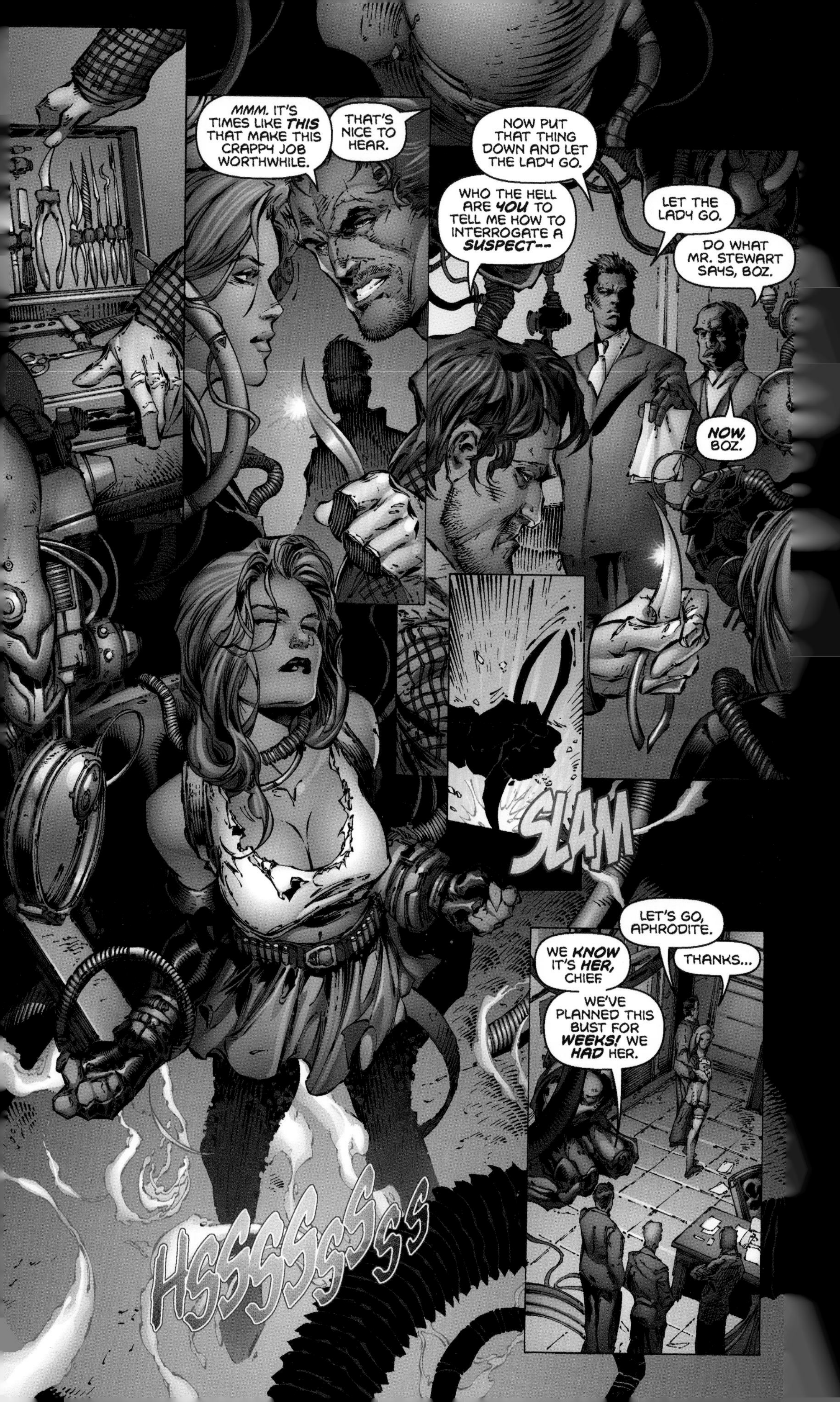
MMM. IT'S TIMES LIKE THIS THAT MAKE THIS CRAPPY JOB WORTHWHILE.
THAT'S NICE TO HEAR.
NOW PUT THAT THING DOWN AND LET THE LADY GO.
WHO THE HELL ARE YOU TO TELL ME HOW TO INTERROGATE A SUSPECT--
LET THE LADY GO.
DO WHAT MR. STEWART SAYS, BOZ.
NOW, BOZ.
SLAM
HSSSSSSSS
LET'S GO, APHRODITE.
WE KNOW IT'S HER, CHIEF.
WE'VE PLANNED THIS BUST FOR WEEKS! WE HAD HER.
THANKS...

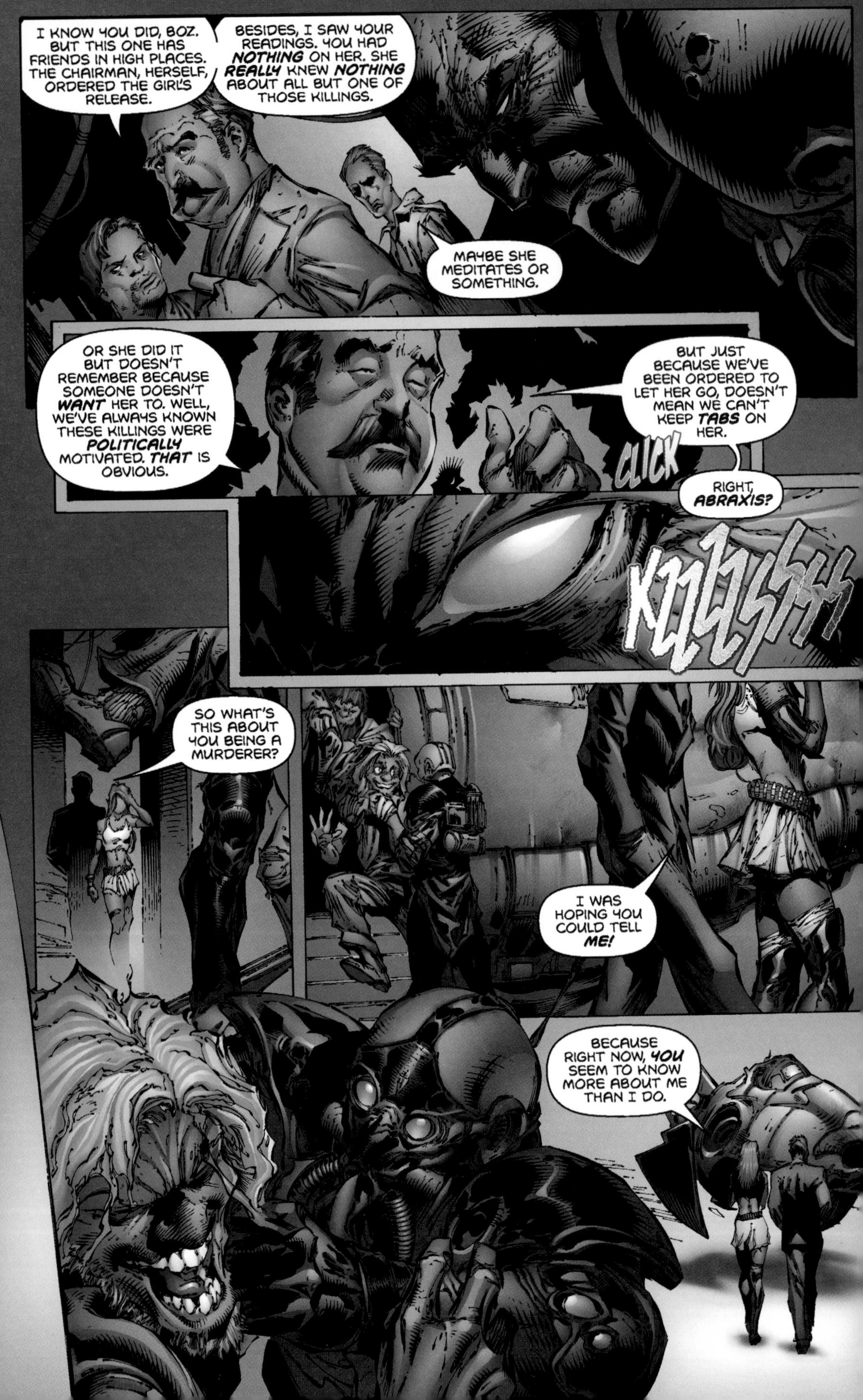

I KNOW YOU DID, BOZ. BUT THIS ONE HAS FRIENDS IN HIGH PLACES. THE CHAIRMAN, HERSELF, ORDERED THE GIRL'S RELEASE.
BESIDES, I SAW YOUR READINGS. YOU HAD NOTHING ON HER. SHE REALLY KNEW NOTHING ABOUT ALL BUT ONE OF THOSE KILLINGS.
MAYBE SHE MEDITATES OR SOMETHING.
OR SHE DID IT BUT DOESN'T REMEMBER BECAUSE SOMEONE DOESN'T WANT HER TO. WELL, WE'VE ALWAYS KNOWN THESE KILLINGS WERE POLITICALLY MOTIVATED. THAT IS OBVIOUS.
BUT JUST BECAUSE WE'VE BEEN ORDERED TO LET HER GO, DOESN'T MEAN WE CAN'T KEEP TABS ON HER.
CLICK
RIGHT, ABRAXIS?
KZZZSSH
SO WHAT'S THIS ABOUT YOU BEING A MURDERER?
I WAS HOPING YOU COULD TELL ME!
BECAUSE RIGHT NOW, YOU SEEM TO KNOW MORE ABOUT ME THAN I DO.

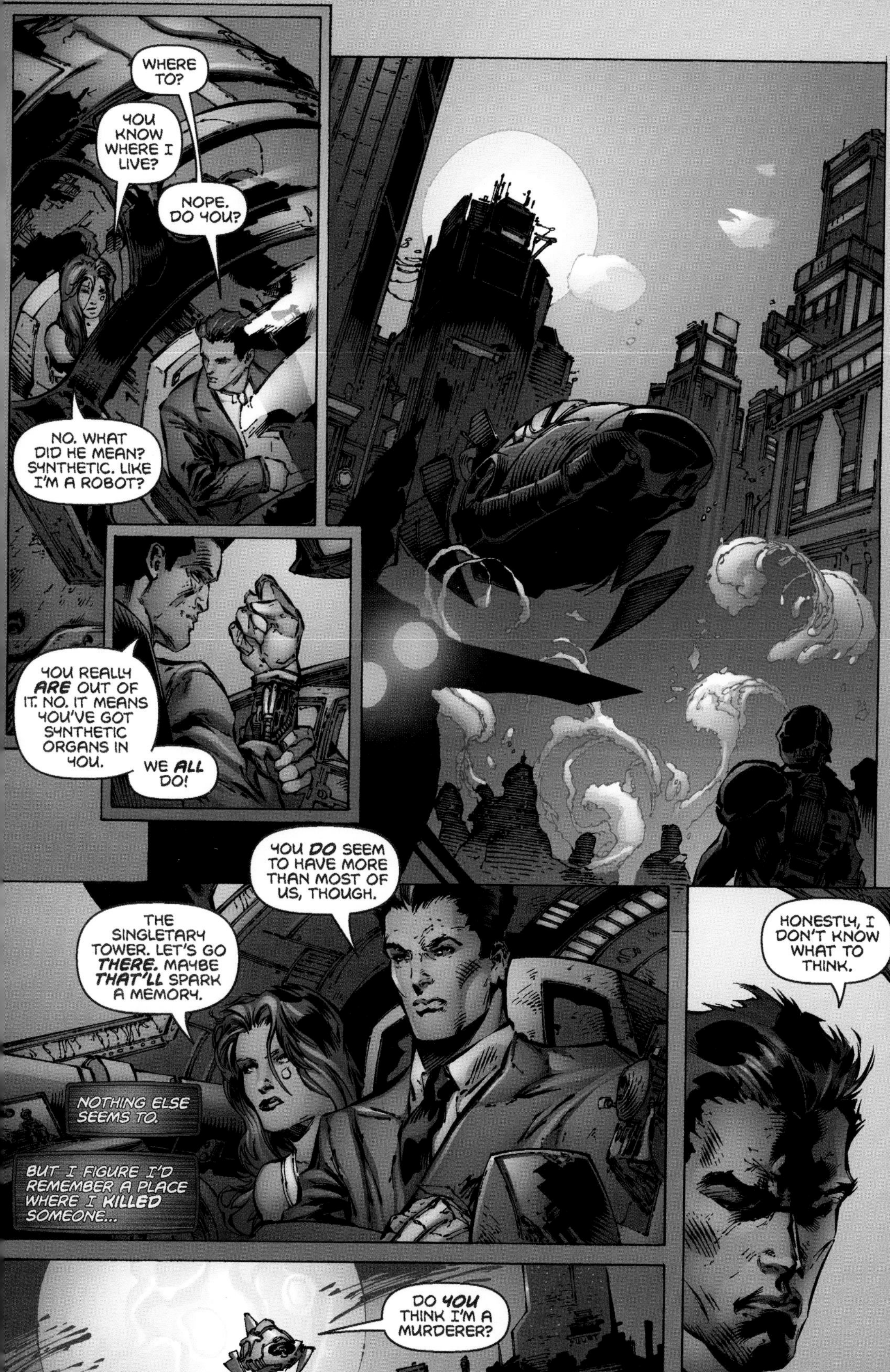

WHERE TO?
YOU KNOW WHERE I LIVE?
NOPE. DO YOU?
NO. WHAT DID HE MEAN? SYNTHETIC. LIKE I'M A ROBOT?
YOU REALLY ARE OUT OF IT. NO. IT MEANS YOU'VE GOT SYNTHETIC ORGANS IN YOU.
WE ALL DO!
YOU DO SEEM TO HAVE MORE THAN MOST OF US, THOUGH.
THE SINGLETARY TOWER. LET'S GO THERE. MAYBE THAT'LL SPARK A MEMORY.
NOTHING ELSE SEEMS TO.
BUT I FIGURE I'D REMEMBER A PLACE WHERE I KILLED SOMEONE...
HONESTLY, I DON'T KNOW WHAT TO THINK.
DO YOU THINK I'M A MURDERER?

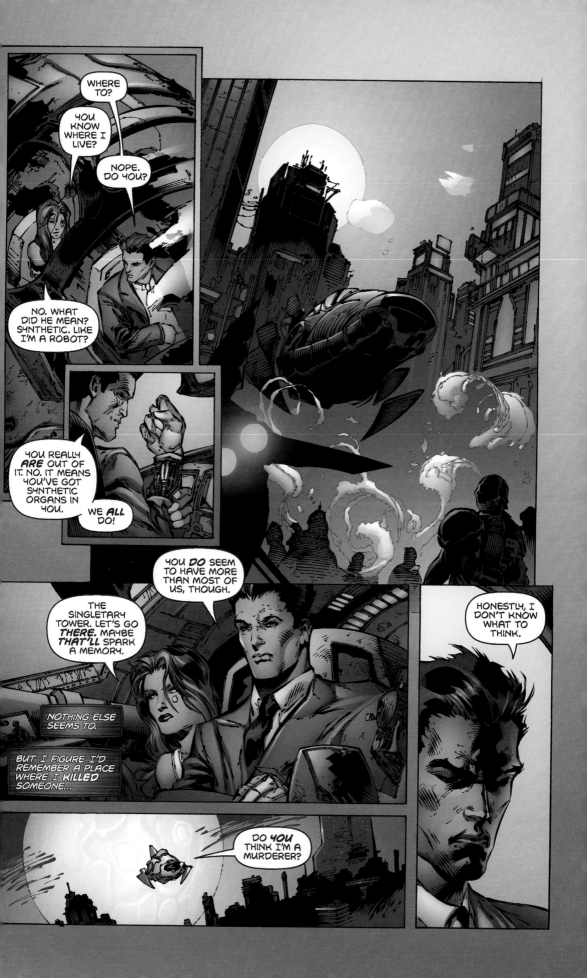

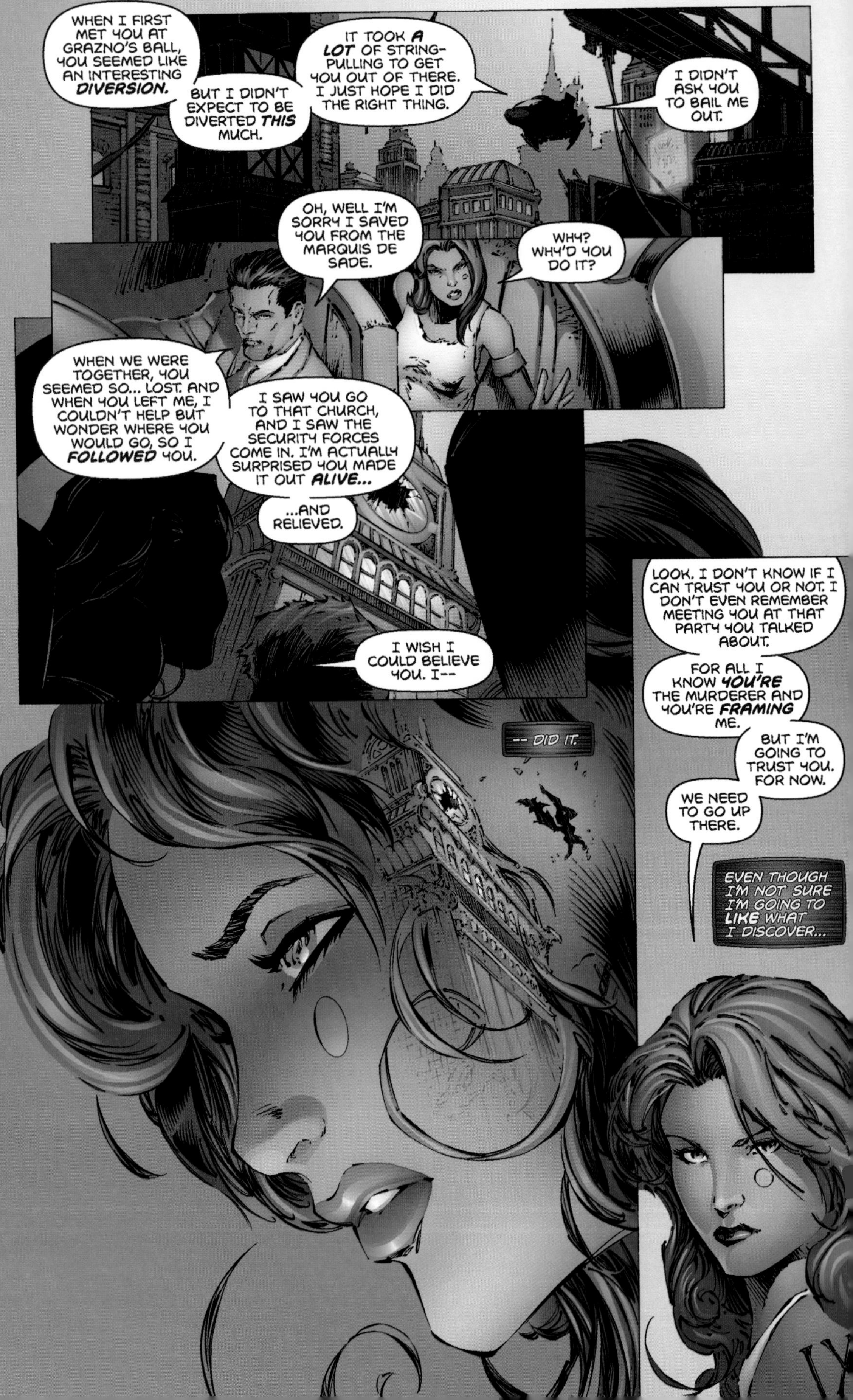

WHEN I FIRST MET YOU AT GRAZNO'S BALL, YOU SEEMED LIKE AN INTERESTING DIVERSION.
BUT I DIDN'T EXPECT TO BE DIVERTED THIS MUCH.
IT TOOK A LOT OF STRING-PULLING TO GET YOU OUT OF THERE. I JUST HOPE I DID THE RIGHT THING.
I DIDN'T ASK YOU TO BAIL ME OUT.
OH, WELL I'M SORRY I SAVED YOU FROM THE MARQUIS DE SADE.
WHY? WHY'D YOU DO IT?
WHEN WE WERE TOGETHER, YOU SEEMED SO... LOST. AND WHEN YOU LEFT ME, I COULDN'T HELP BUT WONDER WHERE YOU WOULD GO, SO I FOLLOWED YOU.
I SAW YOU GO TO THAT CHURCH, AND I SAW THE SECURITY FORCES COME IN. I'M ACTUALLY SURPRISED YOU MADE IT OUT ALIVE...
...AND RELIEVED.
I WISH I COULD BELIEVE YOU. I--
-- DID IT.
LOOK. I DON'T KNOW IF I CAN TRUST YOU OR NOT. I DON'T EVEN REMEMBER MEETING YOU AT THAT PARTY YOU TALKED ABOUT.
FOR ALL I KNOW YOU'RE THE MURDERER AND YOU'RE FRAMING ME.
BUT I'M GOING TO TRUST YOU. FOR NOW.
WE NEED TO GO UP THERE.
EVEN THOUGH I'M NOT SURE I'M GOING TO LIKE WHAT I DISCOVER...

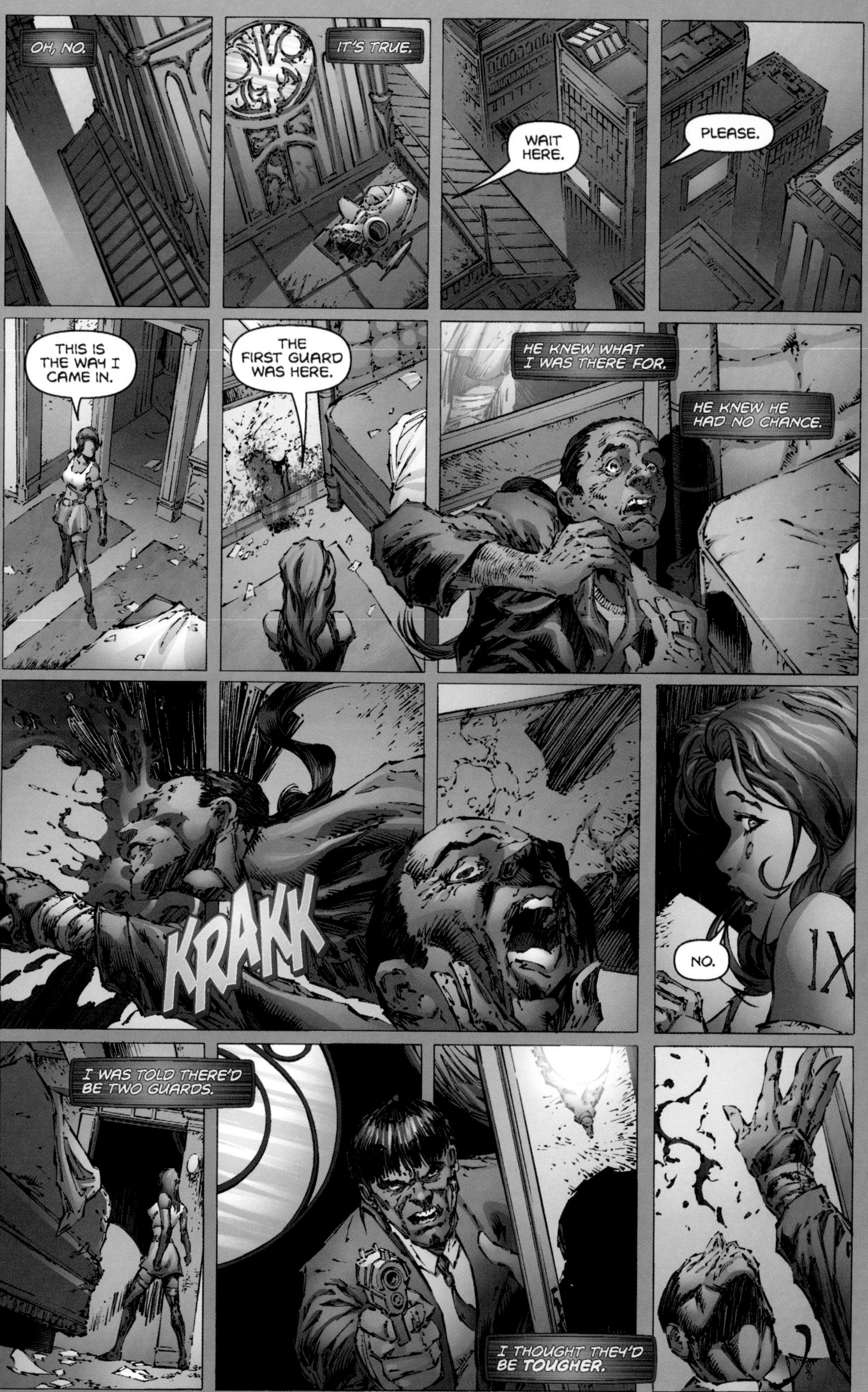

OH, NO.
IT'S TRUE.
WAIT HERE.
PLEASE.
THIS IS THE WAY I CAME IN.
THE FIRST GUARD WAS HERE.
HE KNEW WHAT I WAS THERE FOR.
HE KNEW HE HAD NO CHANCE.
KRAKK
NO.
IX
I WAS TOLD THERE'D BE TWO GUARDS.
I THOUGHT THEY'D BE TOUGHER.

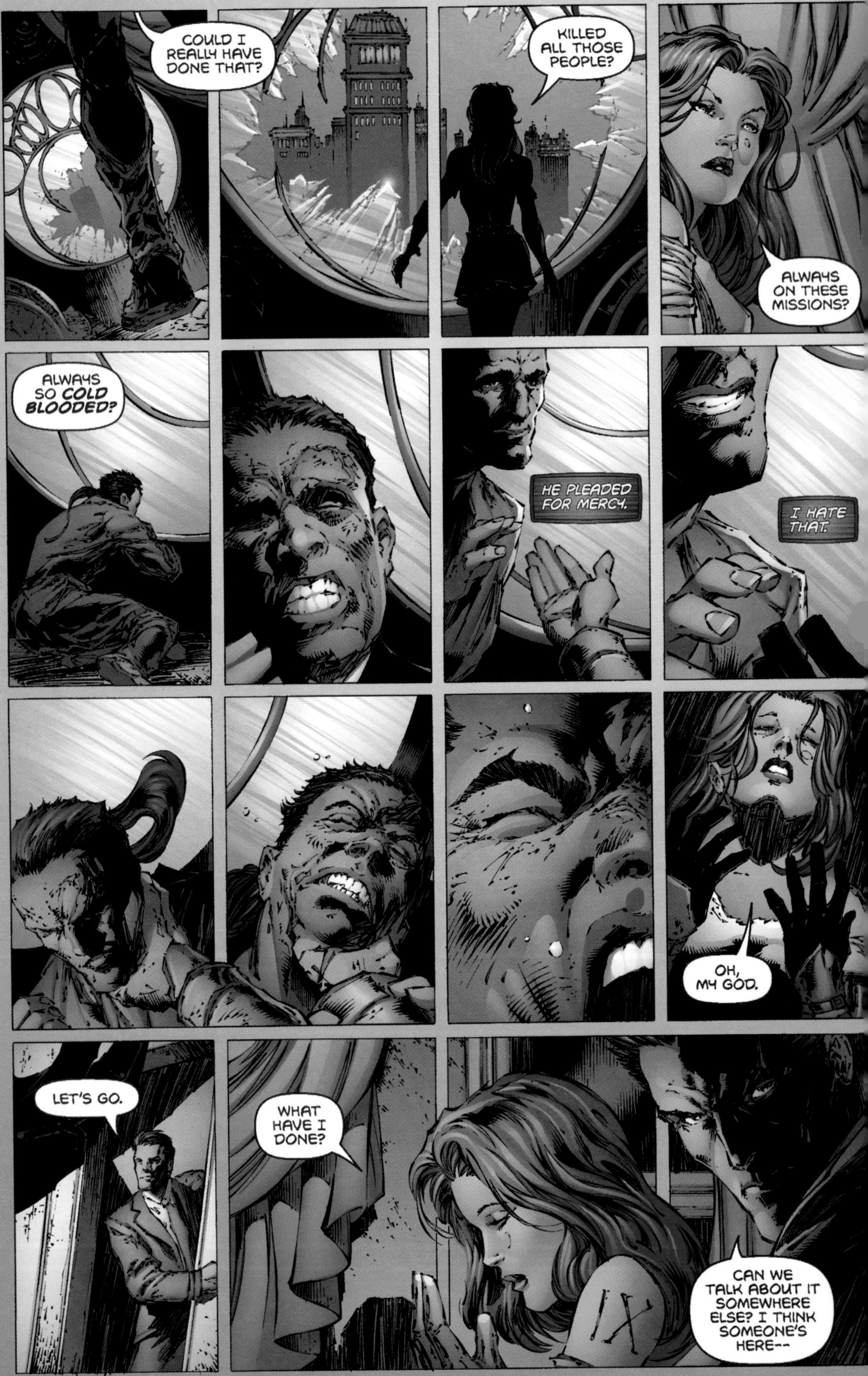
COULD I REALLY HAVE DONE THAT?
KILLED ALL THOSE PEOPLE?
ALWAYS ON THESE MISSIONS?
ALWAYS SO COLD BLOODED?
HE PLEADED FOR MERCY.
I HATE THAT.
OH, MY GOD.
LET'S GO.
WHAT HAVE I DONE?
CAN WE TALK ABOUT IT SOMEWHERE ELSE? I THINK SOMEONE'S HERE--

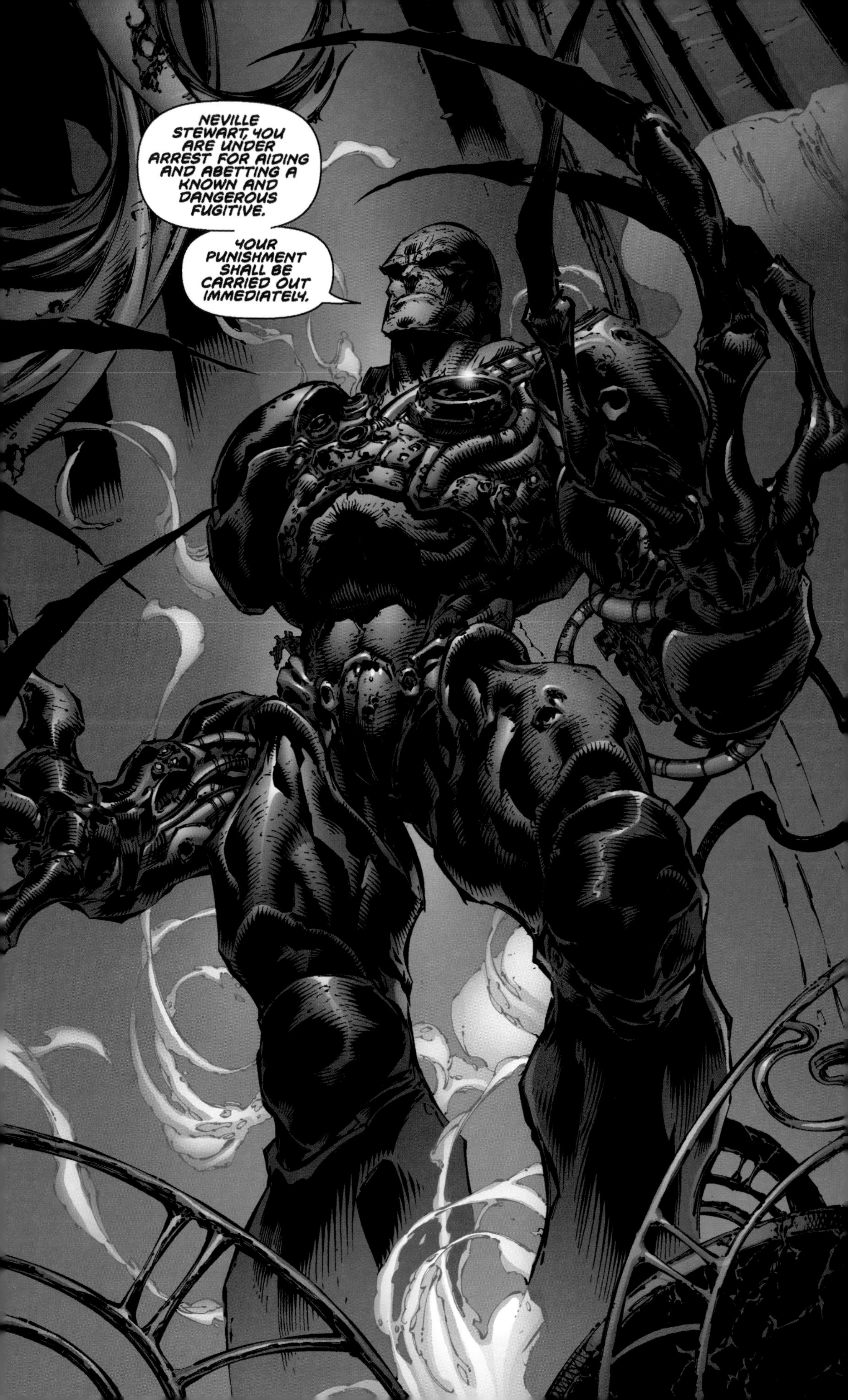
NEVILLE STEWART, YOU ARE UNDER ARREST FOR AIDING AND ABETTING A KNOWN AND DANGEROUS FUGITIVE.
YOUR PUNISHMENT SHALL BE CARRIED OUT IMMEDIATELY.

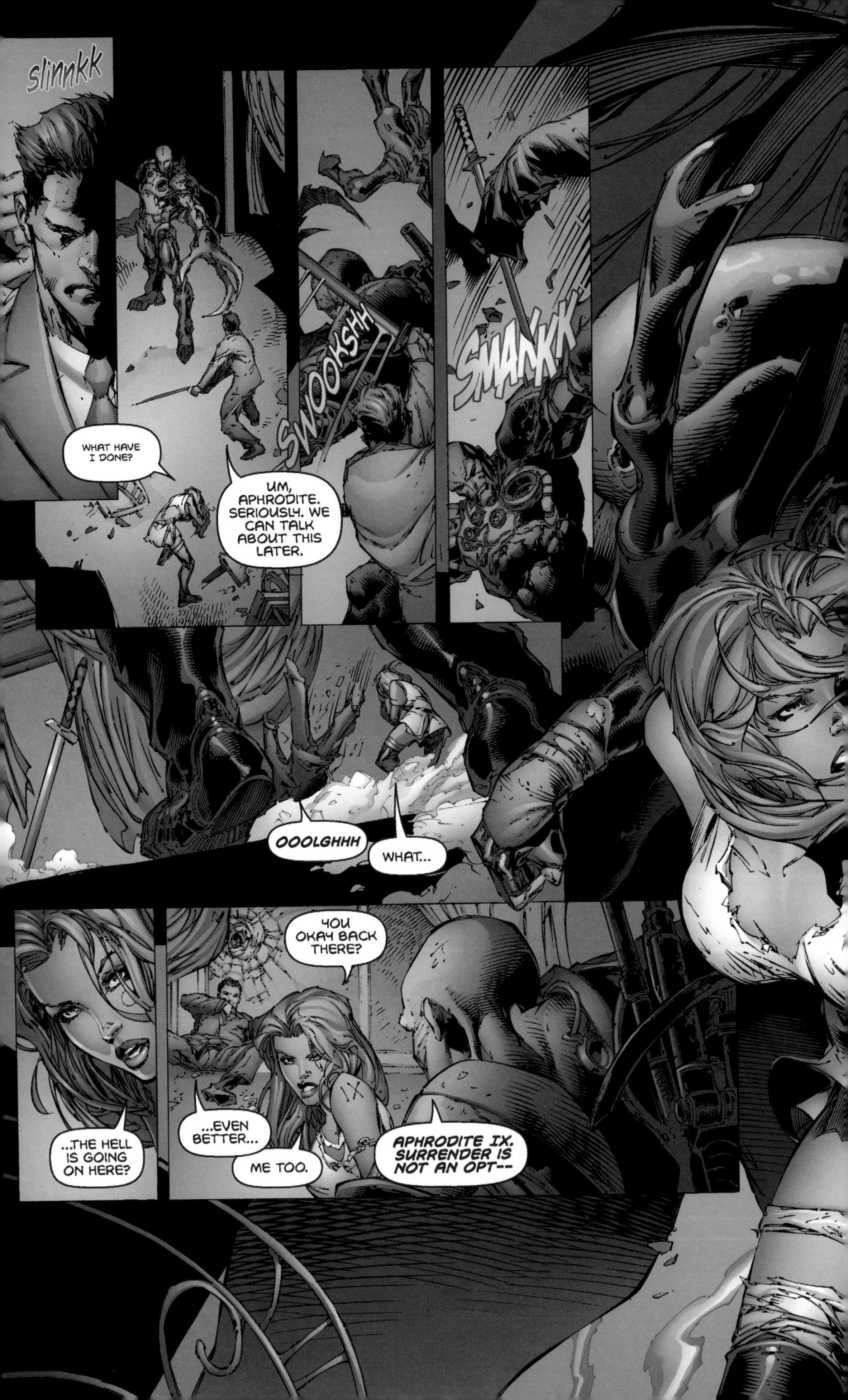
slinnkk
WHAT HAVE I DONE?
UM, APHRODITE. SERIOUSLY. WE CAN TALK ABOUT THIS LATER.
SWOOKSHH
SMANKK
OOOLGHHH
WHAT...
...THE HELL IS GOING ON HERE?
YOU OKAY BACK THERE?
...EVEN BETTER...
ME TOO.
APHRODITE IX. SURRENDER IS NOT AN OPT--

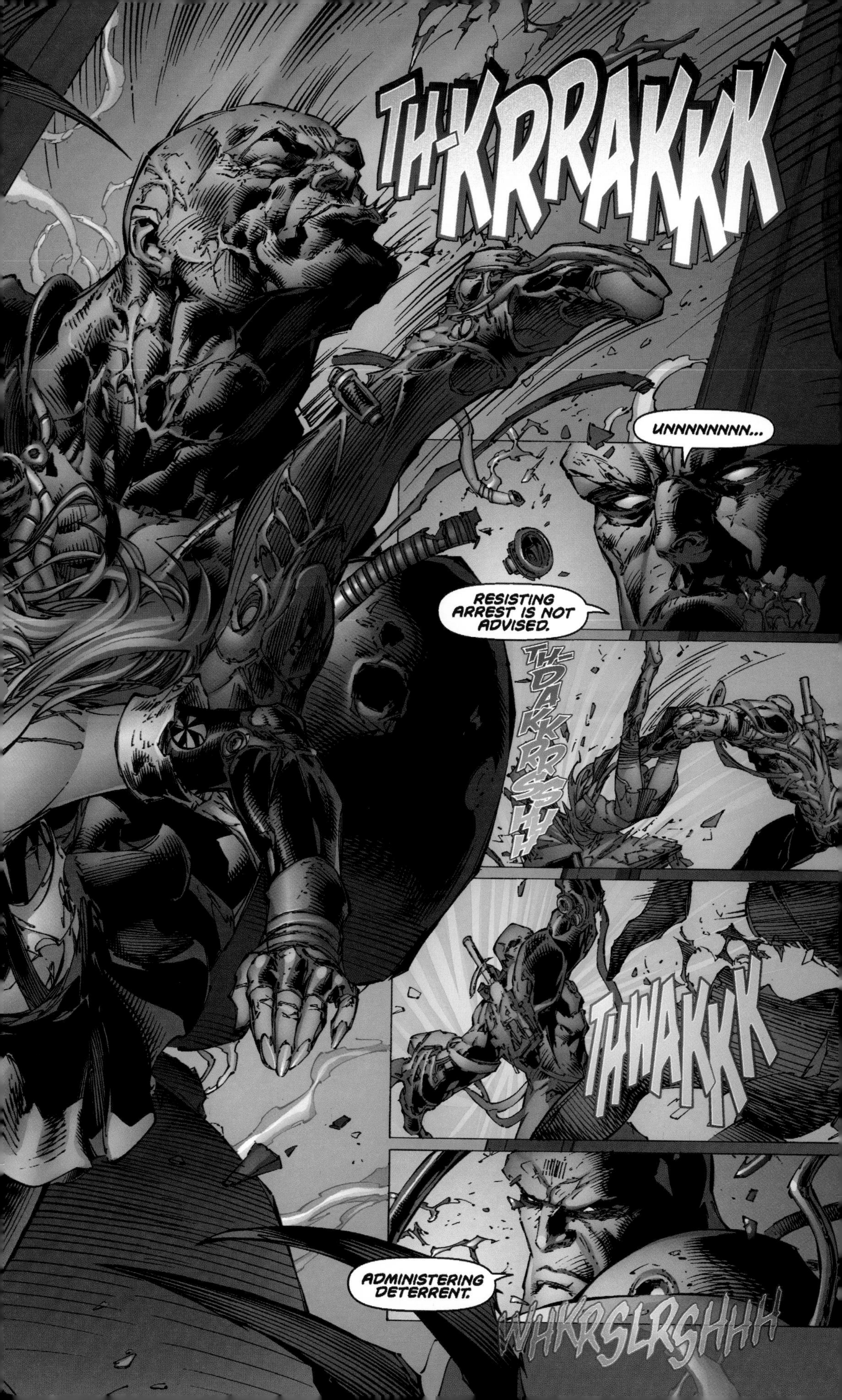
TH-KRRAKKK
UNNNNNNNN...
RESISTING ARREST IS NOT ADVISED.
TH-DAKKRRSSHH
THWAKKK
ADMINISTERING DETERRENT.
WHKRSLRSHHH

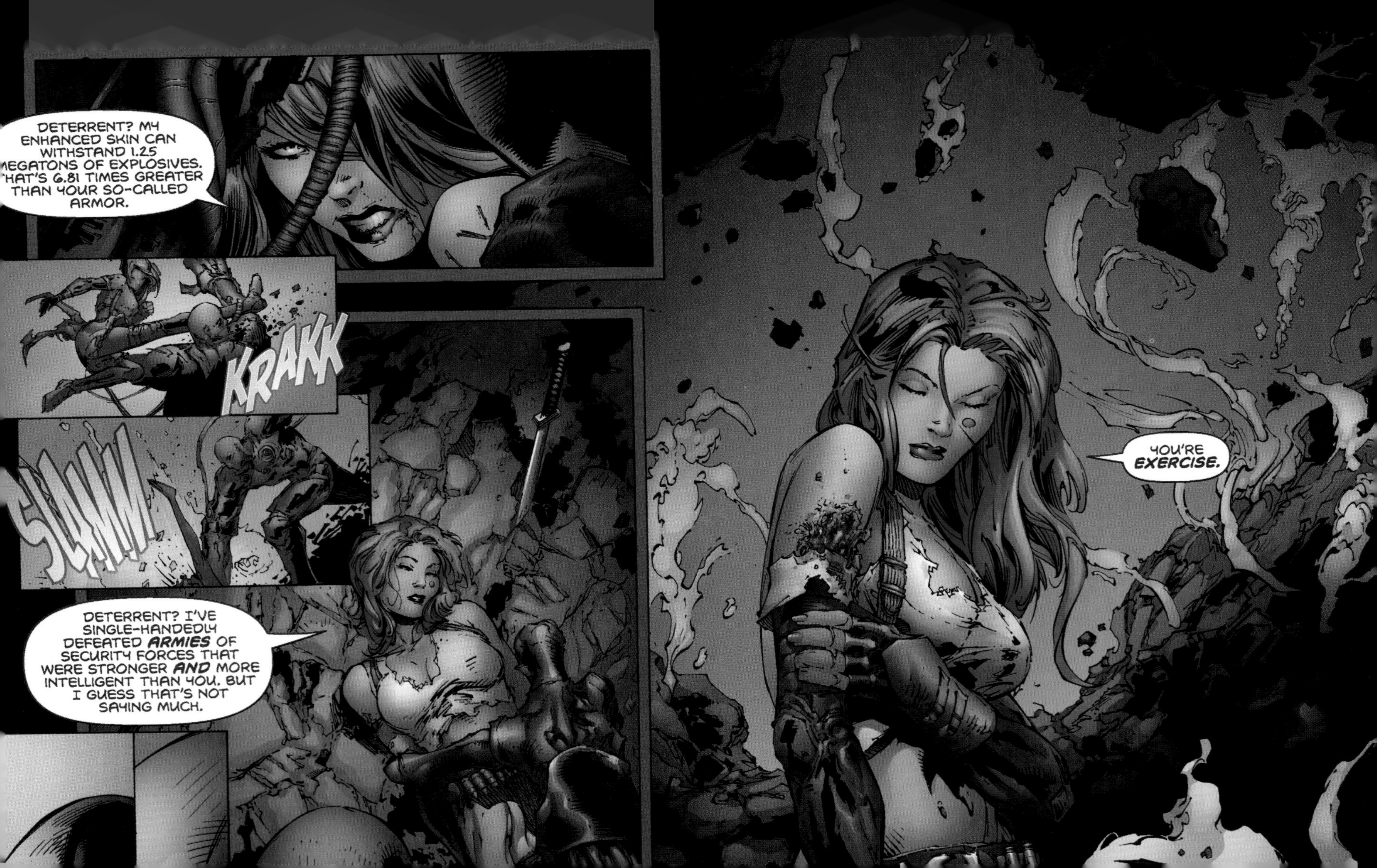

DETERRENT? MY ENHANCED SKIN CAN WITHSTAND 1.25 MEGATONS OF EXPLOSIVES. THAT'S 6.81 TIMES GREATER THAN YOUR SO-CALLED ARMOR.
KRAKK
SLAMM
DETERRENT? I'VE SINGLE-HANDEDLY DEFEATED **ARMIES** OF SECURITY FORCES THAT WERE STRONGER **AND** MORE INTELLIGENT THAN YOU. BUT I GUESS THAT'S NOT SAYING MUCH.
YOU'RE **EXERCISE.**

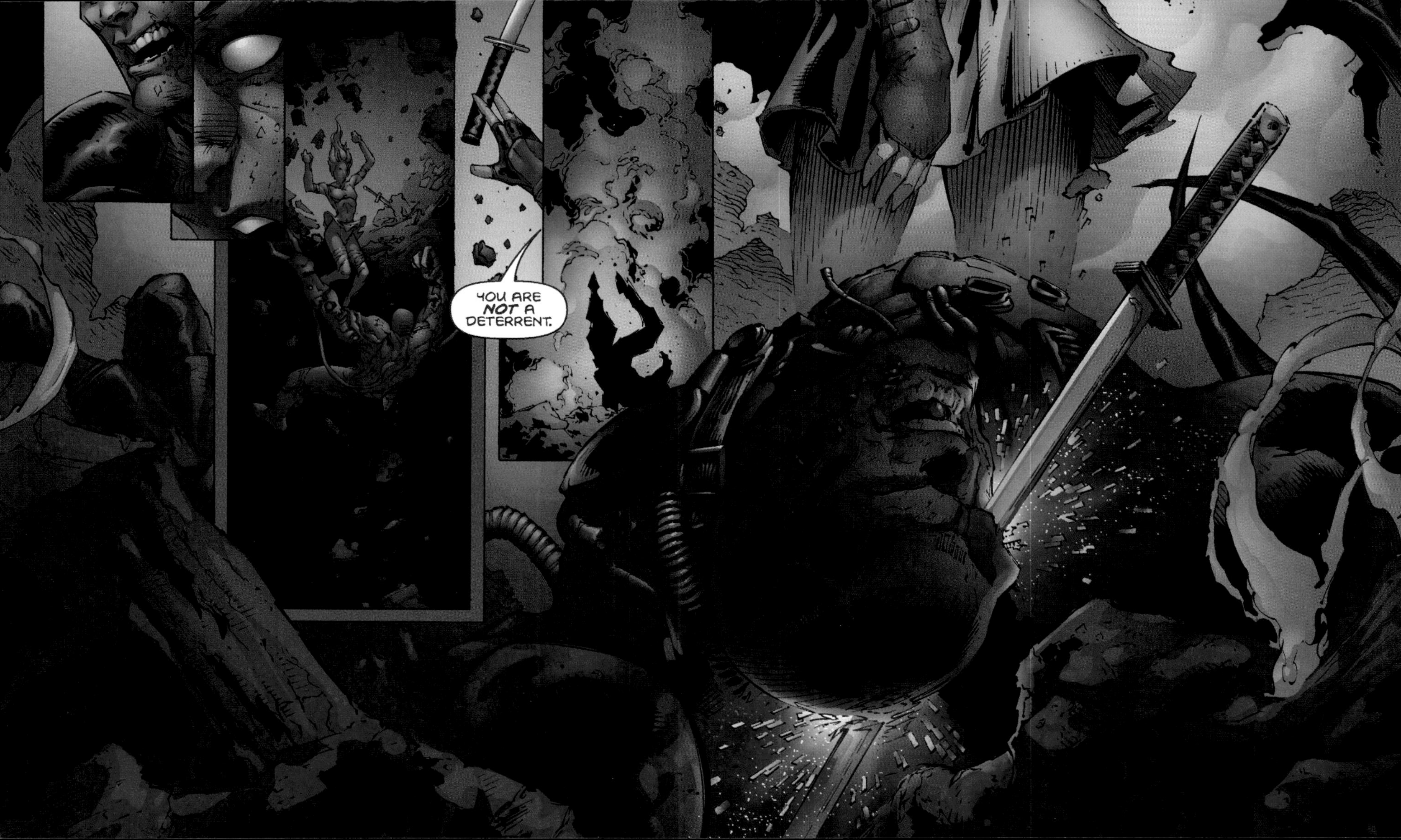
YOU ARE NOT A DETERRENT.

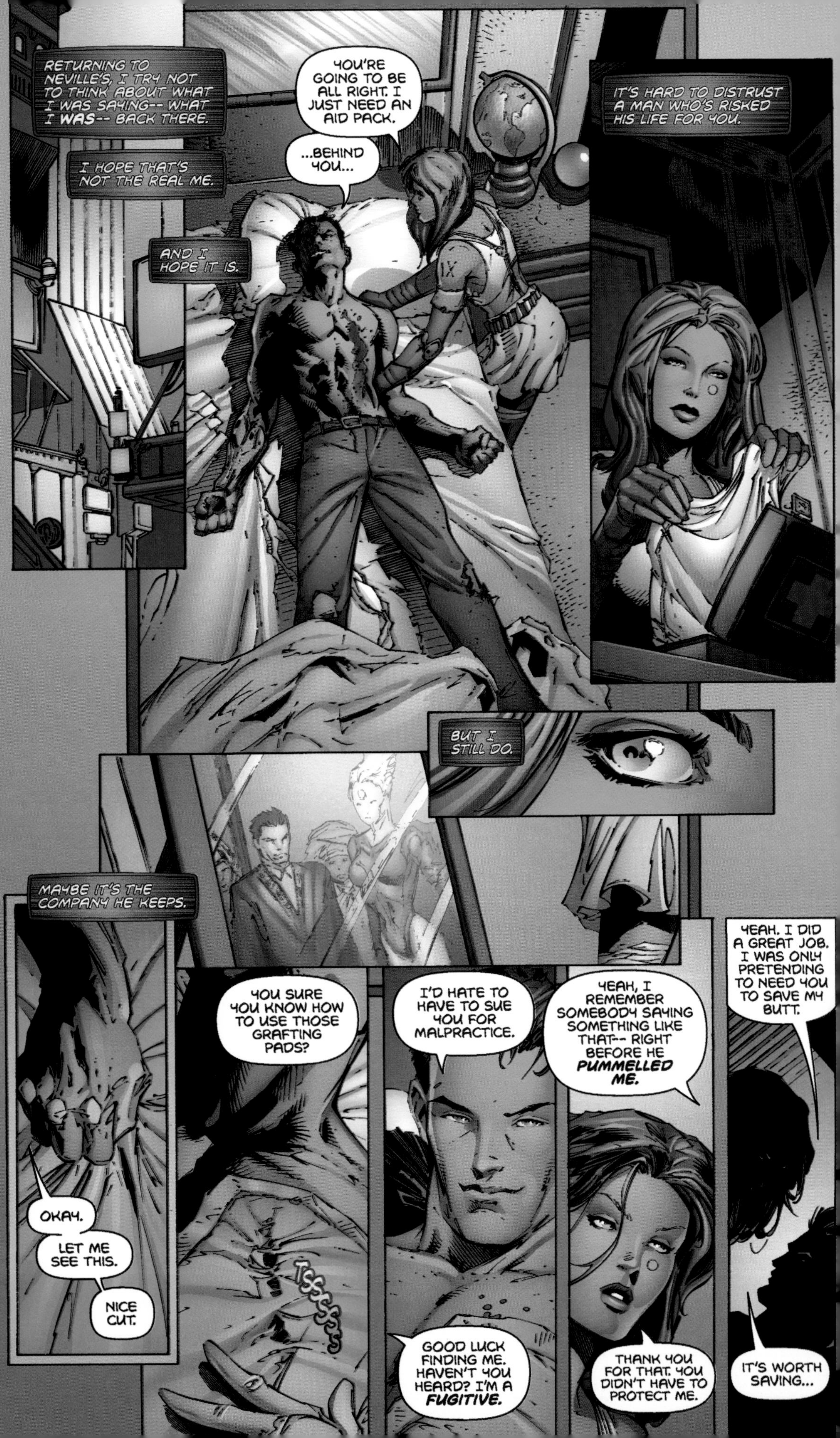
RETURNING TO NEVILLE'S, I TRY NOT TO THINK ABOUT WHAT I WAS SAYING-- WHAT I WAS-- BACK THERE.
I HOPE THAT'S NOT THE REAL ME.
AND I HOPE IT IS.
YOU'RE GOING TO BE ALL RIGHT. I JUST NEED AN AID PACK.
...BEHIND YOU...
IT'S HARD TO DISTRUST A MAN WHO'S RISKED HIS LIFE FOR YOU.
BUT I STILL DO.
MAYBE IT'S THE COMPANY HE KEEPS.
OKAY.
LET ME SEE THIS.
NICE CUT.
YOU SURE YOU KNOW HOW TO USE THOSE GRAFTING PADS?
TSSSSS
I'D HATE TO HAVE TO SUE YOU FOR MALPRACTICE.
GOOD LUCK FINDING ME. HAVEN'T YOU HEARD? I'M A FUGITIVE.
YEAH, I REMEMBER SOMEBODY SAYING SOMETHING LIKE THAT-- RIGHT BEFORE HE PUMMELLED ME.
THANK YOU FOR THAT. YOU DIDN'T HAVE TO PROTECT ME.
YEAH. I DID A GREAT JOB. I WAS ONLY PRETENDING TO NEED YOU TO SAVE MY BUTT.
IT'S WORTH SAVING...

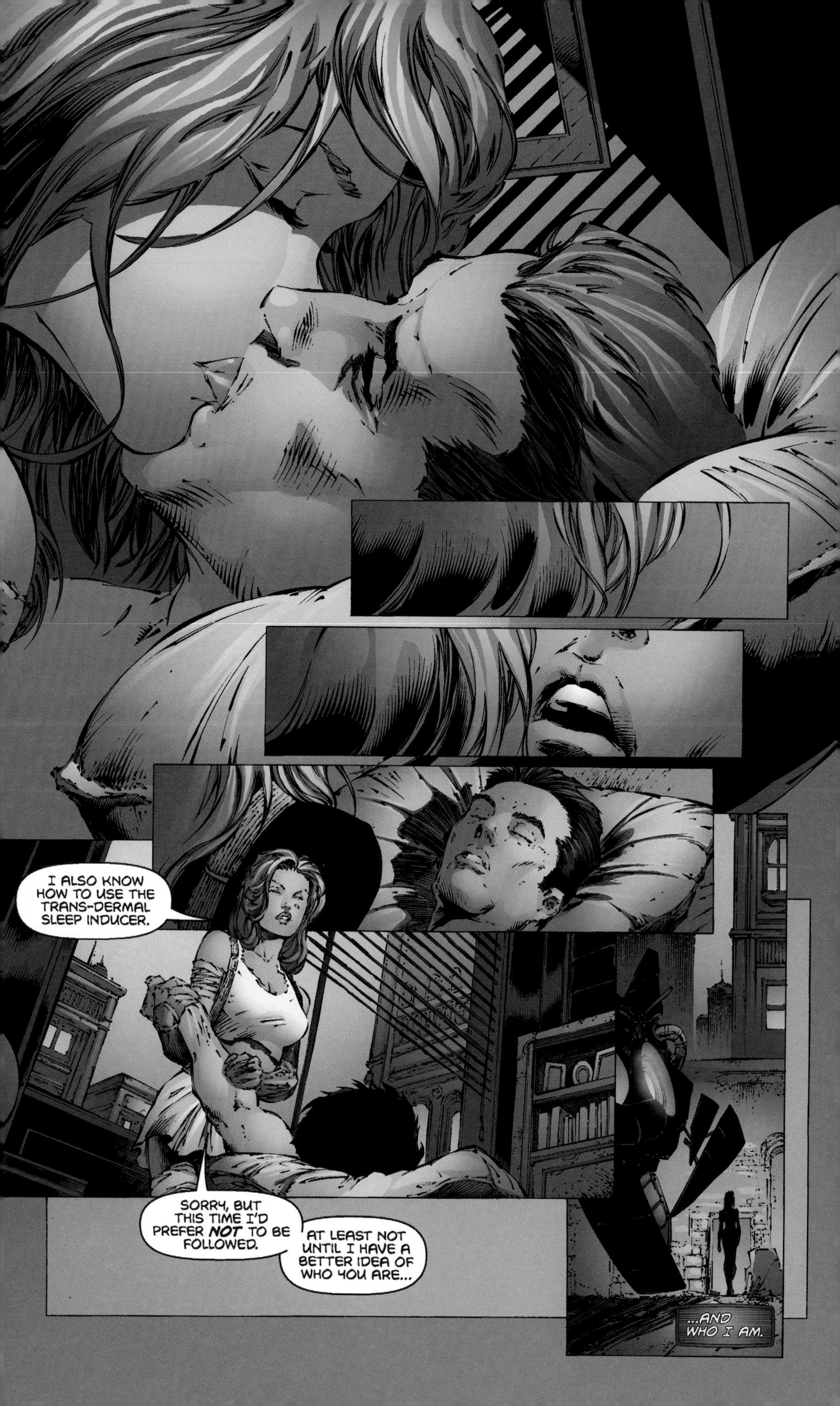

I ALSO KNOW HOW TO USE THE TRANS-DERMAL SLEEP INDUCER.
SORRY, BUT THIS TIME I'D PREFER **NOT** TO BE FOLLOWED.
AT LEAST NOT UNTIL I HAVE A BETTER IDEA OF WHO YOU ARE...
...AND WHO I AM.

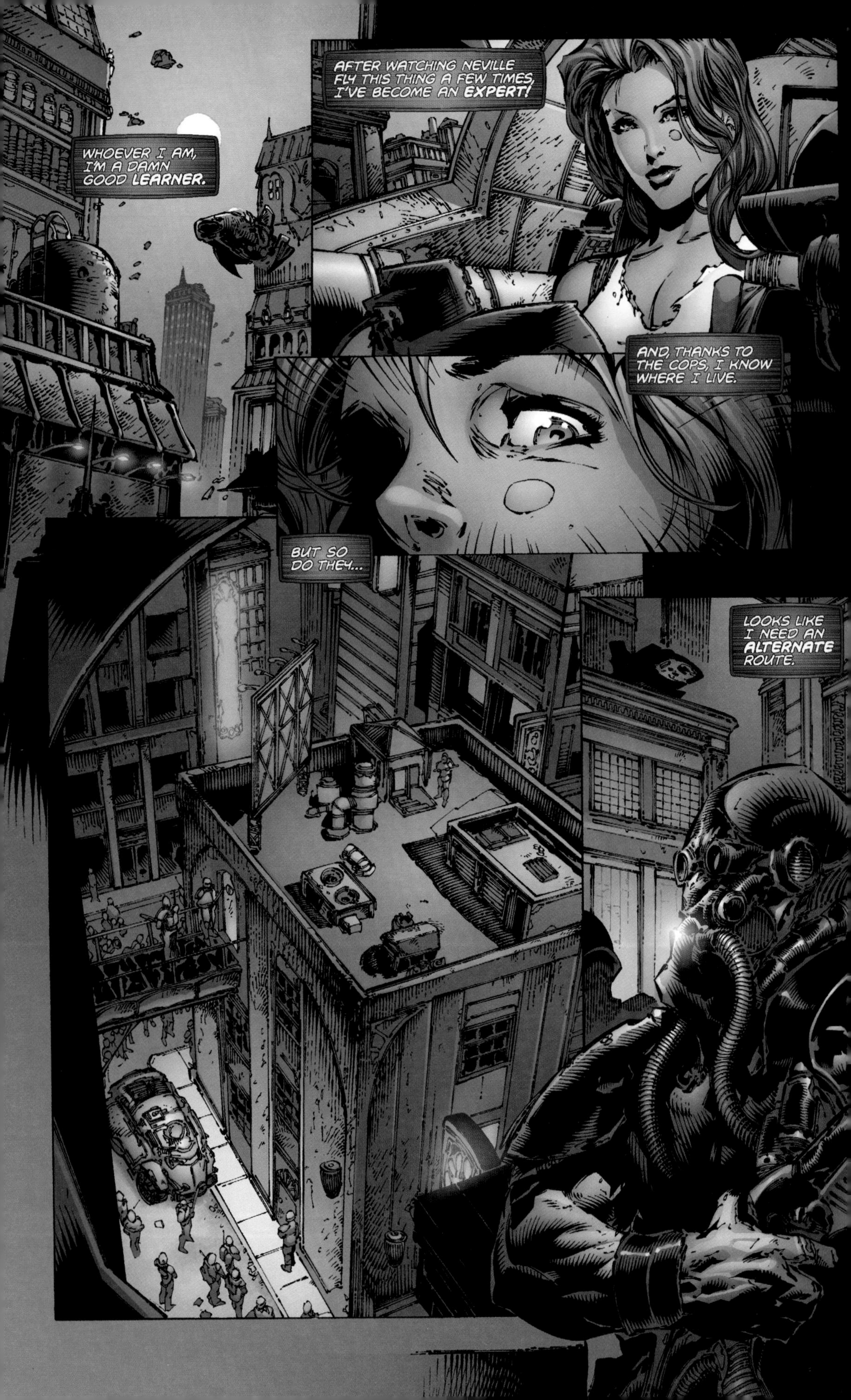
WHOEVER I AM, I'M A DAMN GOOD LEARNER.
AFTER WATCHING NEVILLE FLY THIS THING A FEW TIMES, I'VE BECOME AN EXPERT!
AND, THANKS TO THE COPS, I KNOW WHERE I LIVE.
BUT SO DO THEY...
LOOKS LIKE I NEED AN ALTERNATE ROUTE.

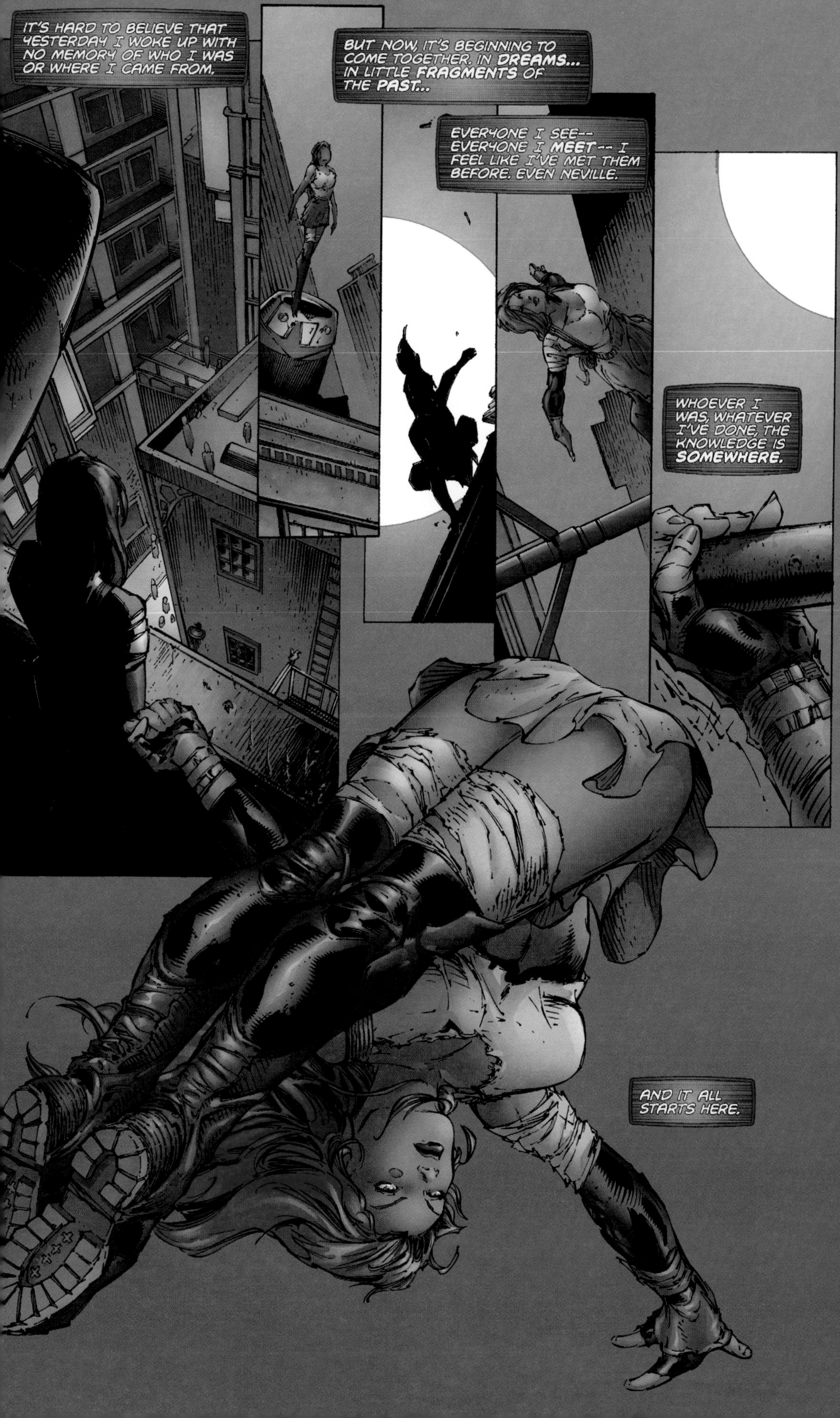
IT'S HARD TO BELIEVE THAT YESTERDAY I WOKE UP WITH NO MEMORY OF WHO I WAS OR WHERE I CAME FROM.
BUT NOW, IT'S BEGINNING TO COME TOGETHER. IN **DREAMS...** IN LITTLE **FRAGMENTS** OF THE **PAST...**
EVERYONE I SEE-- EVERYONE I **MEET**-- I FEEL LIKE I'VE MET THEM BEFORE. EVEN NEVILLE.
WHOEVER I WAS, WHATEVER I'VE DONE, THE KNOWLEDGE IS **SOMEWHERE.**
AND IT ALL STARTS HERE.

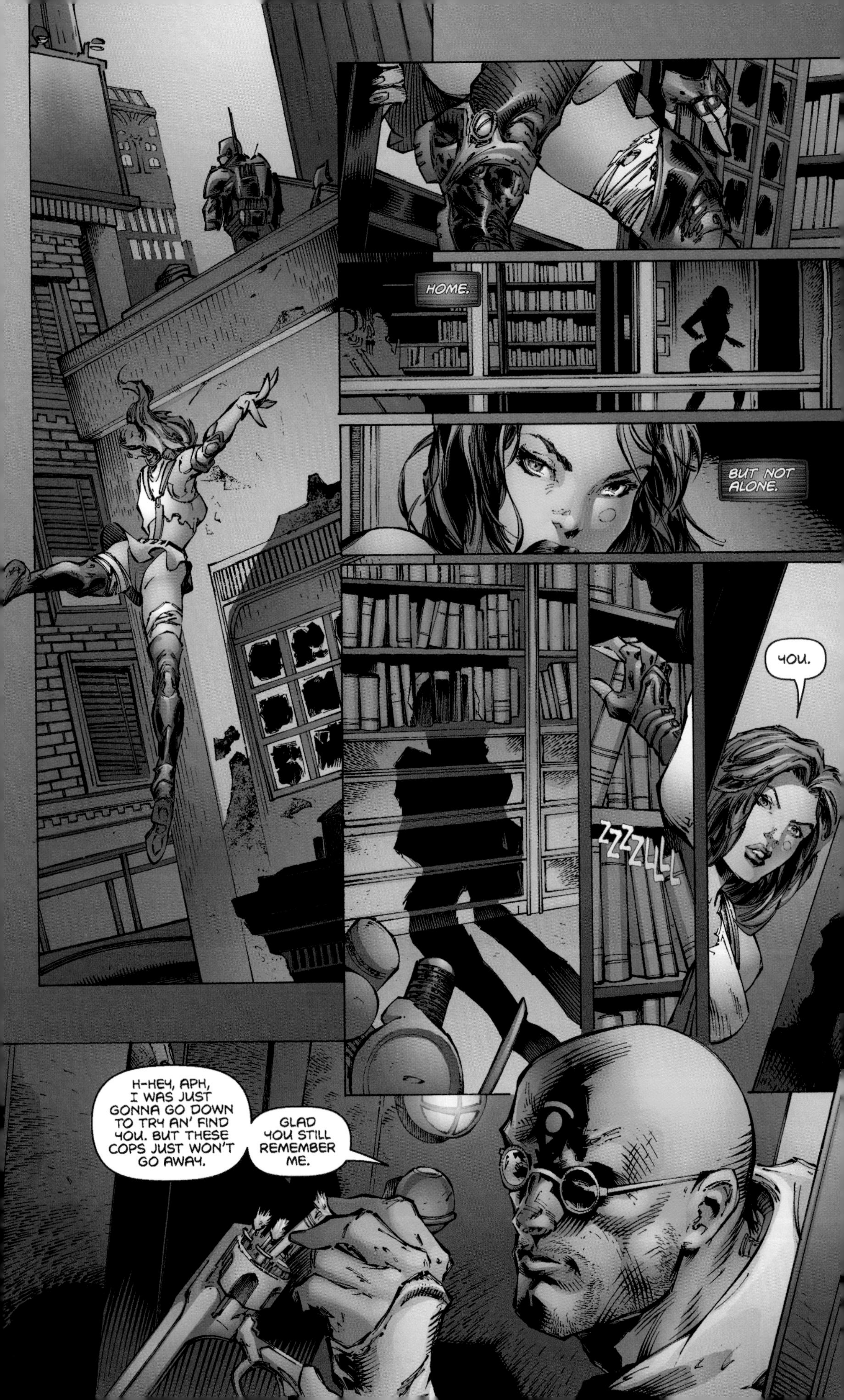
HOME.
BUT NOT ALONE.
ZZZZLLL
YOU.
H-HEY, APH, I WAS JUST GONNA GO DOWN TO TRY AN' FIND YOU. BUT THESE COPS JUST WON'T GO AWAY.
GLAD YOU STILL REMEMBER ME.

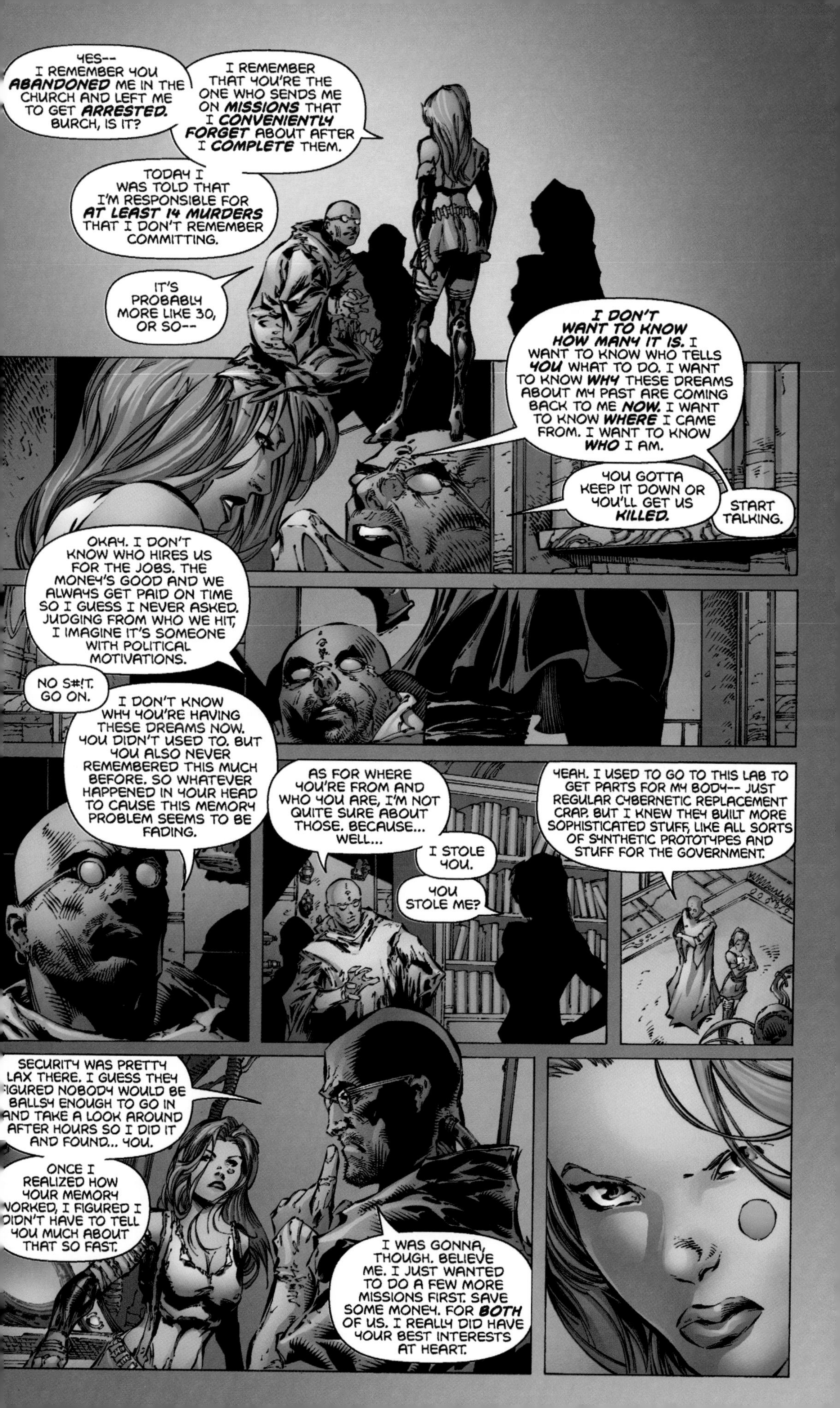

YES-- I REMEMBER YOU ABANDONED ME IN THE CHURCH AND LEFT ME TO GET ARRESTED. BURCH, IS IT?
I REMEMBER THAT YOU'RE THE ONE WHO SENDS ME ON MISSIONS THAT I CONVENIENTLY FORGET ABOUT AFTER I COMPLETE THEM.
TODAY I WAS TOLD THAT I'M RESPONSIBLE FOR AT LEAST 14 MURDERS THAT I DON'T REMEMBER COMMITTING.
IT'S PROBABLY MORE LIKE 30, OR SO--
I DON'T WANT TO KNOW HOW MANY IT IS. I WANT TO KNOW WHO TELLS YOU WHAT TO DO. I WANT TO KNOW WHY THESE DREAMS ABOUT MY PAST ARE COMING BACK TO ME NOW. I WANT TO KNOW WHERE I CAME FROM. I WANT TO KNOW WHO I AM.
YOU GOTTA KEEP IT DOWN OR YOU'LL GET US KILLED.
START TALKING.
OKAY. I DON'T KNOW WHO HIRES US FOR THE JOBS. THE MONEY'S GOOD AND WE ALWAYS GET PAID ON TIME SO I GUESS I NEVER ASKED. JUDGING FROM WHO WE HIT, I IMAGINE IT'S SOMEONE WITH POLITICAL MOTIVATIONS.
NO S#!T. GO ON.
I DON'T KNOW WHY YOU'RE HAVING THESE DREAMS NOW. YOU DIDN'T USED TO. BUT YOU ALSO NEVER REMEMBERED THIS MUCH BEFORE. SO WHATEVER HAPPENED IN YOUR HEAD TO CAUSE THIS MEMORY PROBLEM SEEMS TO BE FADING.
AS FOR WHERE YOU'RE FROM AND WHO YOU ARE, I'M NOT QUITE SURE ABOUT THOSE. BECAUSE... WELL...
I STOLE YOU.
YOU STOLE ME?
YEAH. I USED TO GO TO THIS LAB TO GET PARTS FOR MY BODY-- JUST REGULAR CYBERNETIC REPLACEMENT CRAP. BUT I KNEW THEY BUILT MORE SOPHISTICATED STUFF, LIKE ALL SORTS OF SYNTHETIC PROTOTYPES AND STUFF FOR THE GOVERNMENT.
SECURITY WAS PRETTY LAX THERE. I GUESS THEY FIGURED NOBODY WOULD BE BALLSY ENOUGH TO GO IN AND TAKE A LOOK AROUND AFTER HOURS SO I DID IT AND FOUND... YOU.
ONCE I REALIZED HOW YOUR MEMORY WORKED, I FIGURED I DIDN'T HAVE TO TELL YOU MUCH ABOUT THAT SO FAST.
I WAS GONNA, THOUGH. BELIEVE ME. I JUST WANTED TO DO A FEW MORE MISSIONS FIRST. SAVE SOME MONEY. FOR BOTH OF US. I REALLY DID HAVE YOUR BEST INTERESTS AT HEART.

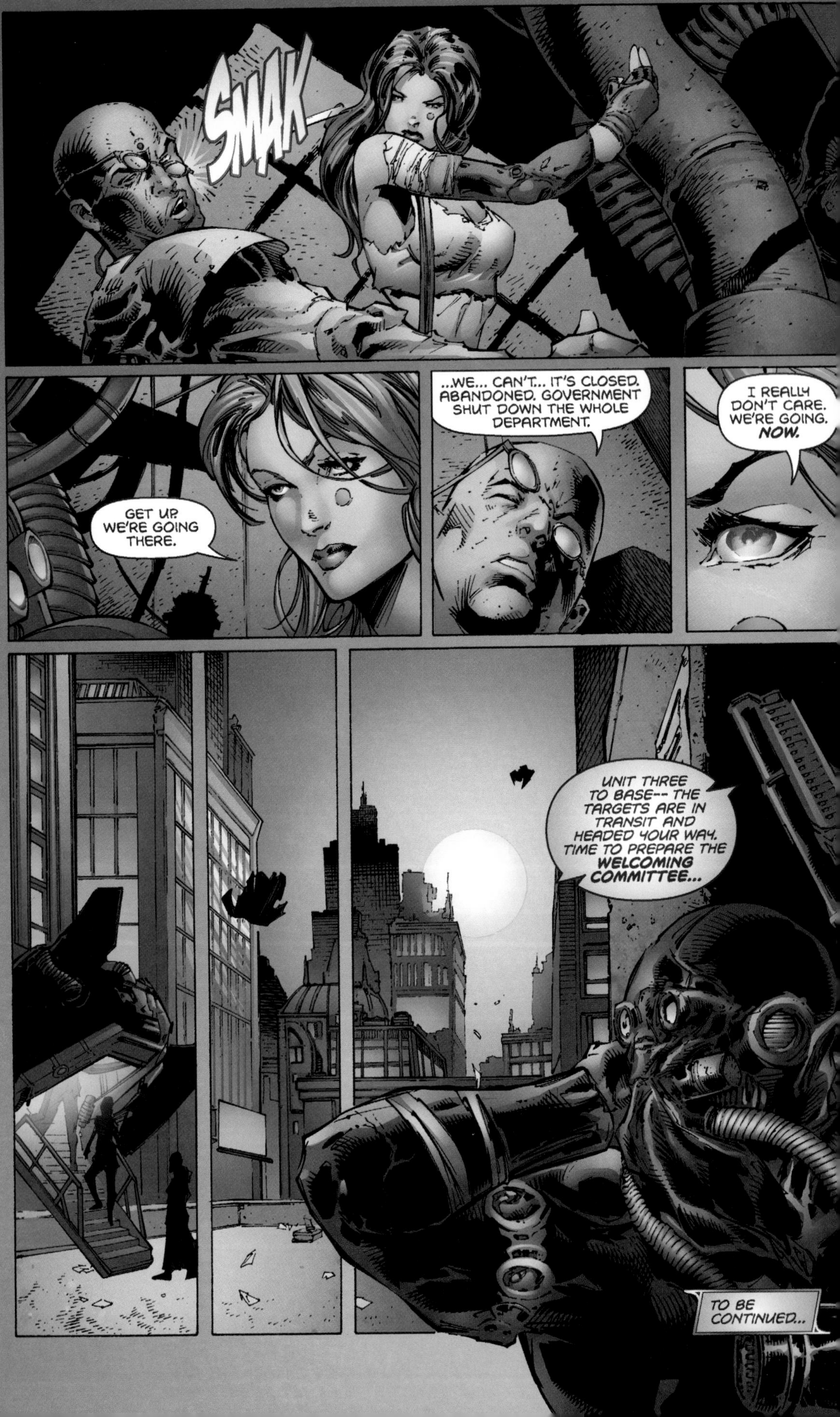
SMAK
GET UP. WE'RE GOING THERE.
...WE... CAN'T... IT'S CLOSED. ABANDONED. GOVERNMENT SHUT DOWN THE WHOLE DEPARTMENT.
I REALLY DON'T CARE. WE'RE GOING. NOW.
UNIT THREE TO BASE-- THE TARGETS ARE IN TRANSIT AND HEADED YOUR WAY. TIME TO PREPARE THE WELCOMING COMMITTEE...
TO BE CONTINUED...

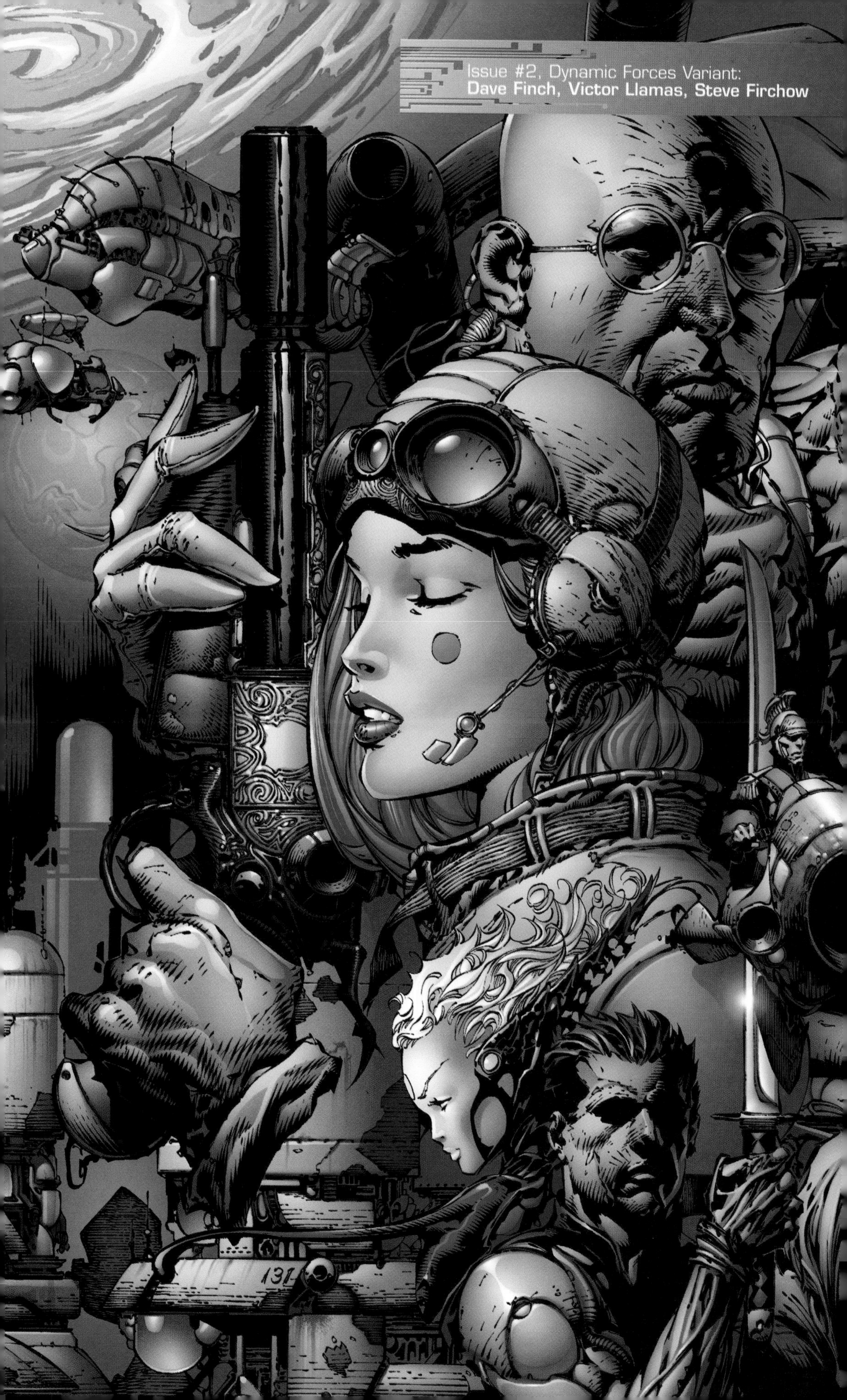

Issue #2, Dynamic Forces Variant:
Dave Finch, Victor Llamas, Steve Firchow

Issue #4:
Dave Finch

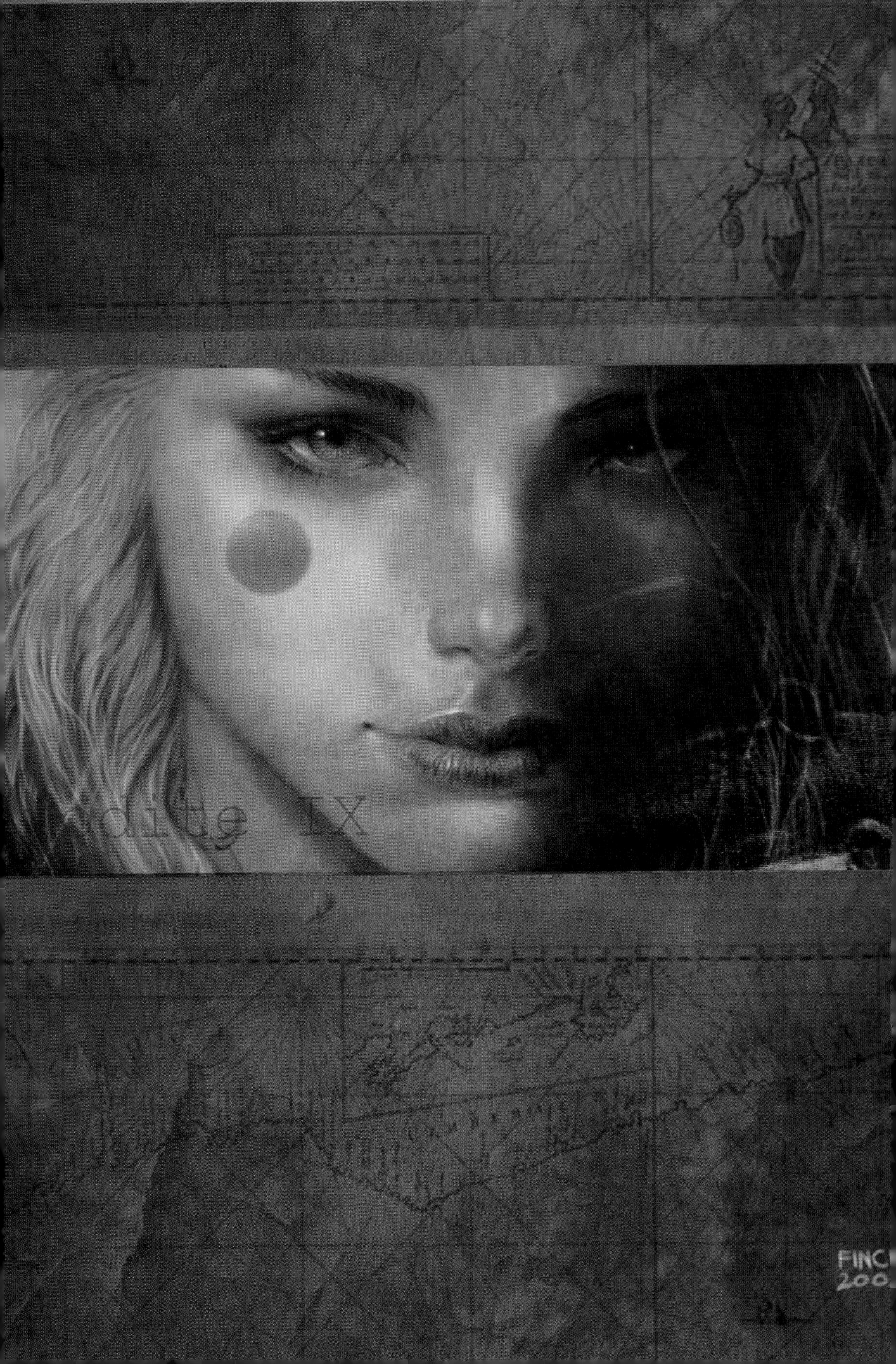

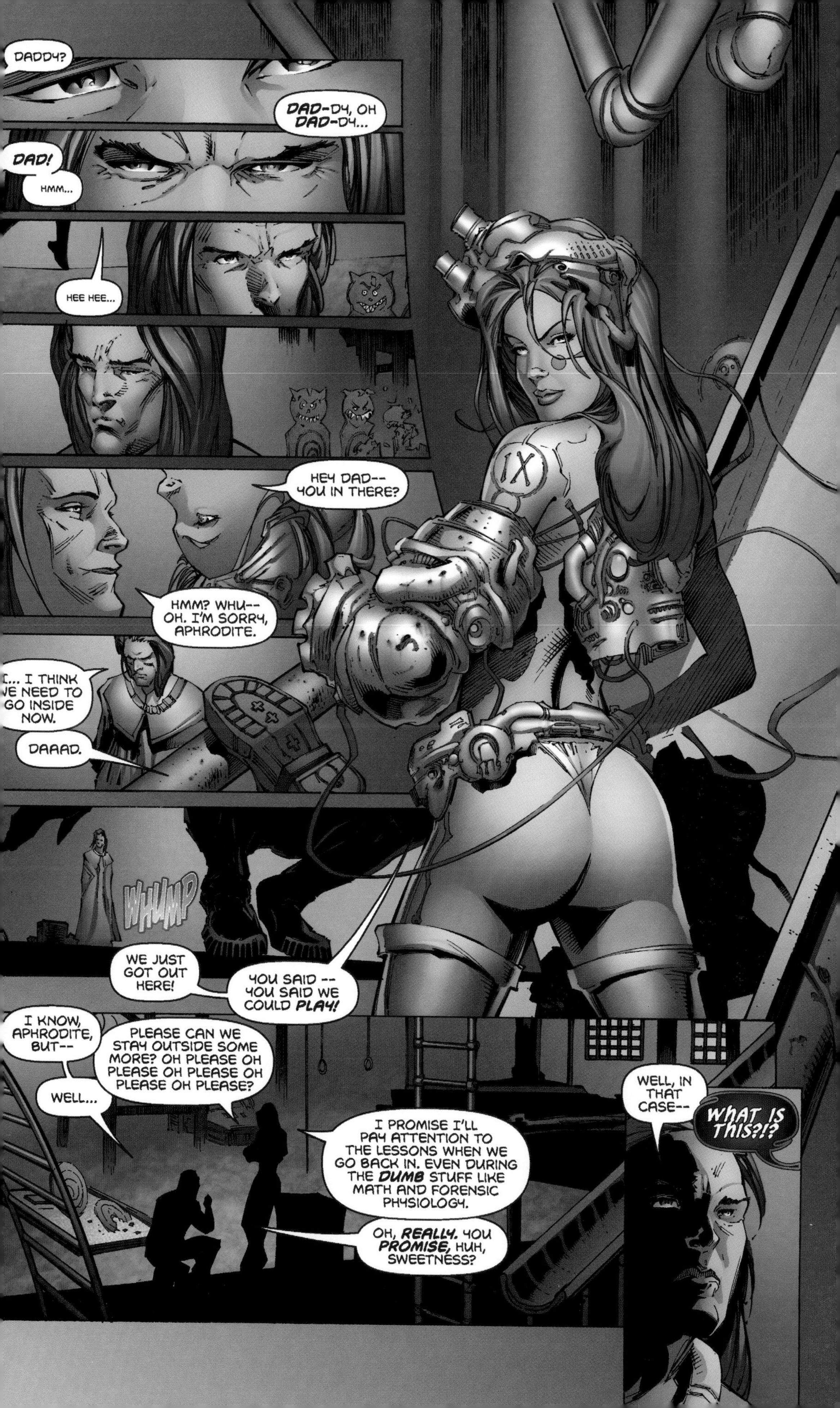

DADDY?
DAD-DY, OH DAD-DY...
DAD!
HMM...
HEE HEE...
HEY DAD-- YOU IN THERE?
HMM? WHU-- OH. I'M SORRY, APHRODITE.
I... I THINK WE NEED TO GO INSIDE NOW.
DAAAD.
WHUMP
WE JUST GOT OUT HERE!
YOU SAID -- YOU SAID WE COULD PLAY!
I KNOW, APHRODITE, BUT--
PLEASE CAN WE STAY OUTSIDE SOME MORE? OH PLEASE OH PLEASE OH PLEASE OH PLEASE OH PLEASE?
WELL...
I PROMISE I'LL PAY ATTENTION TO THE LESSONS WHEN WE GO BACK IN. EVEN DURING THE DUMB STUFF LIKE MATH AND FORENSIC PHYSIOLOGY.
OH, REALLY. YOU PROMISE, HUH, SWEETNESS?
WELL, IN THAT CASE--
WHAT IS THIS?!?

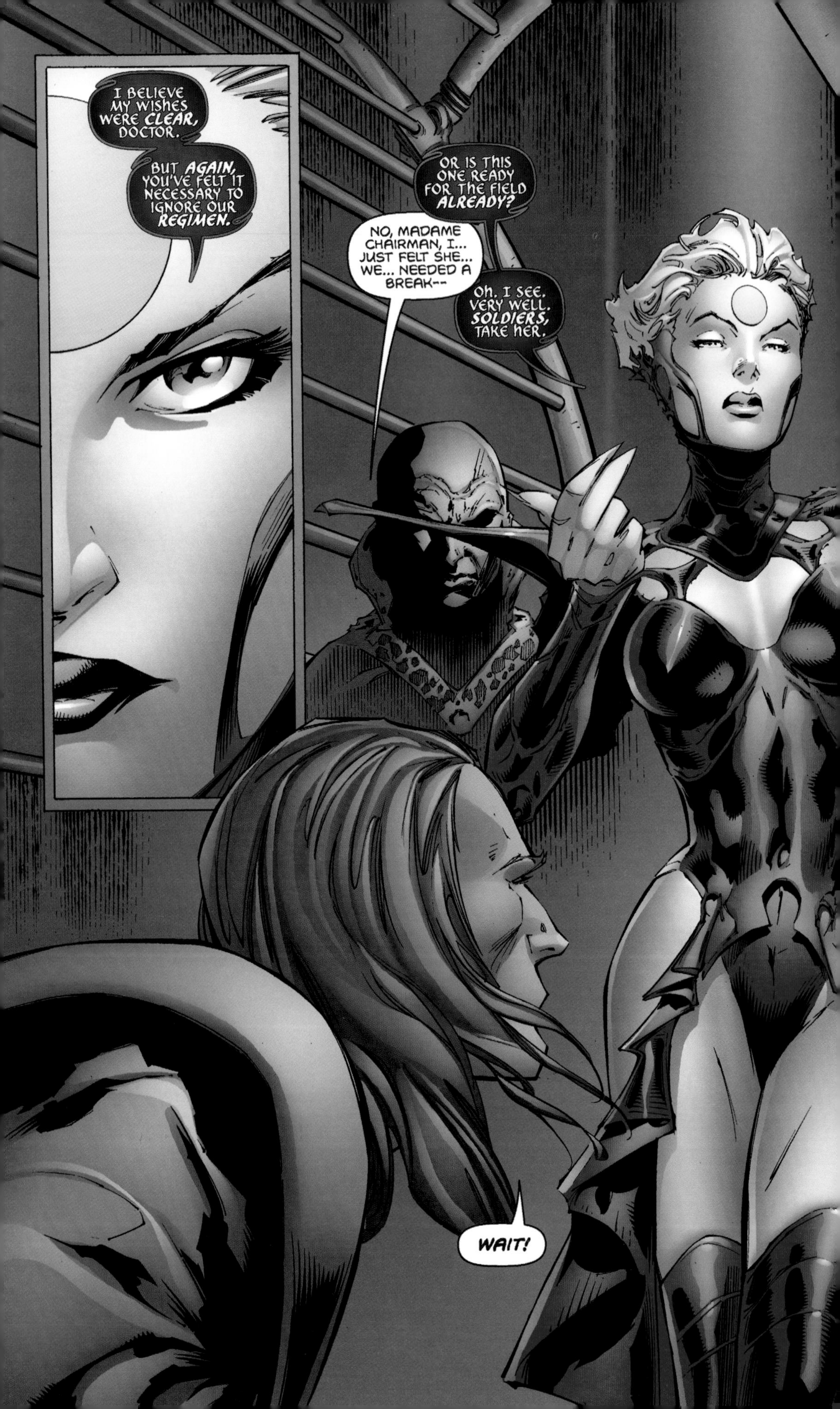
I BELIEVE MY WISHES WERE CLEAR, DOCTOR.
BUT AGAIN, YOU'VE FELT IT NECESSARY TO IGNORE OUR REGIMEN.
OR IS THIS ONE READY FOR THE FIELD ALREADY?
NO, MADAME CHAIRMAN, I... JUST FELT SHE... WE... NEEDED A BREAK--
Oh. I SEE. VERY WELL. SOLDIERS, TAKE HER.
WAIT!

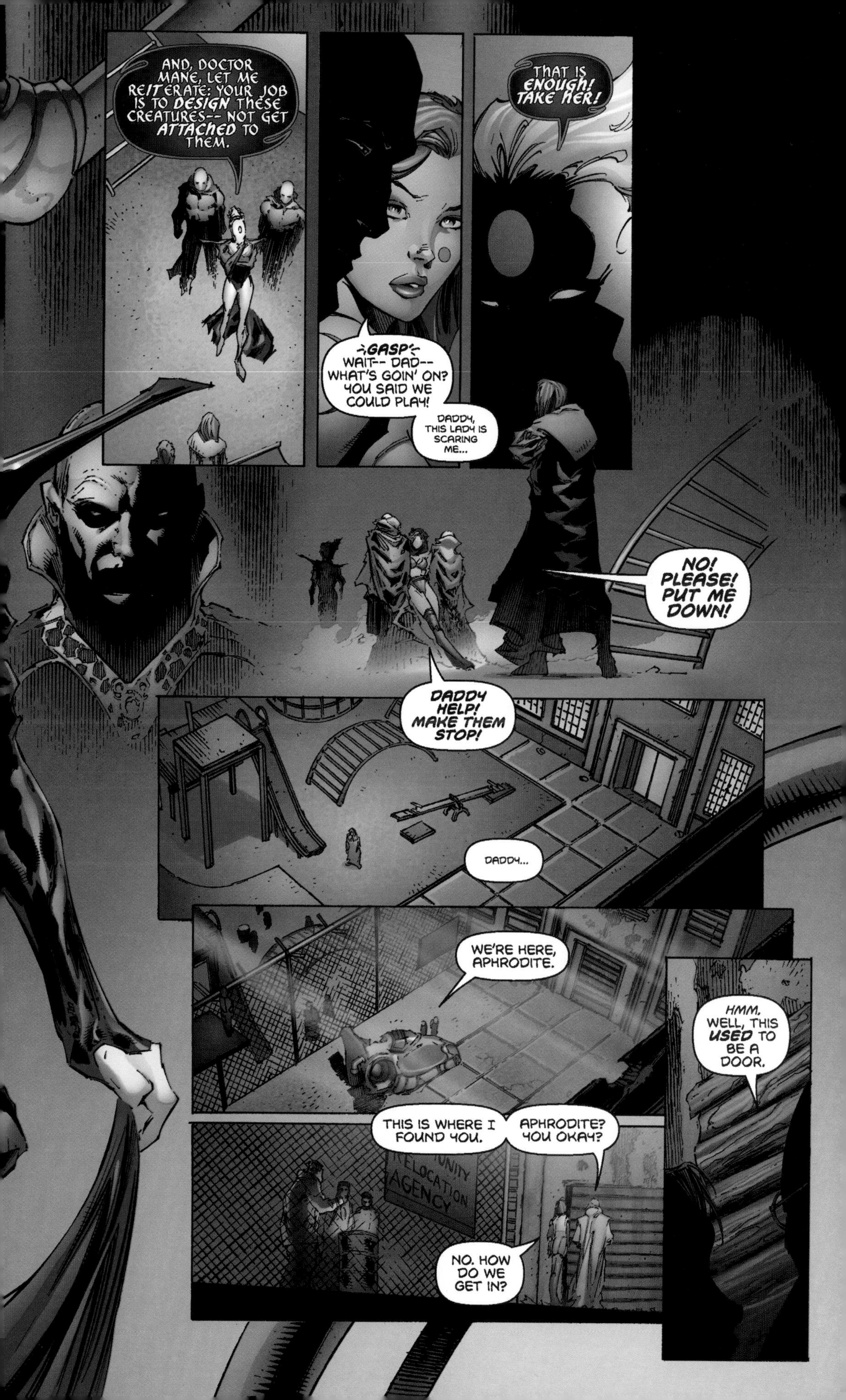
AND, DOCTOR MANE, LET ME REITERATE: YOUR JOB IS TO DESIGN THESE CREATURES-- NOT GET ATTACHED TO THEM.
GASP
WAIT-- DAD-- WHAT'S GOIN' ON? YOU SAID WE COULD PLAY!
DADDY, THIS LADY IS SCARING ME...
THAT IS ENOUGH! TAKE HER!
NO! PLEASE! PUT ME DOWN!
DADDY HELP! MAKE THEM STOP!
DADDY...
WE'RE HERE, APHRODITE.
HMM. WELL, THIS USED TO BE A DOOR.
THIS IS WHERE I FOUND YOU.
APHRODITE? YOU OKAY?
RELOCATION AGENCY
NO. HOW DO WE GET IN?

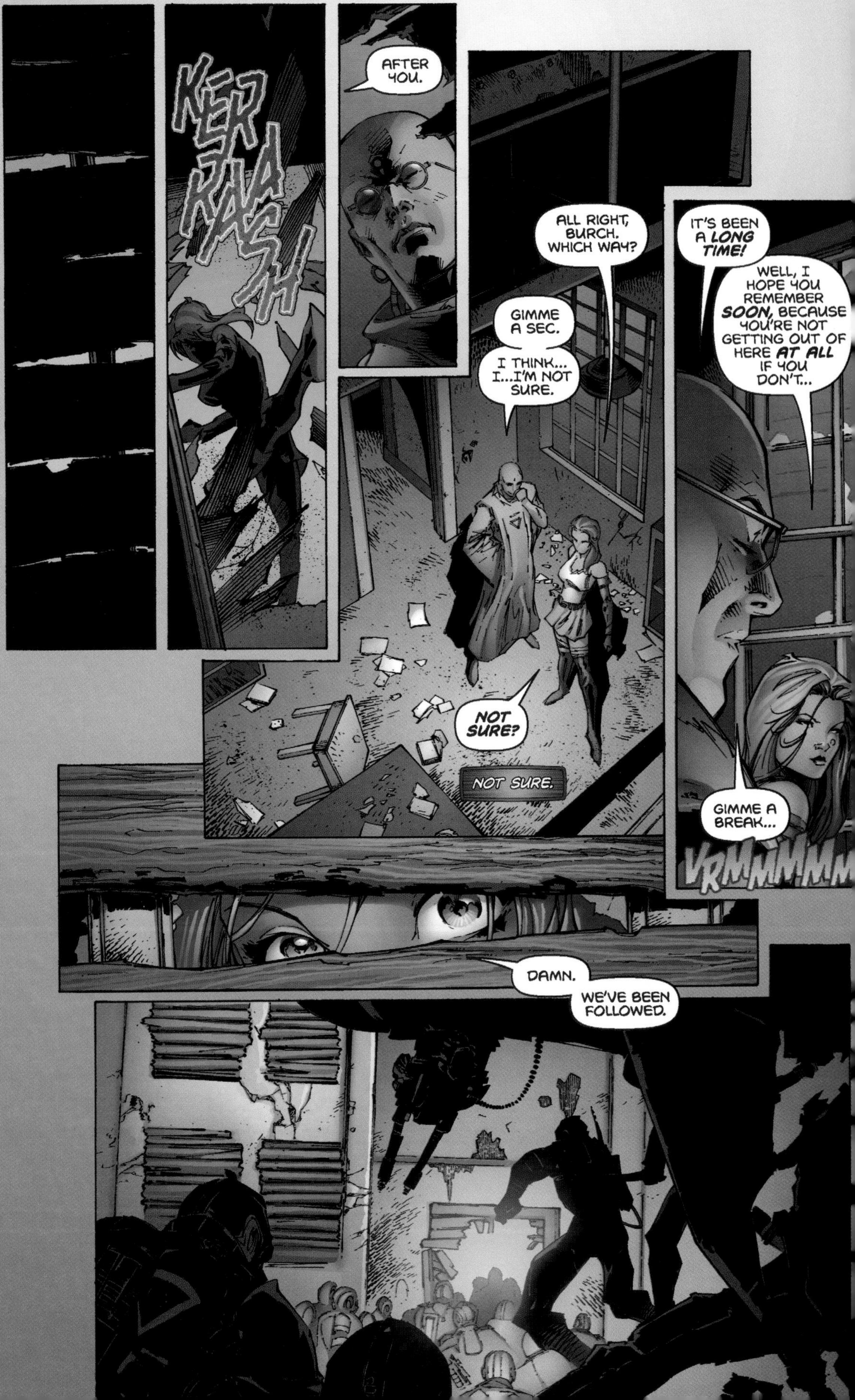

KERRAKASH
AFTER YOU.
ALL RIGHT, BURCH. WHICH WAY?
GIMME A SEC.
I THINK... I...I'M NOT SURE.
NOT SURE?
NOT SURE.
IT'S BEEN A LONG TIME!
WELL, I HOPE YOU REMEMBER SOON, BECAUSE YOU'RE NOT GETTING OUT OF HERE AT ALL IF YOU DON'T...
GIMME A BREAK...
VRMMMMM
DAMN.
WE'VE BEEN FOLLOWED.

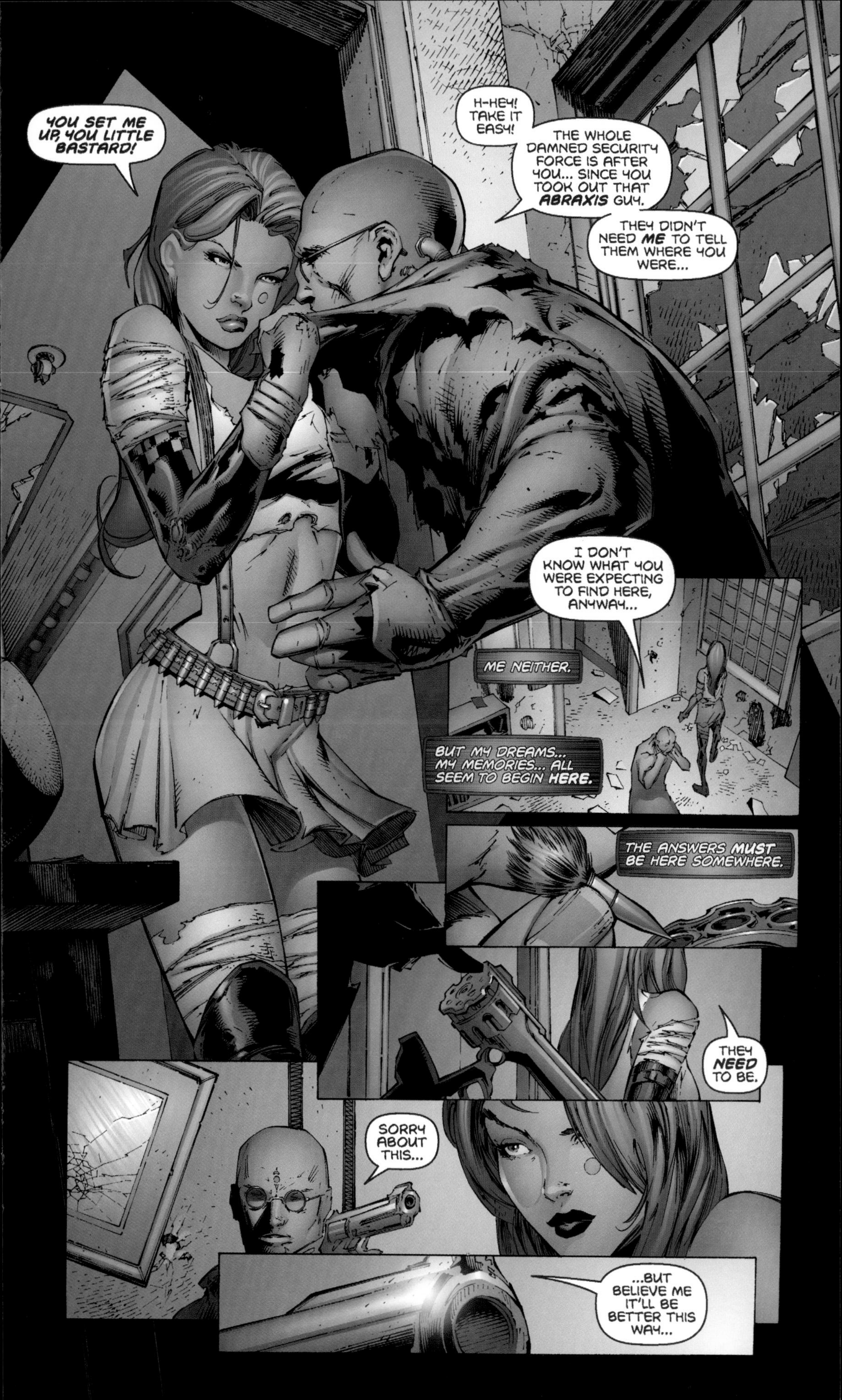
YOU SET ME UP, YOU LITTLE BASTARD!
H-HEY! TAKE IT EASY!
THE WHOLE DAMNED SECURITY FORCE IS AFTER YOU... SINCE YOU TOOK OUT THAT ABRAXIS GUY.
THEY DIDN'T NEED ME TO TELL THEM WHERE YOU WERE...
I DON'T KNOW WHAT YOU WERE EXPECTING TO FIND HERE, ANYWAY...
ME NEITHER.
BUT MY DREAMS... MY MEMORIES... ALL SEEM TO BEGIN HERE.
THE ANSWERS MUST BE HERE SOMEWHERE.
THEY NEED TO BE.
SORRY ABOUT THIS...
...BUT BELIEVE ME IT'LL BE BETTER THIS WAY...

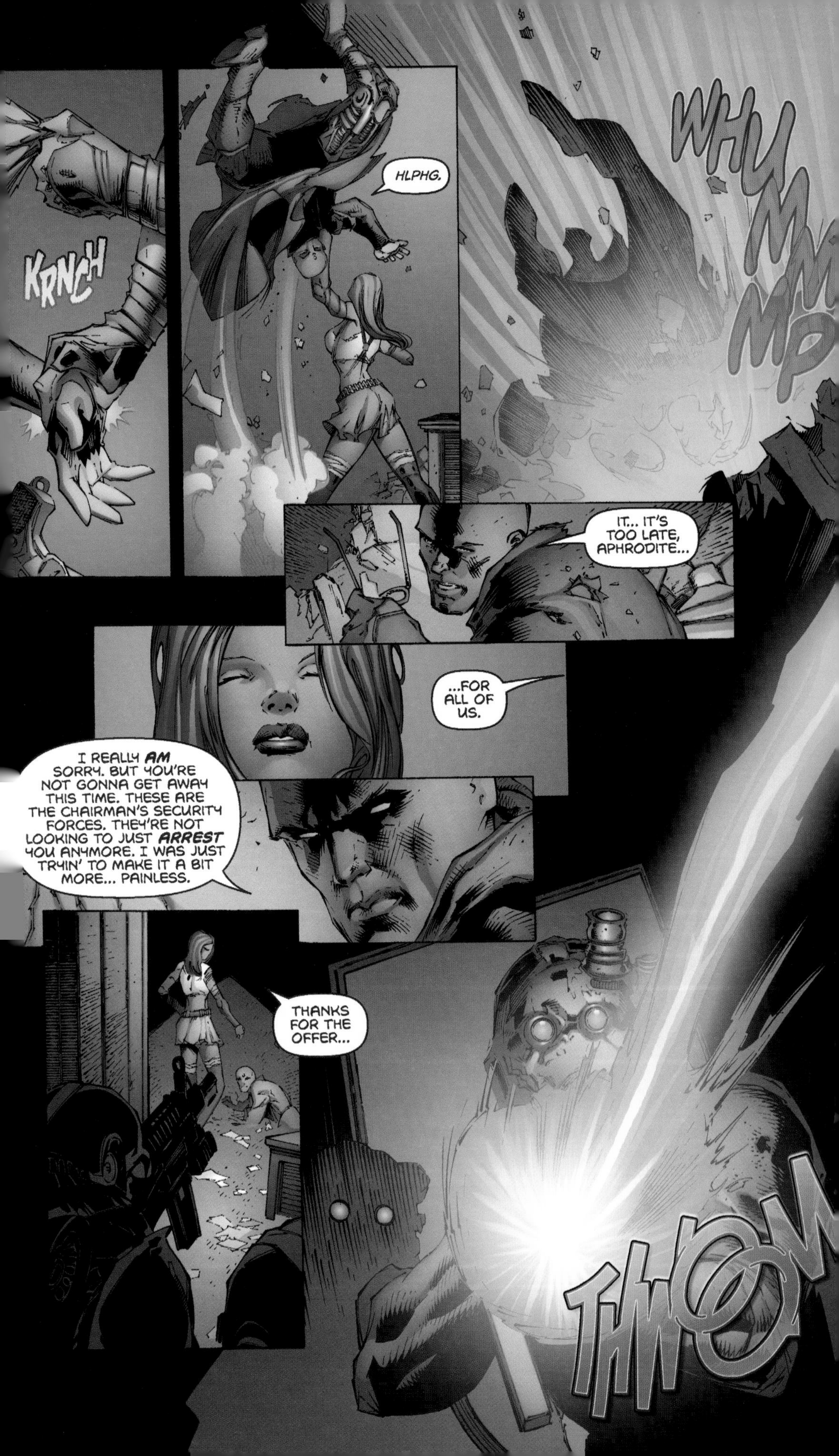
KRNCH
HLPHG.
WHUMMMMMP
IT... IT'S TOO LATE, APHRODITE...
...FOR ALL OF US.
I REALLY AM SORRY. BUT YOU'RE NOT GONNA GET AWAY THIS TIME. THESE ARE THE CHAIRMAN'S SECURITY FORCES. THEY'RE NOT LOOKING TO JUST ARREST YOU ANYMORE. I WAS JUST TRYIN' TO MAKE IT A BIT MORE... PAINLESS.
THANKS FOR THE OFFER...
THWOOM

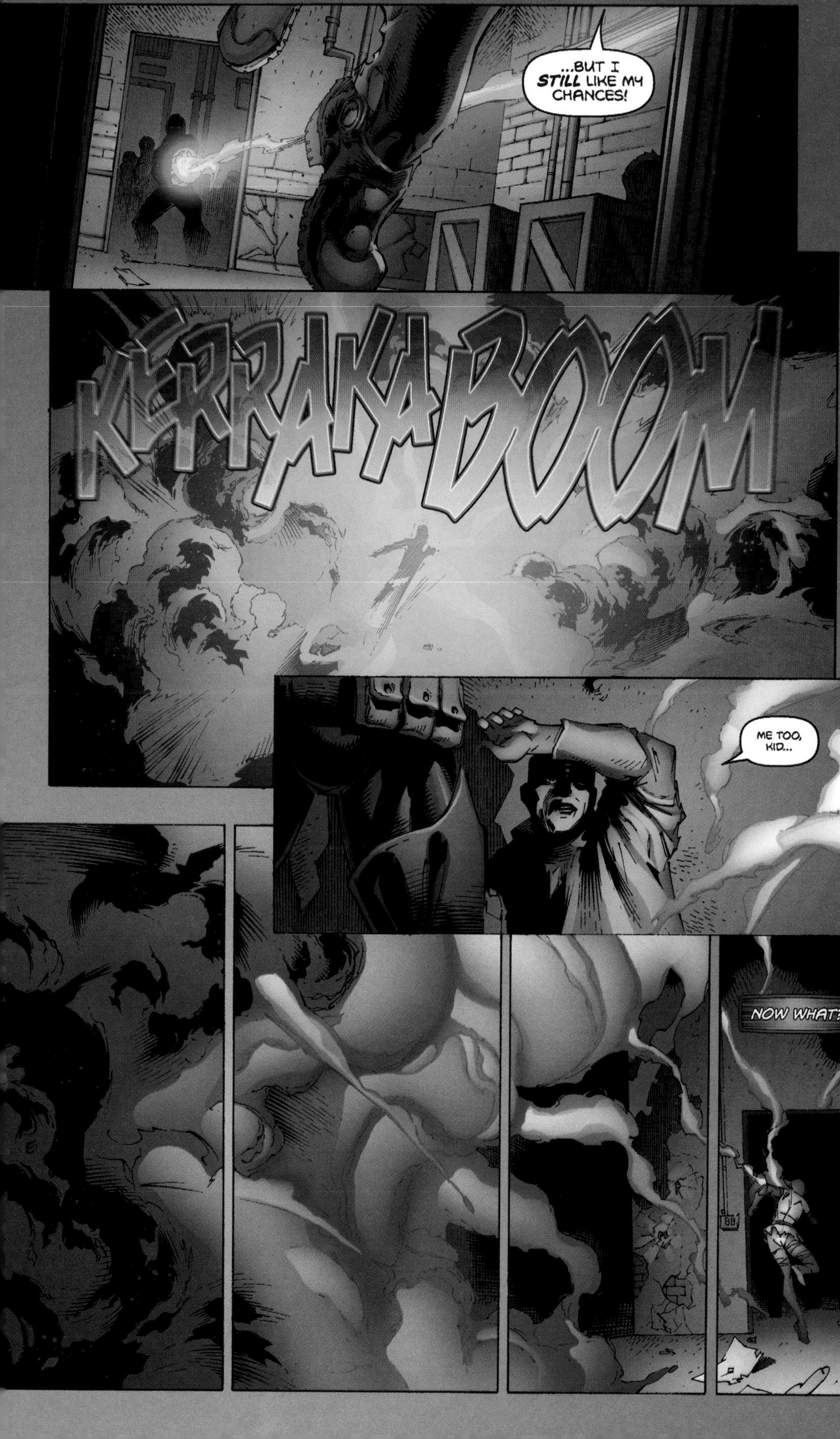
...BUT I STILL LIKE MY CHANCES!
KERRAKABOOM
ME TOO, KID...
NOW WHAT?

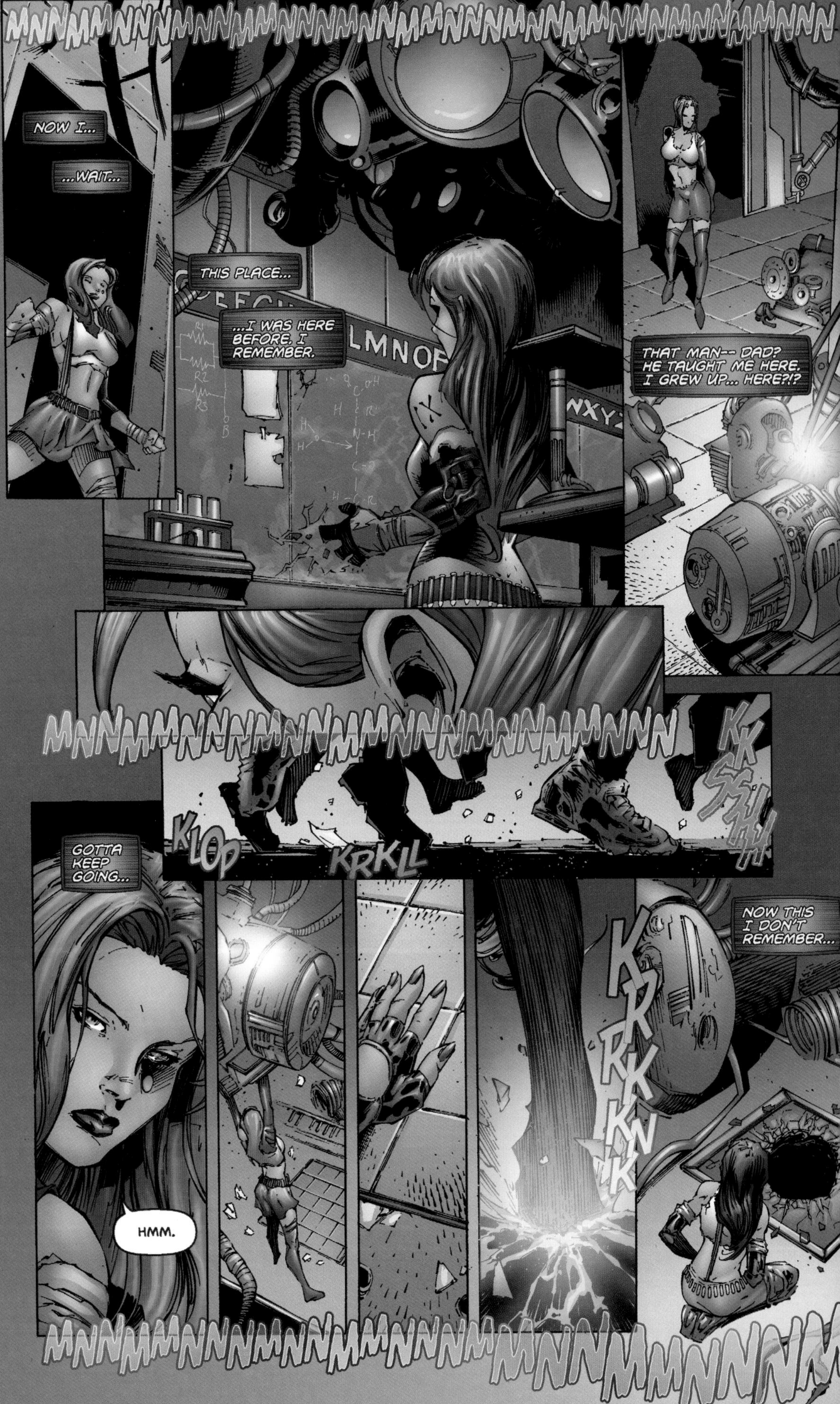
MNNMMNNNMNNNMMNNNMNNMMNNNMNNNMMNNNMNNNMNNNMMNNNMMNNN
NOW I...
...WAIT...
THIS PLACE...
...I WAS HERE BEFORE. I REMEMBER.
LMNOP
WXYZ
THAT MAN-- DAD? HE TAUGHT ME HERE. I GREW UP... HERE?!?
MNNMMNNNMNNNMMNNNMNNMMNNNMNNNMMNNN
KK SSHH
KLOP
KRKLL
GOTTA KEEP GOING...
HMM.
KRRKKNK
NOW THIS I DON'T REMEMBER...
MNNMMNNNMNNNMMNNNMNNMMNNNMNNNMMNNNMNNNMMNNN

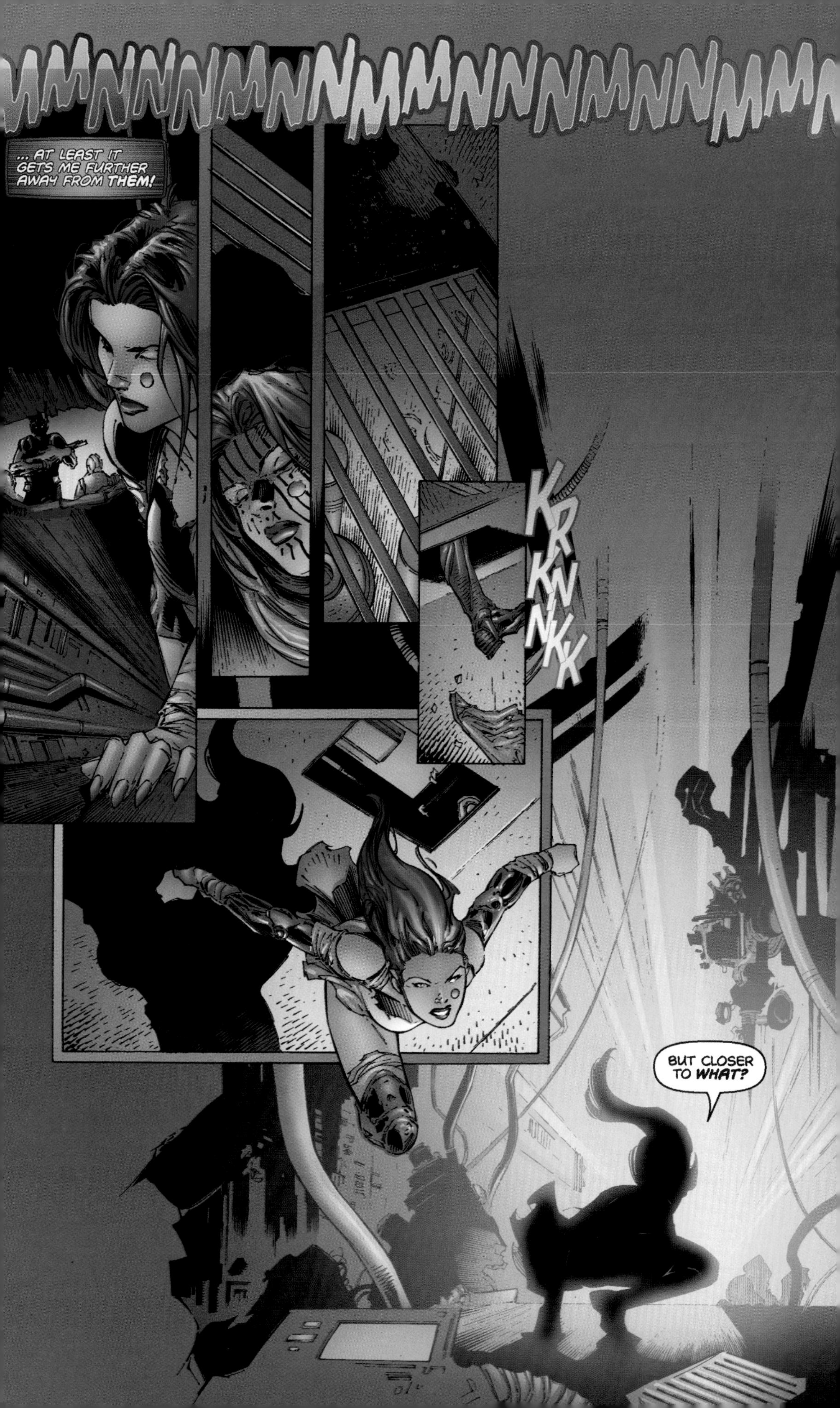
MMNNNMMNNNMMNNNMMNNNMM
... AT LEAST IT GETS ME FURTHER AWAY FROM THEM!
KRKNNKK
BUT CLOSER TO WHAT?

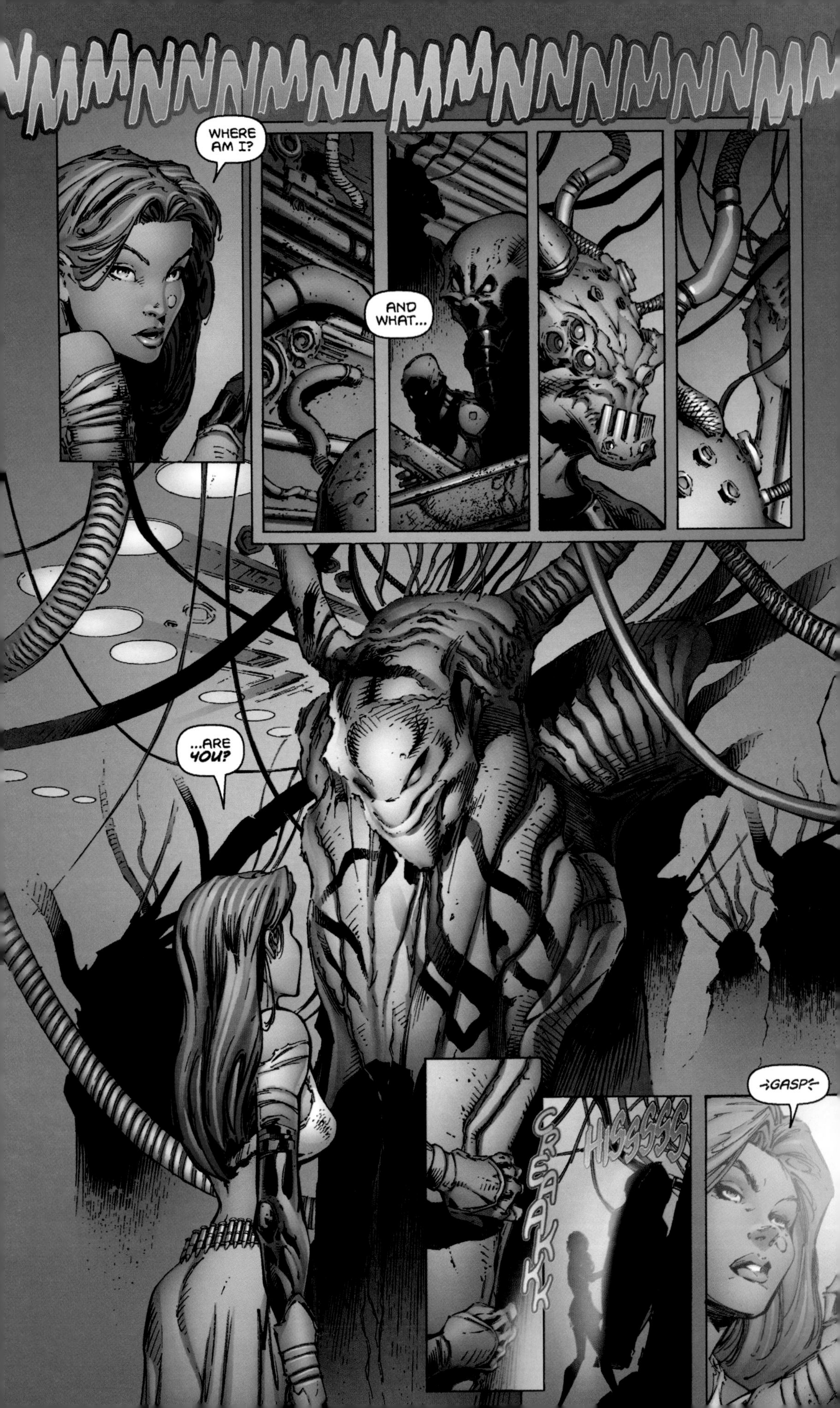

VMMMNNNMMNNMMMNNNMMNNNMM
WHERE AM I?
AND WHAT...
...ARE YOU?
CREAKKK
HISSSSS
-GASP-

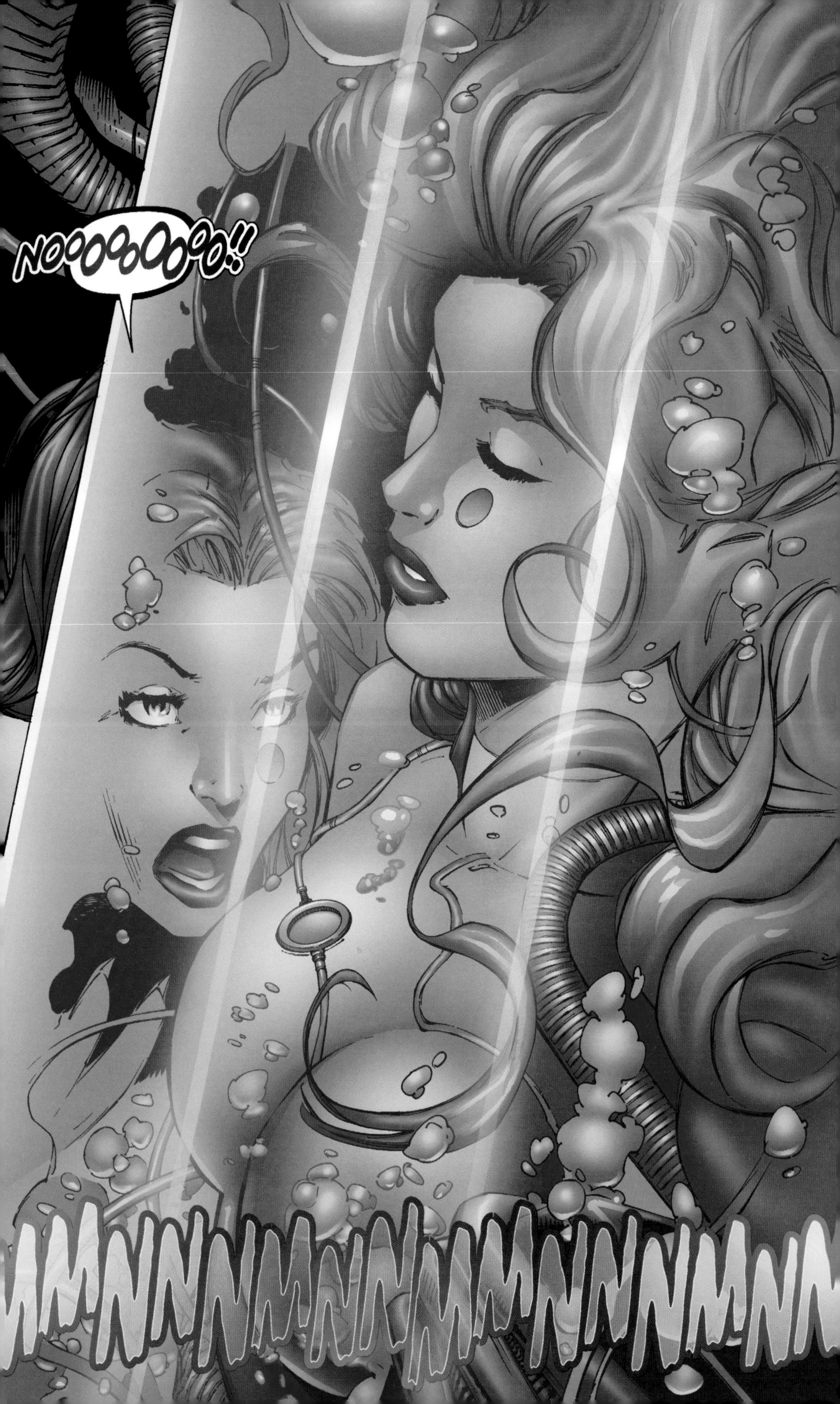
NOOOOOOOO!!
MMNNNMMNNNMMMNNNNMMNNA

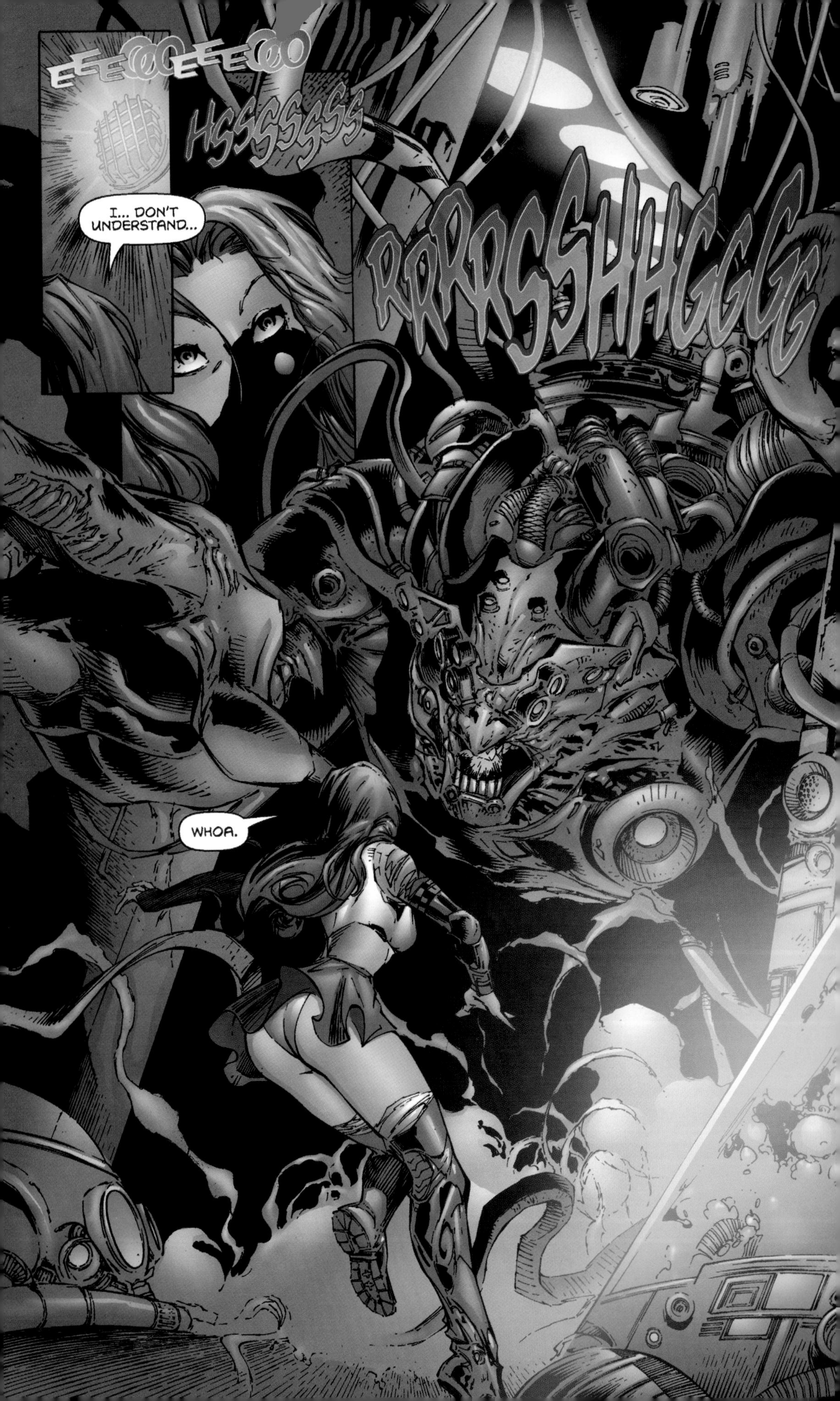
EEEOOOEEEEOO
HSSSSSSS
I... DON'T UNDERSTAND...
RRRRSSHHGGG
WHOA.

Issue #1, Black & White Sketch Cover
Dave Finch

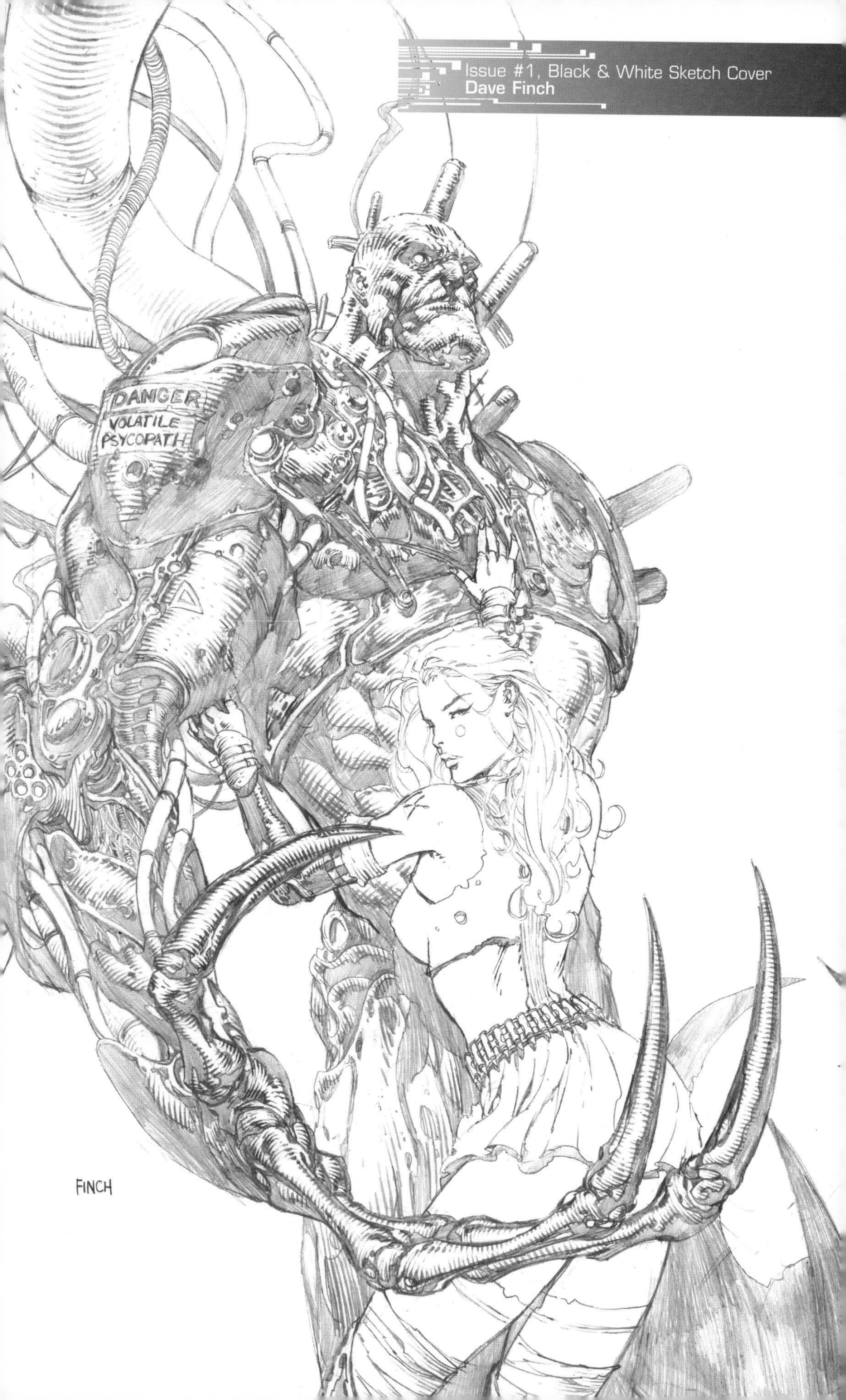
DANGER
VOLATILE
PSYCOPATH
FINCH

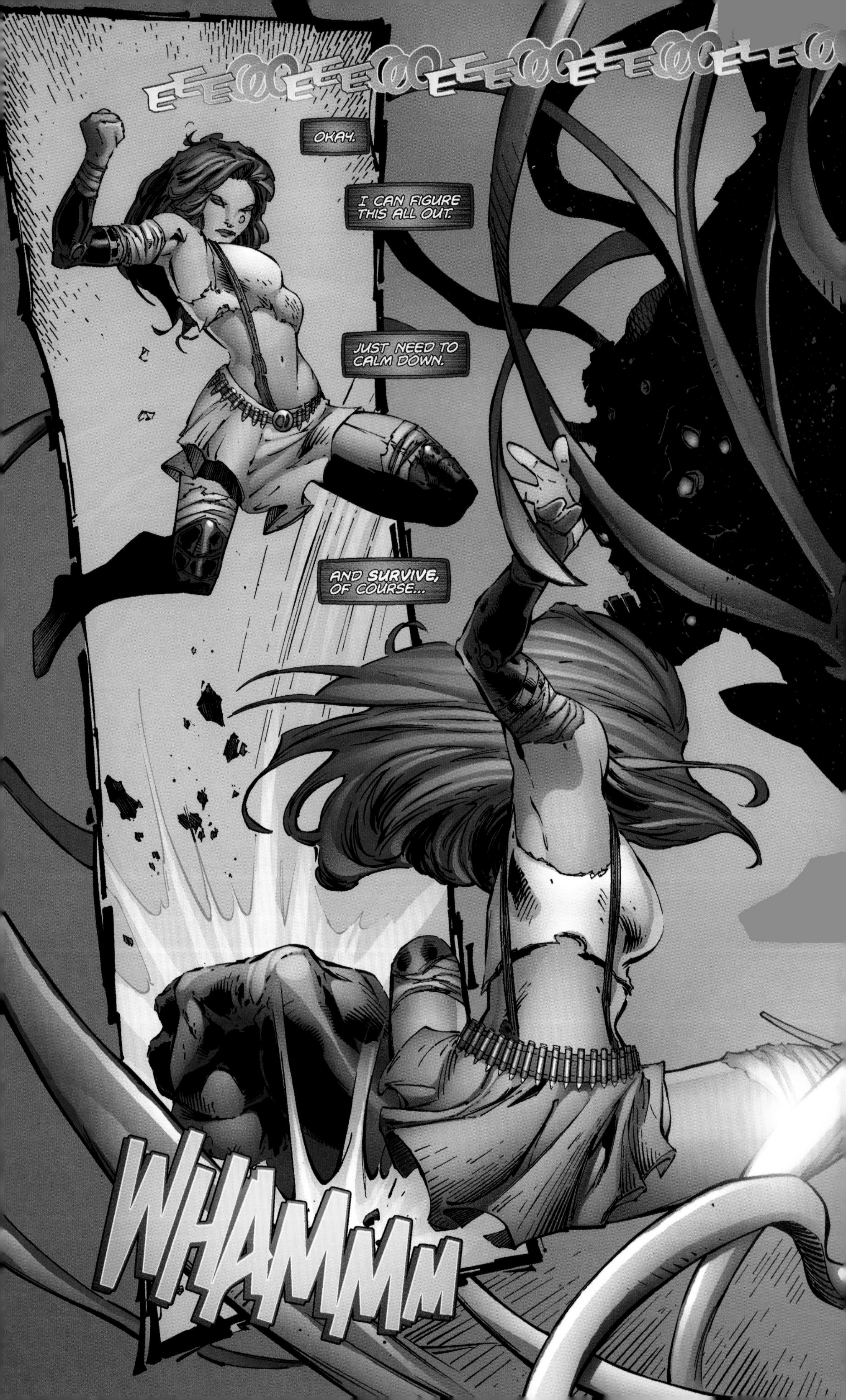
OKAY.
I CAN FIGURE THIS ALL OUT.
JUST NEED TO CALM DOWN.
AND SURVIVE, OF COURSE...
WHAMMMM

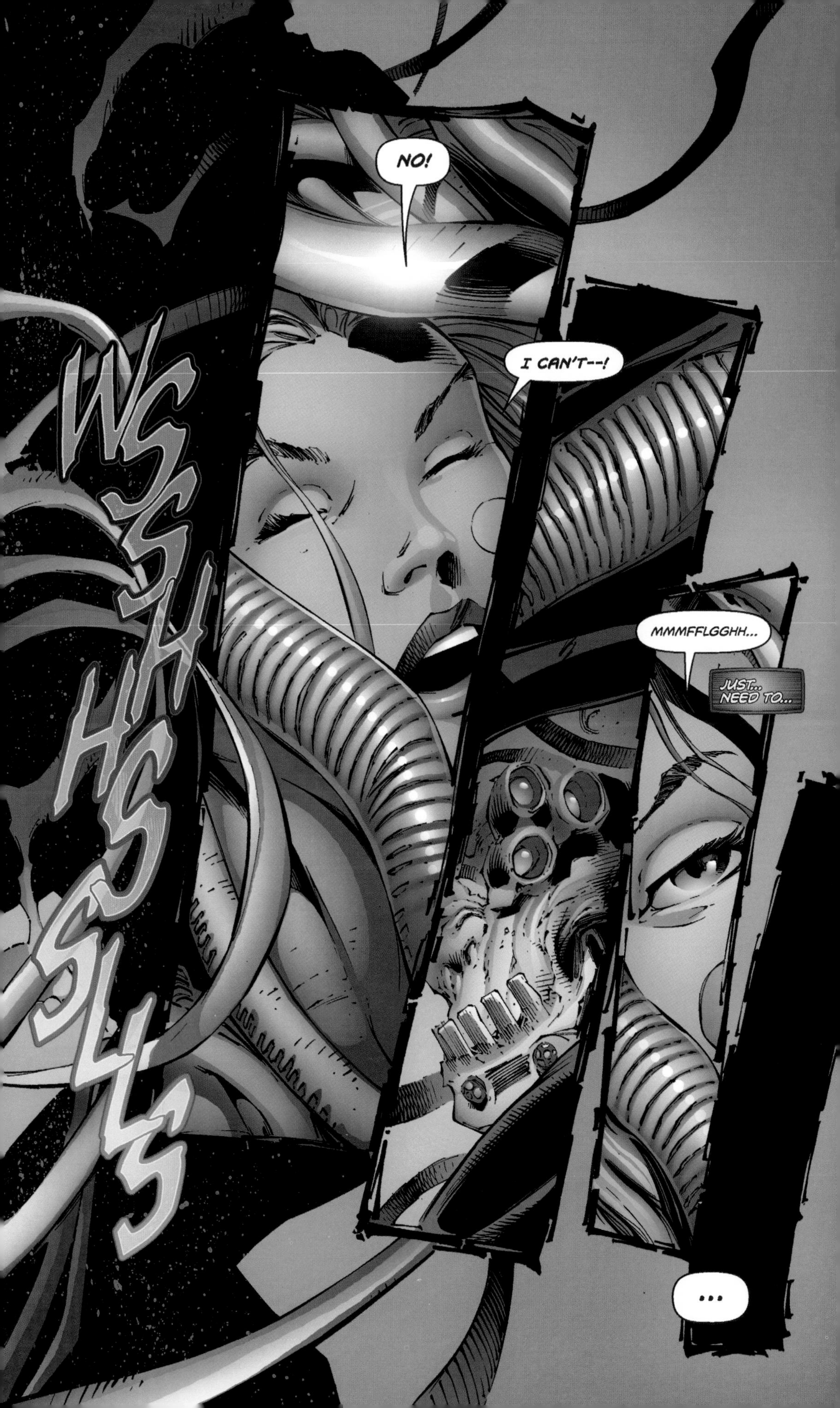
NO!
I CAN'T--!
MMMFFLGGHH...
JUST... NEED TO...
...

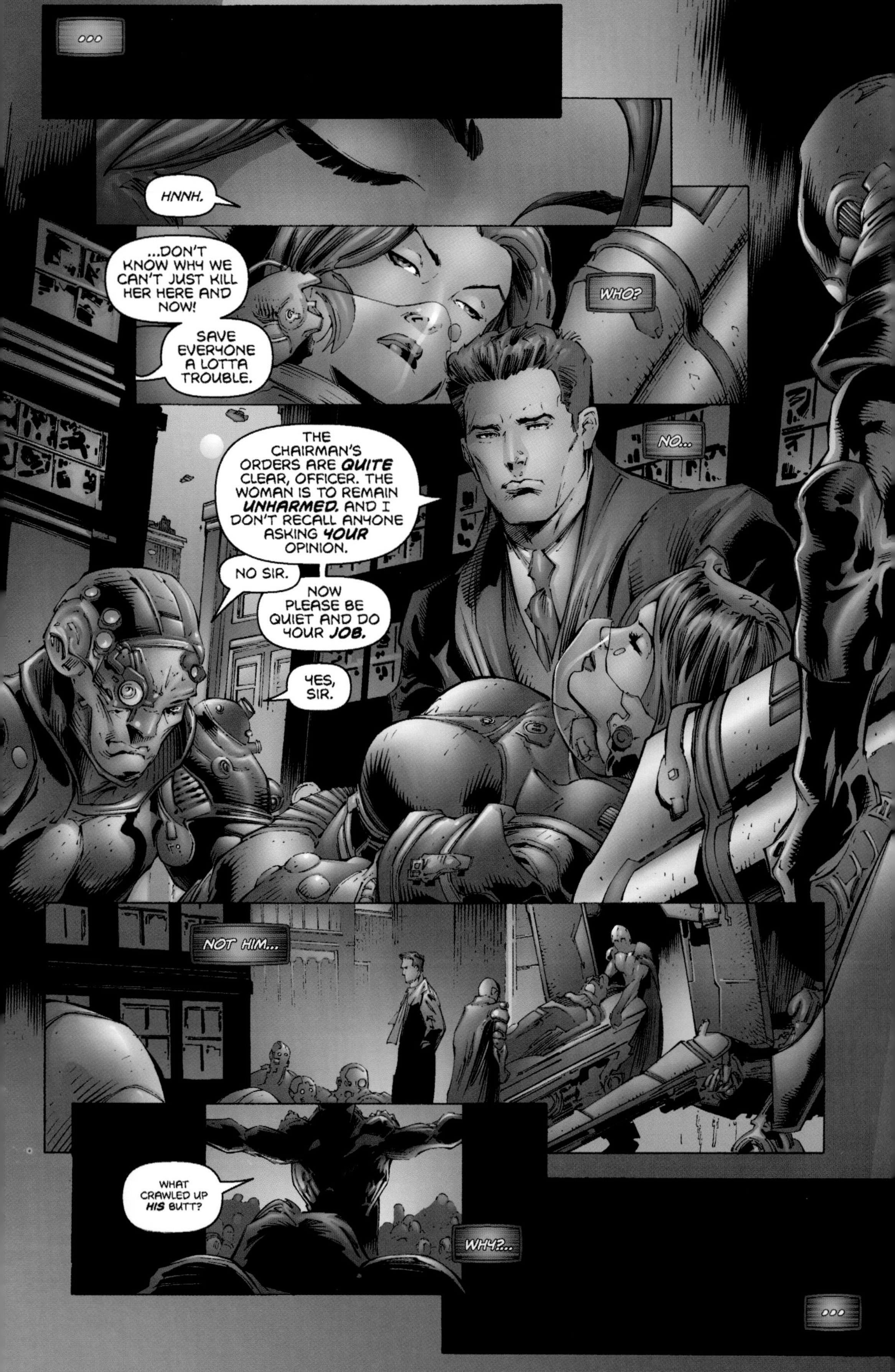

ooo
HNNH.
...DON'T KNOW WHY WE CAN'T JUST KILL HER HERE AND NOW!
SAVE EVERYONE A LOTTA TROUBLE.
WHO?
NO...
THE CHAIRMAN'S ORDERS ARE QUITE CLEAR, OFFICER. THE WOMAN IS TO REMAIN UNHARMED. AND I DON'T RECALL ANYONE ASKING YOUR OPINION.
NO SIR.
NOW PLEASE BE QUIET AND DO YOUR JOB.
YES, SIR.
NOT HIM...
WHAT CRAWLED UP HIS BUTT?
WHY?...
ooo

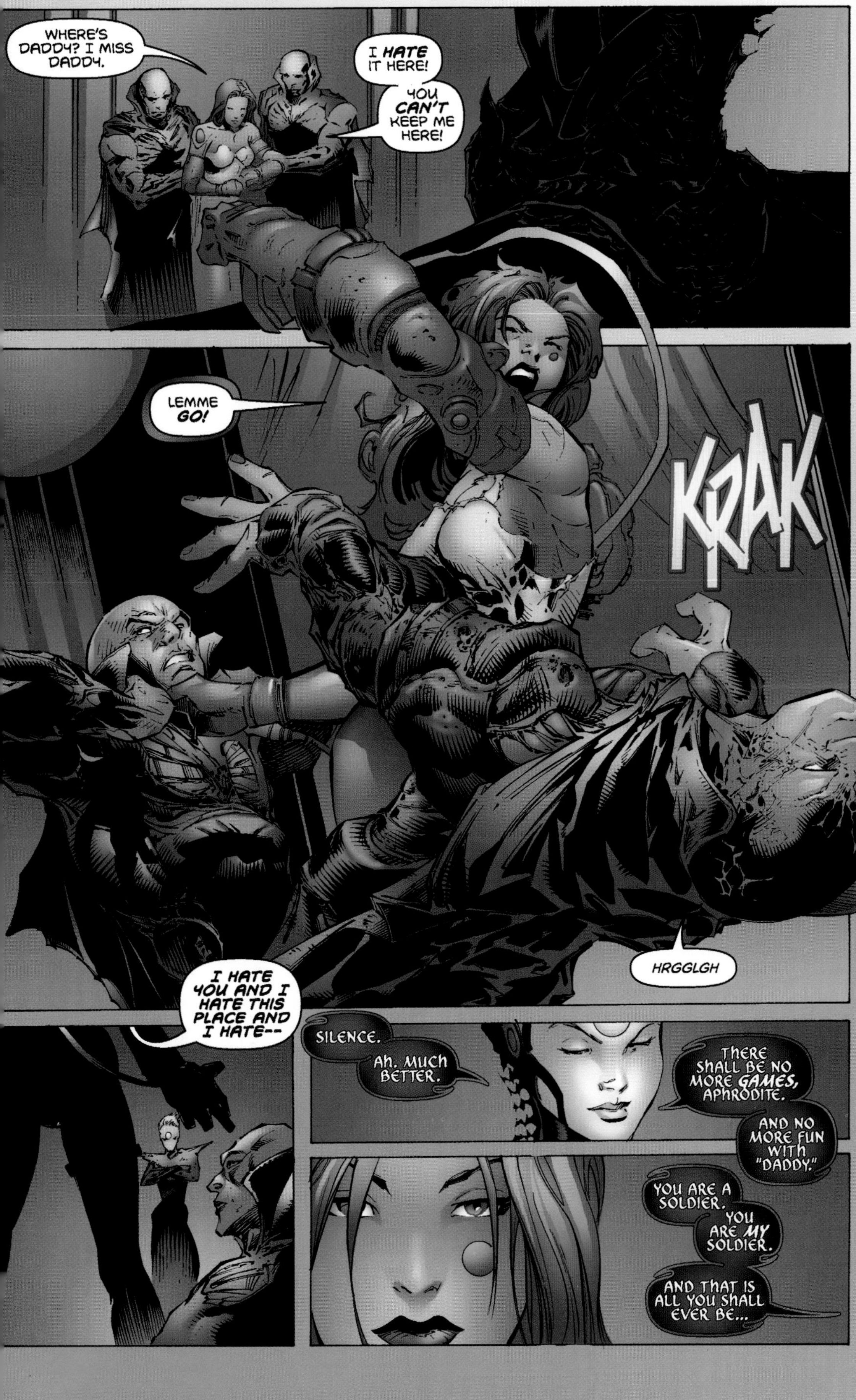
WHERE'S DADDY? I MISS DADDY.
I HATE IT HERE!
YOU CAN'T KEEP ME HERE!
LEMME GO!
KRAK
HRGGLGH
I HATE YOU AND I HATE THIS PLACE AND I HATE--
SILENCE.
Ah. MUCH BETTER.
THERE SHALL BE NO MORE GAMES, APHRODITE.
AND NO MORE FUN WITH "DADDY."
YOU ARE A SOLDIER.
YOU ARE MY SOLDIER.
AND THAT IS ALL YOU SHALL EVER BE...

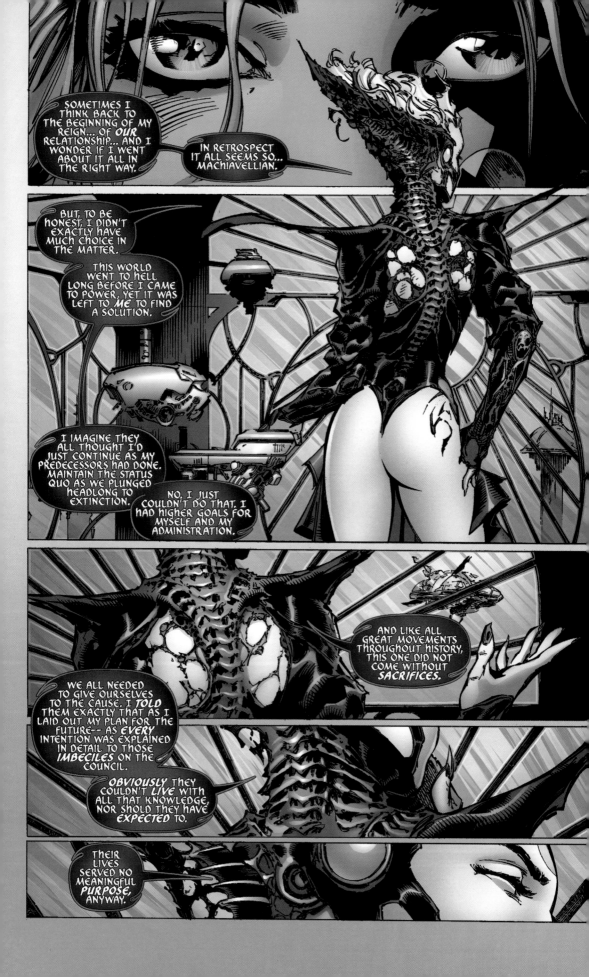

SOMETIMES I THINK BACK TO THE BEGINNING OF MY REIGN... OF *OUR* RELATIONSHIP... AND I WONDER IF I WENT ABOUT IT ALL IN THE RIGHT WAY.

IN RETROSPECT IT ALL SEEMS SO... MACHIAVELLIAN.

BUT, TO BE HONEST, I DIDN'T EXACTLY HAVE MUCH CHOICE IN THE MATTER.

THIS WORLD WENT TO HELL LONG BEFORE I CAME TO POWER, YET IT WAS LEFT TO *ME* TO FIND A SOLUTION.

I IMAGINE THEY ALL THOUGHT I'D JUST CONTINUE AS MY PREDECESSORS HAD DONE. MAINTAIN THE STATUS QUO AS WE PLUNGED HEADLONG TO EXTINCTION.

NO, I JUST COULDN'T DO THAT. I HAD HIGHER GOALS FOR MYSELF AND MY ADMINISTRATION.

AND LIKE ALL GREAT MOVEMENTS THROUGHOUT HISTORY, THIS ONE DID NOT COME WITHOUT *SACRIFICES.*

WE ALL NEEDED TO GIVE OURSELVES TO THE CAUSE. I *TOLD* THEM EXACTLY THAT AS I LAID OUT MY PLAN FOR THE FUTURE-- AS *EVERY* INTENTION WAS EXPLAINED IN DETAIL TO THOSE *IMBECILES* ON THE COUNCIL.

OBVIOUSLY THEY COULDN'T *LIVE* WITH ALL THAT KNOWLEDGE, NOR SHOLD THEY HAVE *EXPECTED* TO.

THEIR LIVES SERVED NO MEANINGFUL *PURPOSE,* ANYWAY.

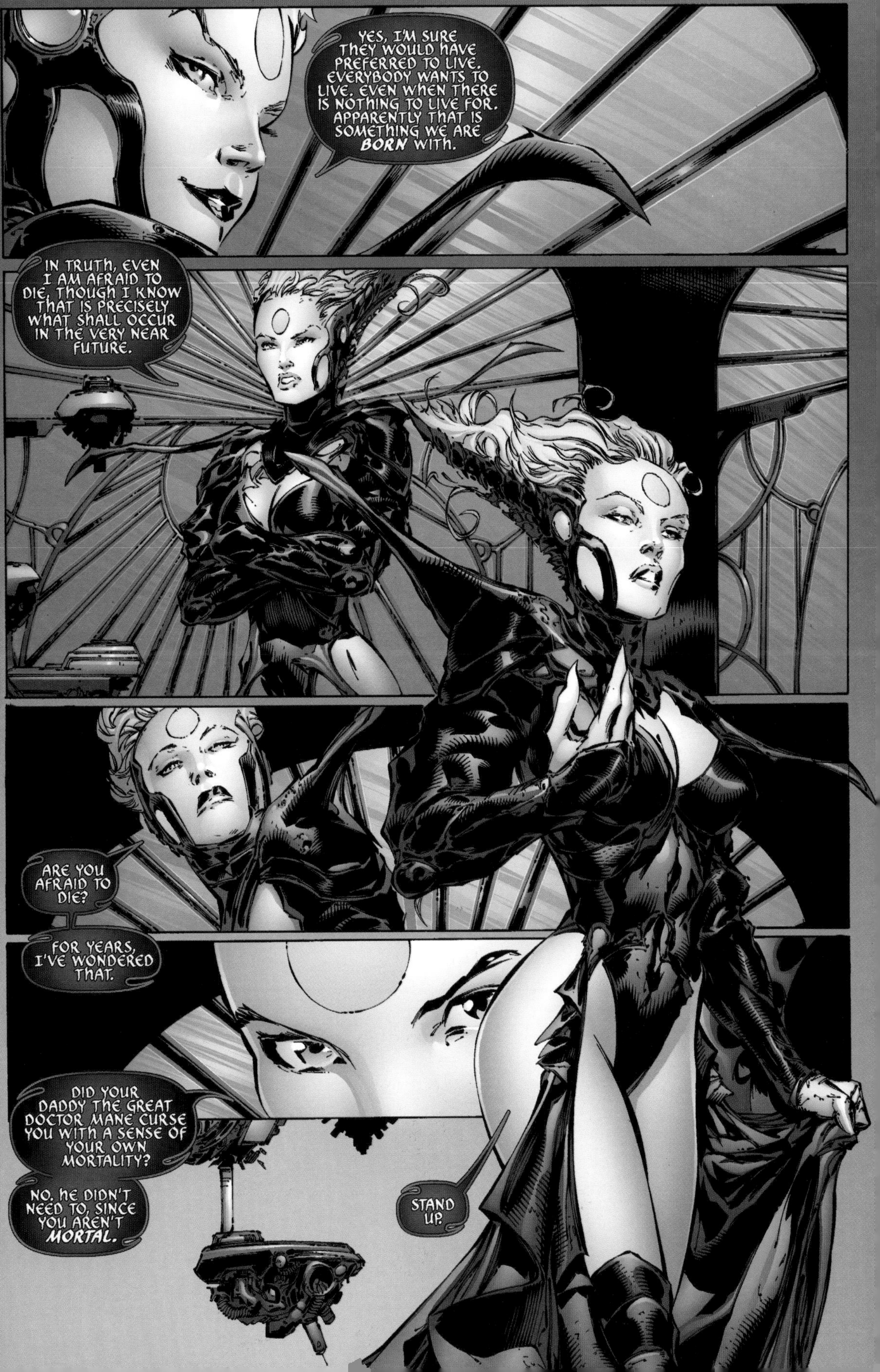
YES, I'M SURE THEY WOULD HAVE PREFERRED TO LIVE. EVERYBODY WANTS TO LIVE. EVEN WHEN THERE IS NOTHING TO LIVE FOR. APPARENTLY THAT IS SOMETHING WE ARE BORN WITH.
IN TRUTH, EVEN I AM AFRAID TO DIE, THOUGH I KNOW THAT IS PRECISELY WHAT SHALL OCCUR IN THE VERY NEAR FUTURE.
ARE YOU AFRAID TO DIE?
FOR YEARS, I'VE WONDERED THAT.
DID YOUR DADDY THE GREAT DOCTOR MANE CURSE YOU WITH A SENSE OF YOUR OWN MORTALITY?
NO, HE DIDN'T NEED TO, SINCE YOU AREN'T MORTAL.
STAND UP.

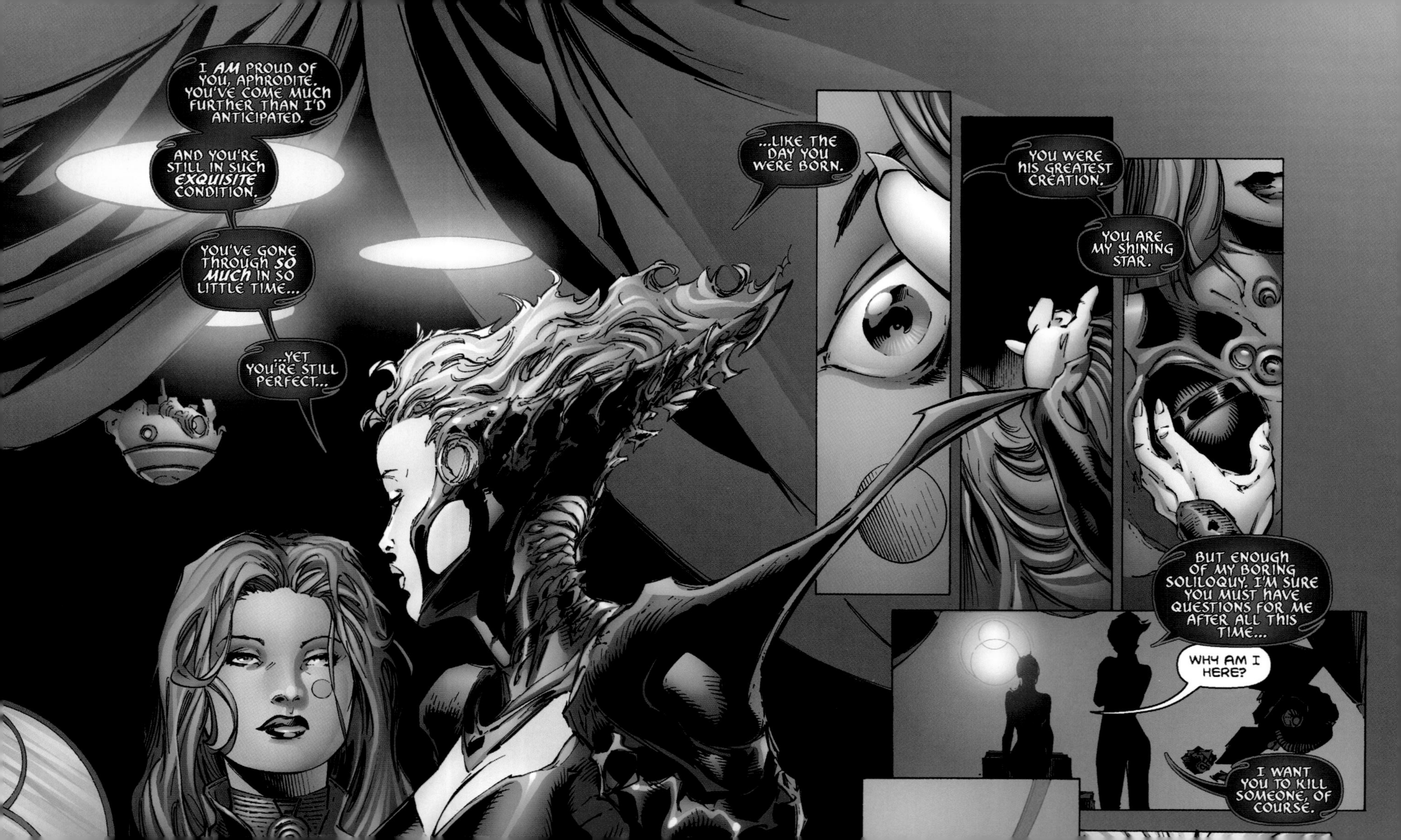
I AM PROUD OF YOU, APHRODITE. YOU'VE COME MUCH FURTHER THAN I'D ANTICIPATED.
AND YOU'RE STILL IN SUCH EXQUISITE CONDITION.
YOU'VE GONE THROUGH SO MUCH IN SO LITTLE TIME...
...YET YOU'RE STILL PERFECT...
...LIKE THE DAY YOU WERE BORN.
YOU WERE HIS GREATEST CREATION.
YOU ARE MY SHINING STAR.
BUT ENOUGH OF MY BORING SOLILOQUY. I'M SURE YOU MUST HAVE QUESTIONS FOR ME AFTER ALL THIS TIME...
WHY AM I HERE?
I WANT YOU TO KILL SOMEONE, OF COURSE.

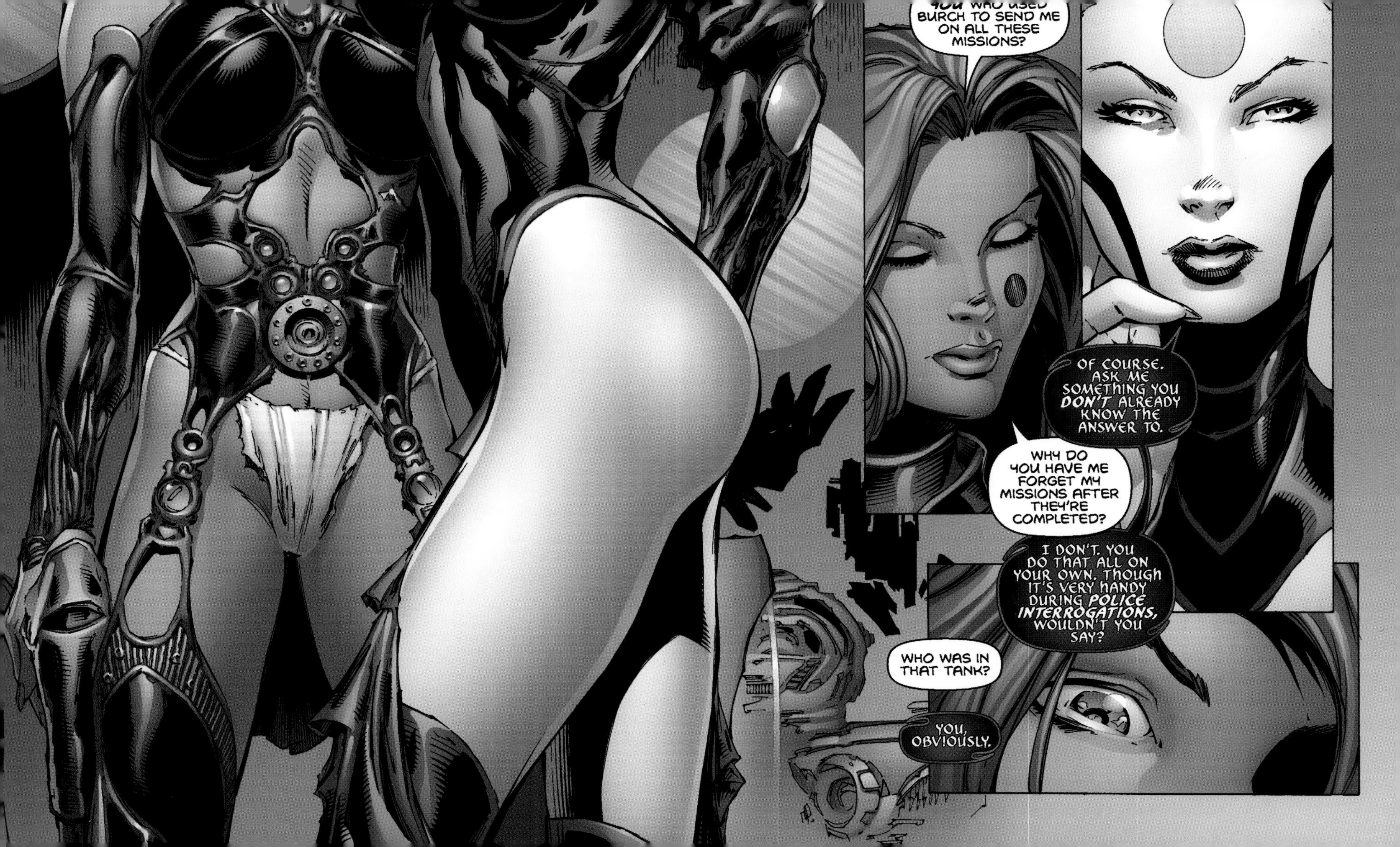
BURCH TO SEND ME ON ALL THESE MISSIONS?
OF COURSE. ASK ME SOMETHING YOU DON'T ALREADY KNOW THE ANSWER TO.
WHY DO YOU HAVE ME FORGET MY MISSIONS AFTER THEY'RE COMPLETED?
I DON'T. YOU DO THAT ALL ON YOUR OWN. THOUGH IT'S VERY HANDY DURING POLICE INTERROGATIONS, WOULDN'T YOU SAY?
WHO WAS IN THAT TANK?
YOU, OBVIOUSLY.

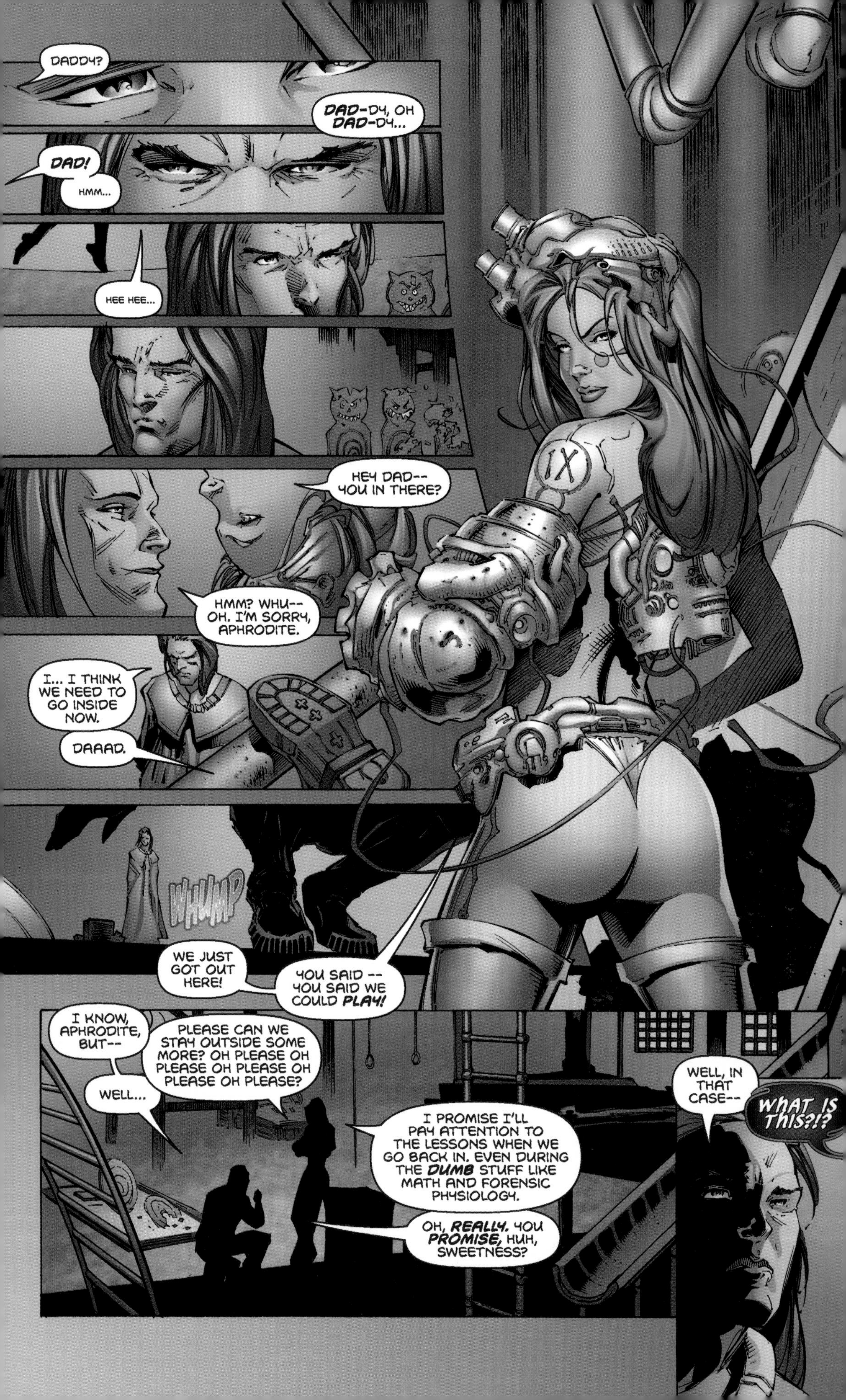
DADDY?
DAD-DY, OH DAD-DY...
DAD!
HMM...
HEE HEE...
HEY DAD-- YOU IN THERE?
HMM? WHU-- OH. I'M SORRY, APHRODITE.
I... I THINK WE NEED TO GO INSIDE NOW.
DAAAD.
WHUMP
WE JUST GOT OUT HERE!
YOU SAID -- YOU SAID WE COULD PLAY!
I KNOW, APHRODITE, BUT--
PLEASE CAN WE STAY OUTSIDE SOME MORE? OH PLEASE OH PLEASE OH PLEASE OH PLEASE OH PLEASE?
WELL...
I PROMISE I'LL PAY ATTENTION TO THE LESSONS WHEN WE GO BACK IN. EVEN DURING THE DUMB STUFF LIKE MATH AND FORENSIC PHYSIOLOGY.
OH, REALLY. YOU PROMISE, HUH, SWEETNESS?
WELL, IN THAT CASE--
WHAT IS THIS?!?

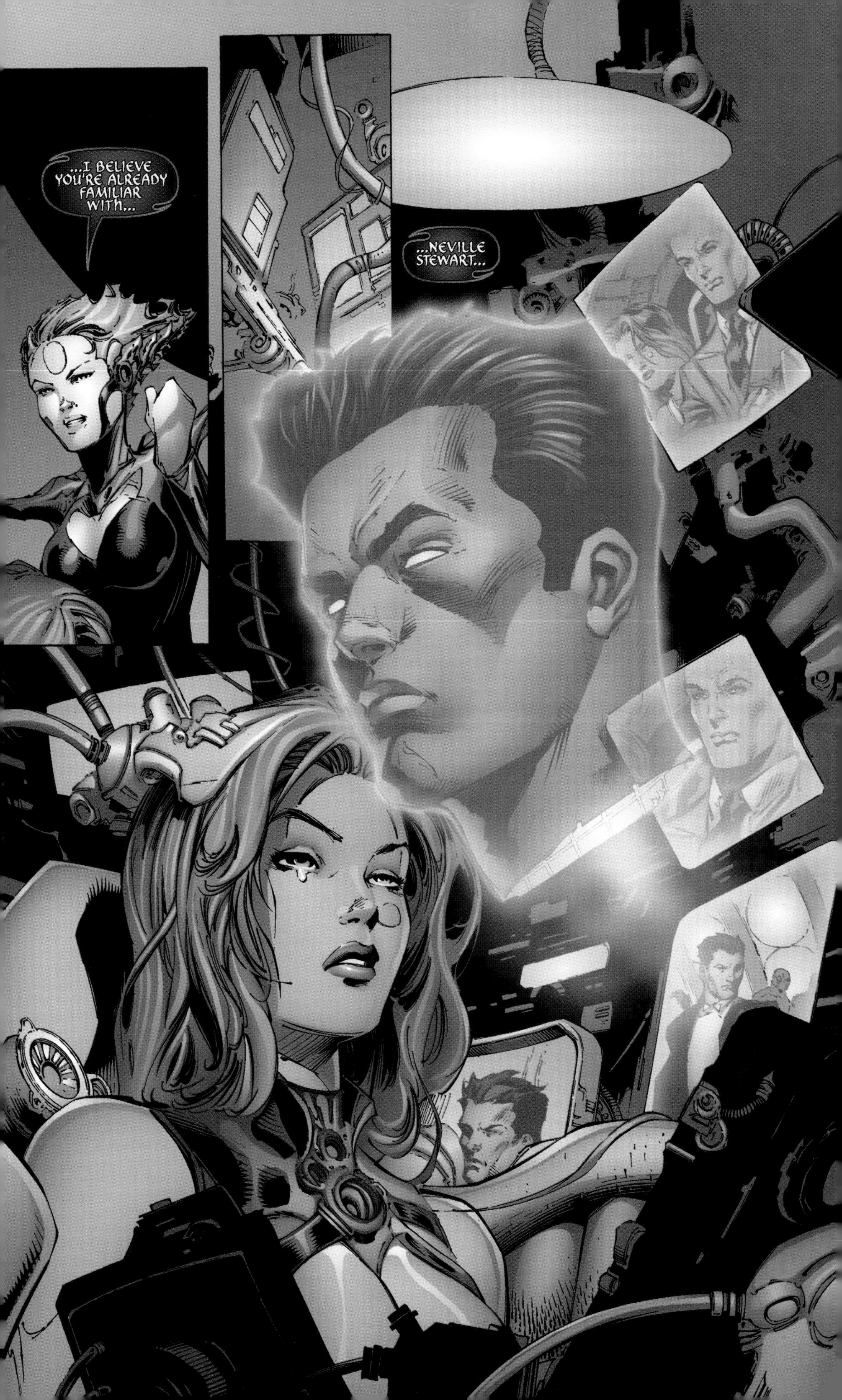
...I BELIEVE YOU'RE ALREADY FAMILIAR WITH...
...NEVILLE STEWART...

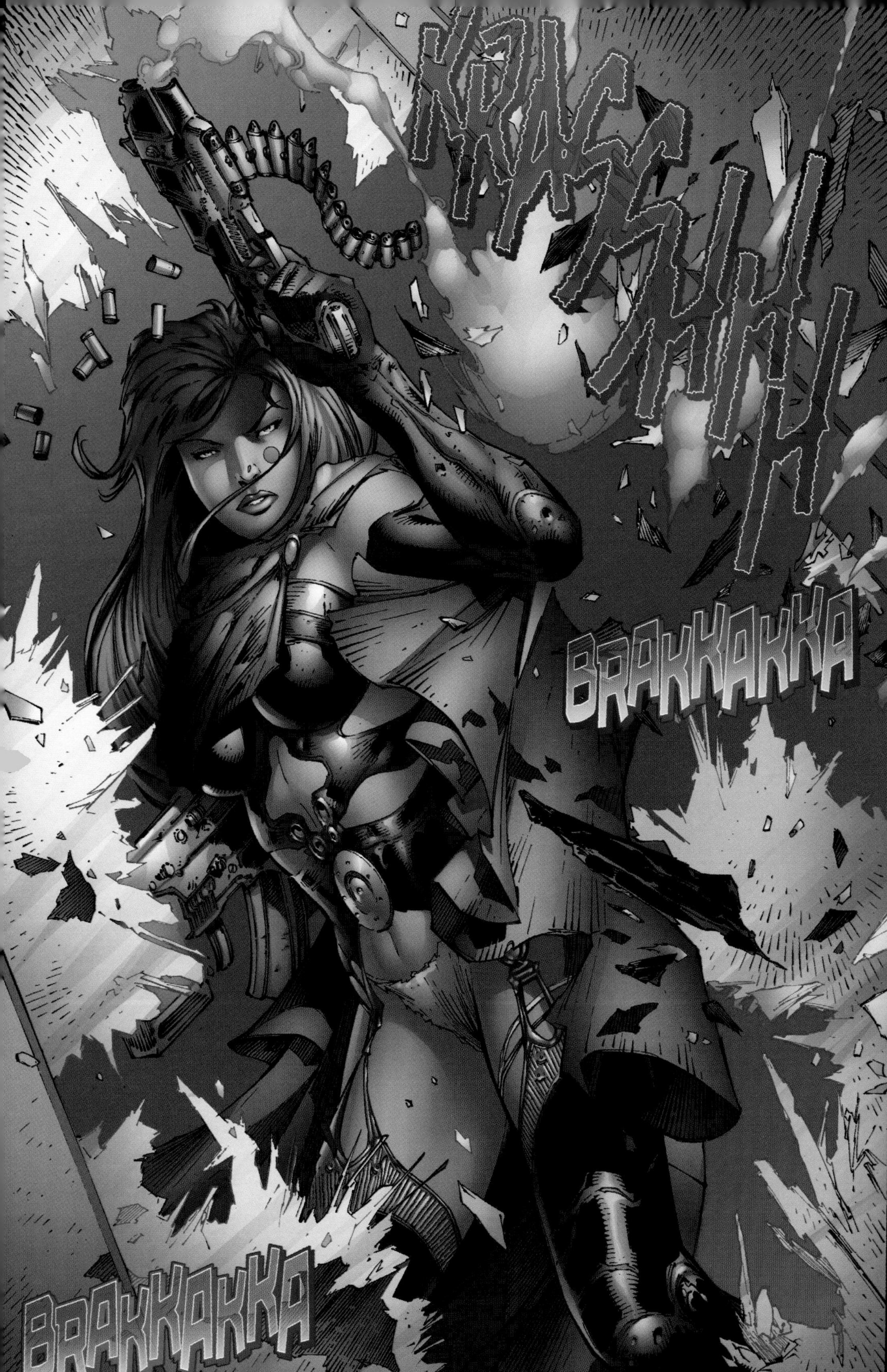
KRASSHHH
BRAKKAKKA
BRAKKAKKA

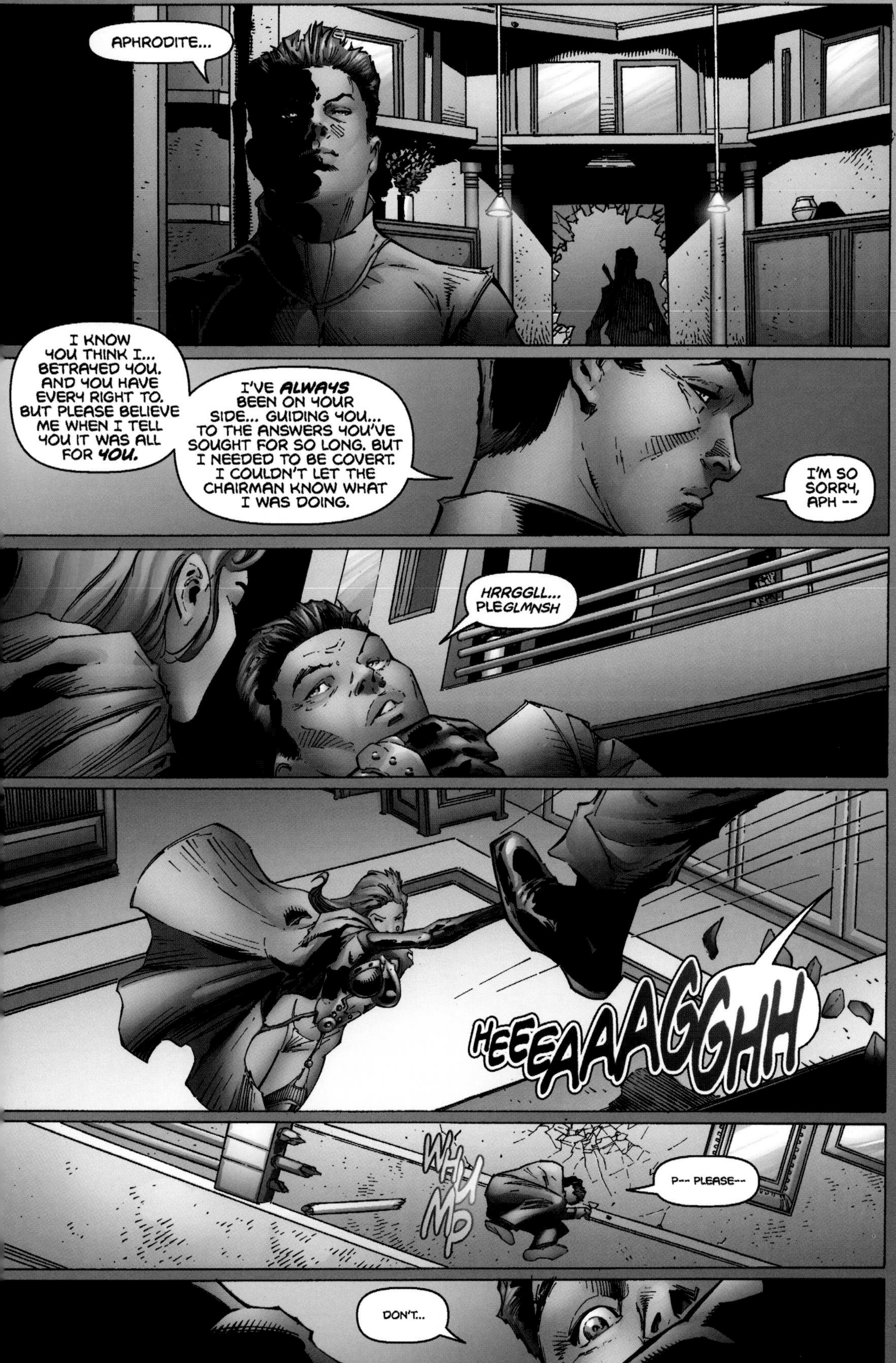

APHRODITE...
I KNOW YOU THINK I... BETRAYED YOU. AND YOU HAVE EVERY RIGHT TO. BUT PLEASE BELIEVE ME WHEN I TELL YOU IT WAS ALL FOR *YOU.*
I'VE *ALWAYS* BEEN ON YOUR SIDE... GUIDING YOU... TO THE ANSWERS YOU'VE SOUGHT FOR SO LONG. BUT I NEEDED TO BE COVERT. I COULDN'T LET THE CHAIRMAN KNOW WHAT I WAS DOING.
I'M SO SORRY, APH --
HRRGGLL... PLEGLMNSH
HEEEAAAAGGHH
WHUMP
P-- PLEASE--
DON'T...

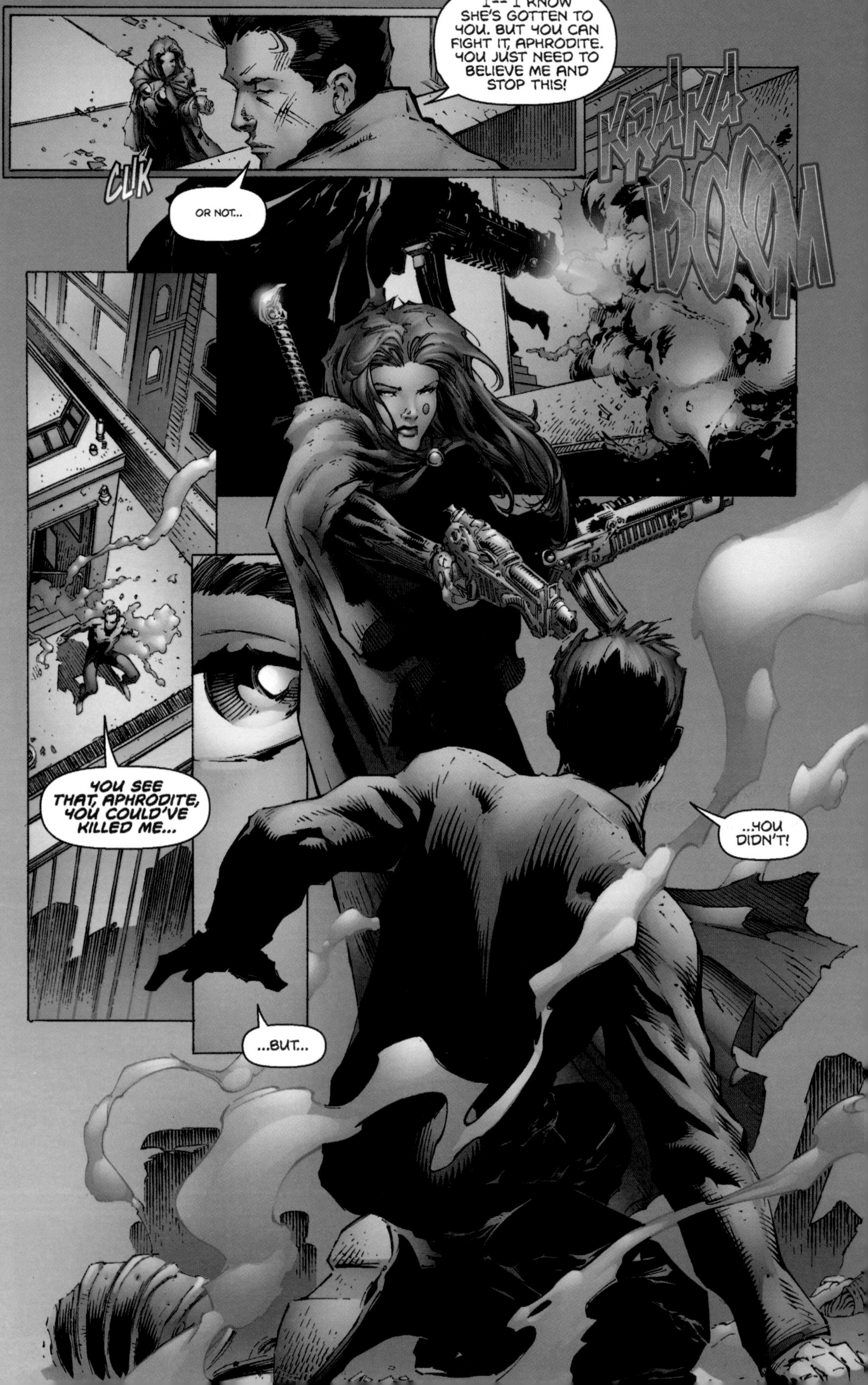
I-- I KNOW SHE'S GOTTEN TO YOU. BUT YOU CAN FIGHT IT, APHRODITE. YOU JUST NEED TO BELIEVE ME AND STOP THIS!
CLIK
OR NOT...
KRAKA BOOM
YOU SEE THAT, APHRODITE, YOU COULD'VE KILLED ME...
...BUT...
...YOU DIDN'T!

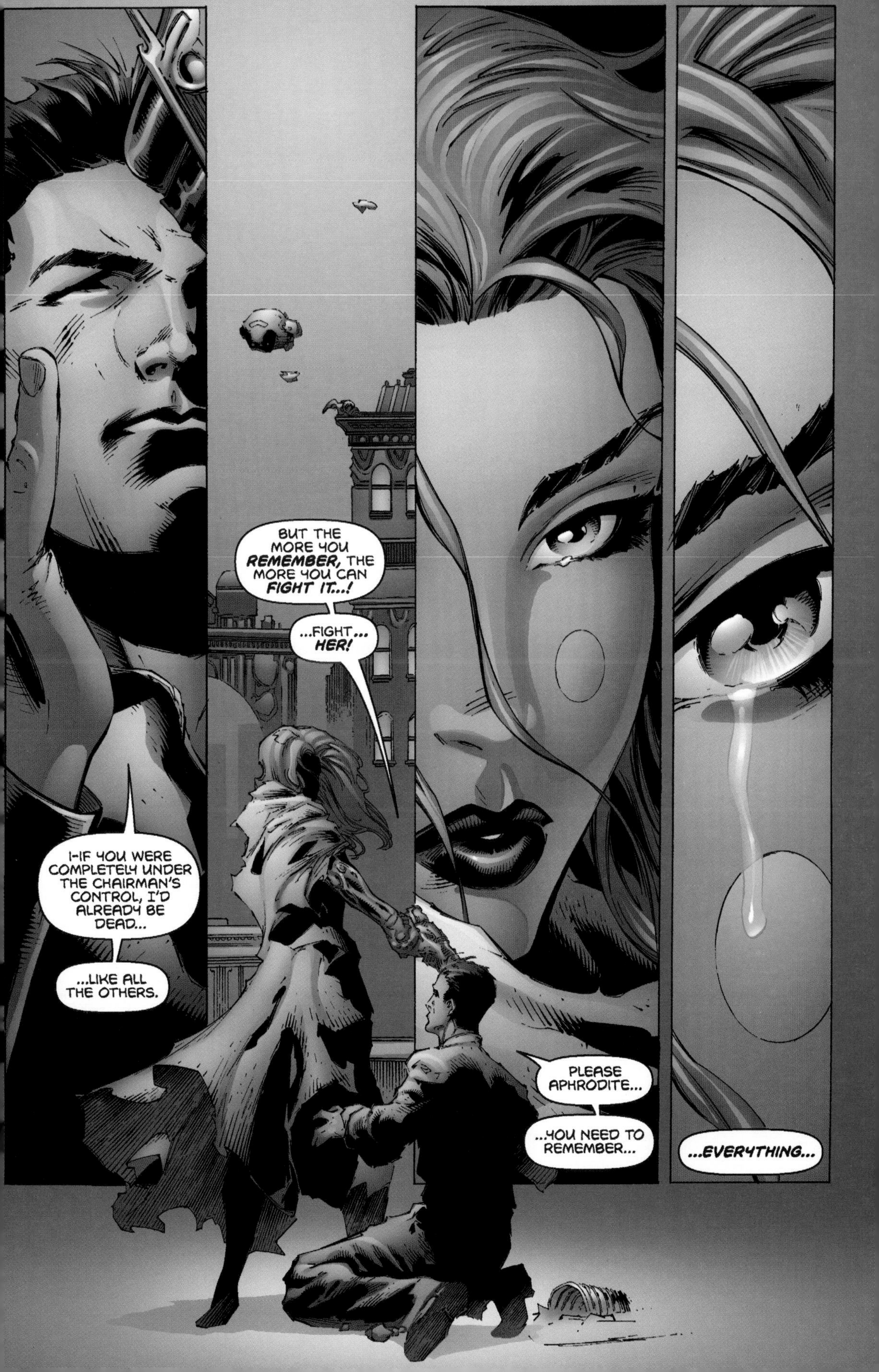
I-IF YOU WERE COMPLETELY UNDER THE CHAIRMAN'S CONTROL, I'D ALREADY BE DEAD...
...LIKE ALL THE OTHERS.
BUT THE MORE YOU REMEMBER, THE MORE YOU CAN FIGHT IT...!
...FIGHT... HER!
PLEASE APHRODITE...
...YOU NEED TO REMEMBER...
...EVERYTHING...

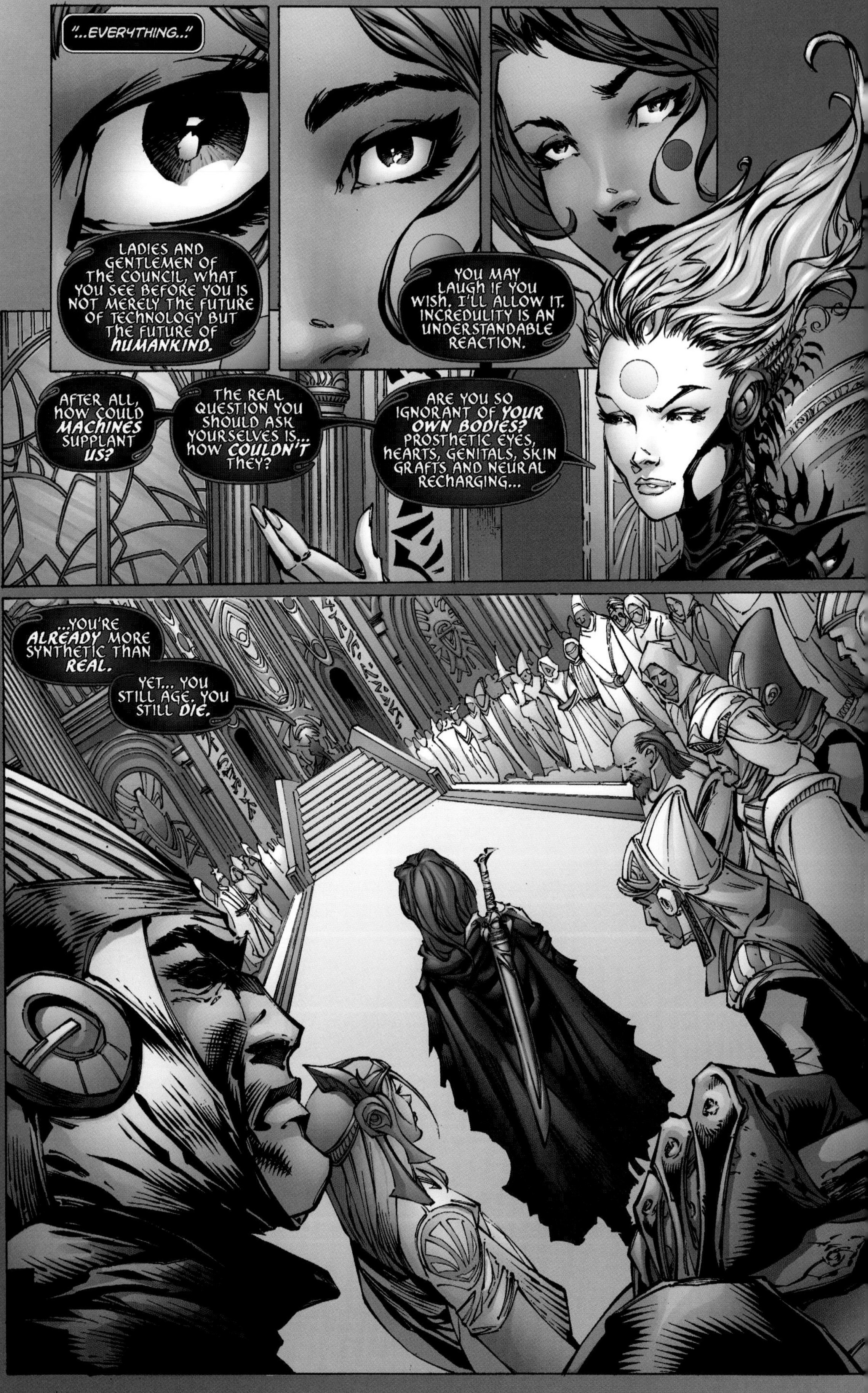
"...EVERYTHING..."
LADIES AND GENTLEMEN OF THE COUNCIL, WHAT YOU SEE BEFORE YOU IS NOT MERELY THE FUTURE OF TECHNOLOGY BUT THE FUTURE OF HUMANKIND.
YOU MAY LAUGH IF YOU WISH. I'LL ALLOW IT. INCREDULITY IS AN UNDERSTANDABLE REACTION.
AFTER ALL, HOW COULD MACHINES SUPPLANT US?
THE REAL QUESTION YOU SHOULD ASK YOURSELVES IS... HOW COULDN'T THEY?
ARE YOU SO IGNORANT OF YOUR OWN BODIES? PROSTHETIC EYES, HEARTS, GENITALS, SKIN GRAFTS AND NEURAL RECHARGING...
...YOU'RE ALREADY MORE SYNTHETIC THAN REAL.
YET... YOU STILL AGE. YOU STILL DIE.

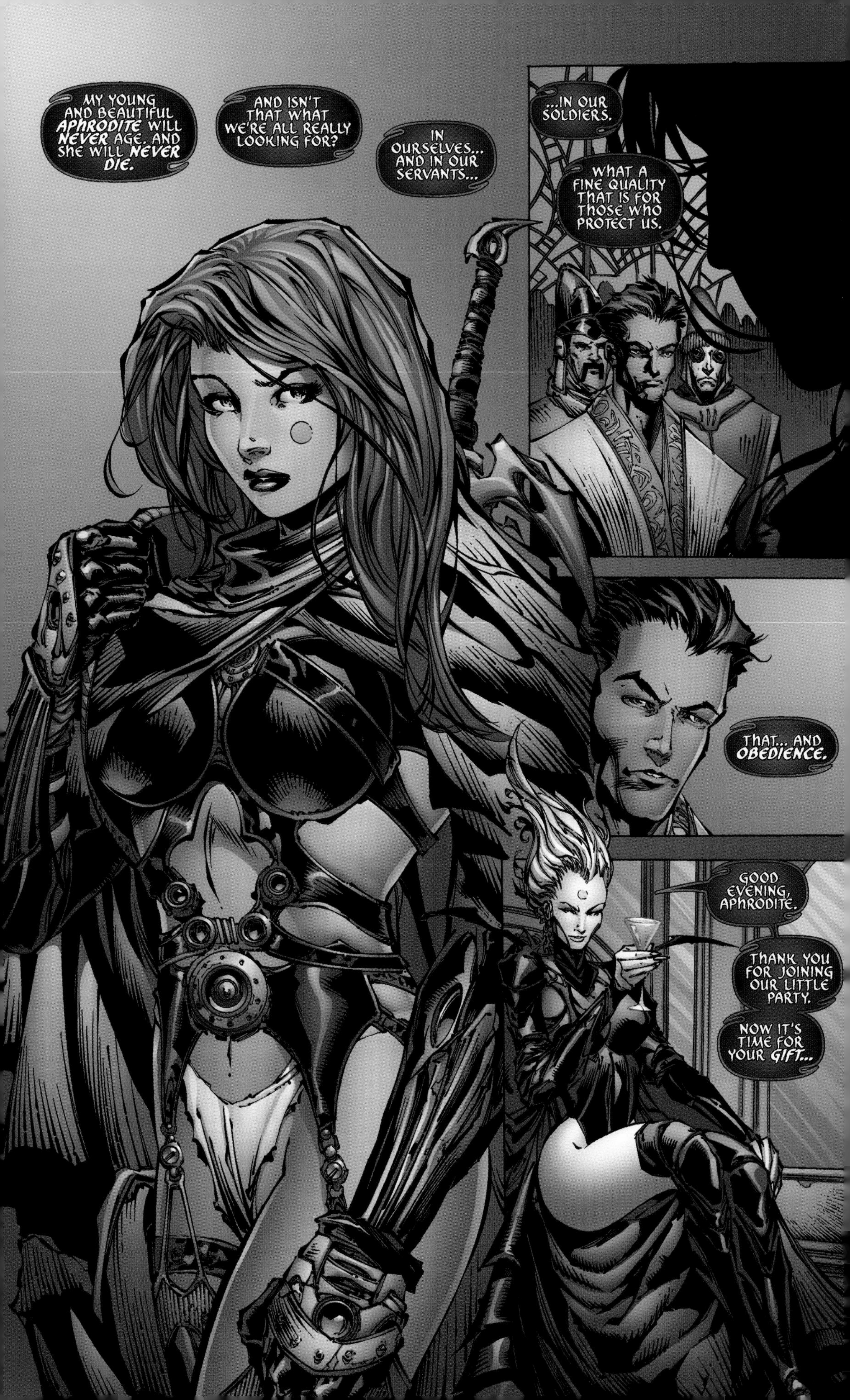
MY YOUNG AND BEAUTIFUL APHRODITE WILL NEVER AGE. AND SHE WILL NEVER DIE.
AND ISN'T THAT WHAT WE'RE ALL REALLY LOOKING FOR?
IN OURSELVES... AND IN OUR SERVANTS...
...IN OUR SOLDIERS.
WHAT A FINE QUALITY THAT IS FOR THOSE WHO PROTECT US.
THAT... AND OBEDIENCE.
GOOD EVENING, APHRODITE.
THANK YOU FOR JOINING OUR LITTLE PARTY.
NOW IT'S TIME FOR YOUR GIFT...

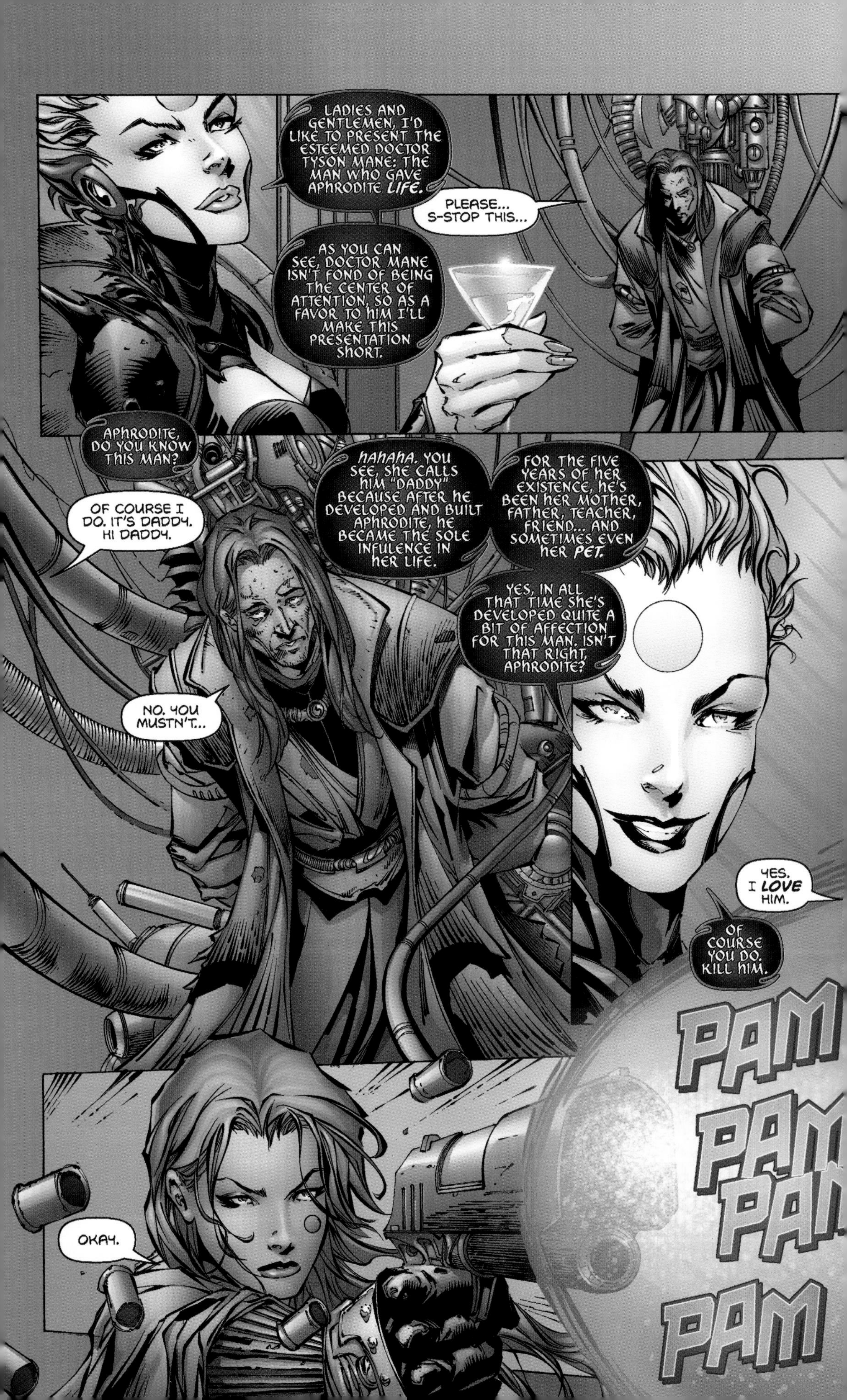
LADIES AND GENTLEMEN, I'D LIKE TO PRESENT THE ESTEEMED DOCTOR TYSON MANE: THE MAN WHO GAVE APHRODITE LIFE.
PLEASE... S-STOP THIS...
AS YOU CAN SEE, DOCTOR MANE ISN'T FOND OF BEING THE CENTER OF ATTENTION, SO AS A FAVOR TO HIM I'LL MAKE THIS PRESENTATION SHORT.
APHRODITE, DO YOU KNOW THIS MAN?
OF COURSE I DO. IT'S DADDY. HI DADDY.
HAHAHA. YOU SEE, SHE CALLS HIM "DADDY" BECAUSE AFTER HE DEVELOPED AND BUILT APHRODITE, HE BECAME THE SOLE INFULENCE IN HER LIFE.
FOR THE FIVE YEARS OF HER EXISTENCE, HE'S BEEN HER MOTHER, FATHER, TEACHER, FRIEND... AND SOMETIMES EVEN HER PET.
YES, IN ALL THAT TIME SHE'S DEVELOPED QUITE A BIT OF AFFECTION FOR THIS MAN. ISN'T THAT RIGHT, APHRODITE?
NO. YOU MUSTN'T...
YES. I LOVE HIM.
OF COURSE YOU DO. KILL HIM.
OKAY.
PAM
PAM
PAM
PAM

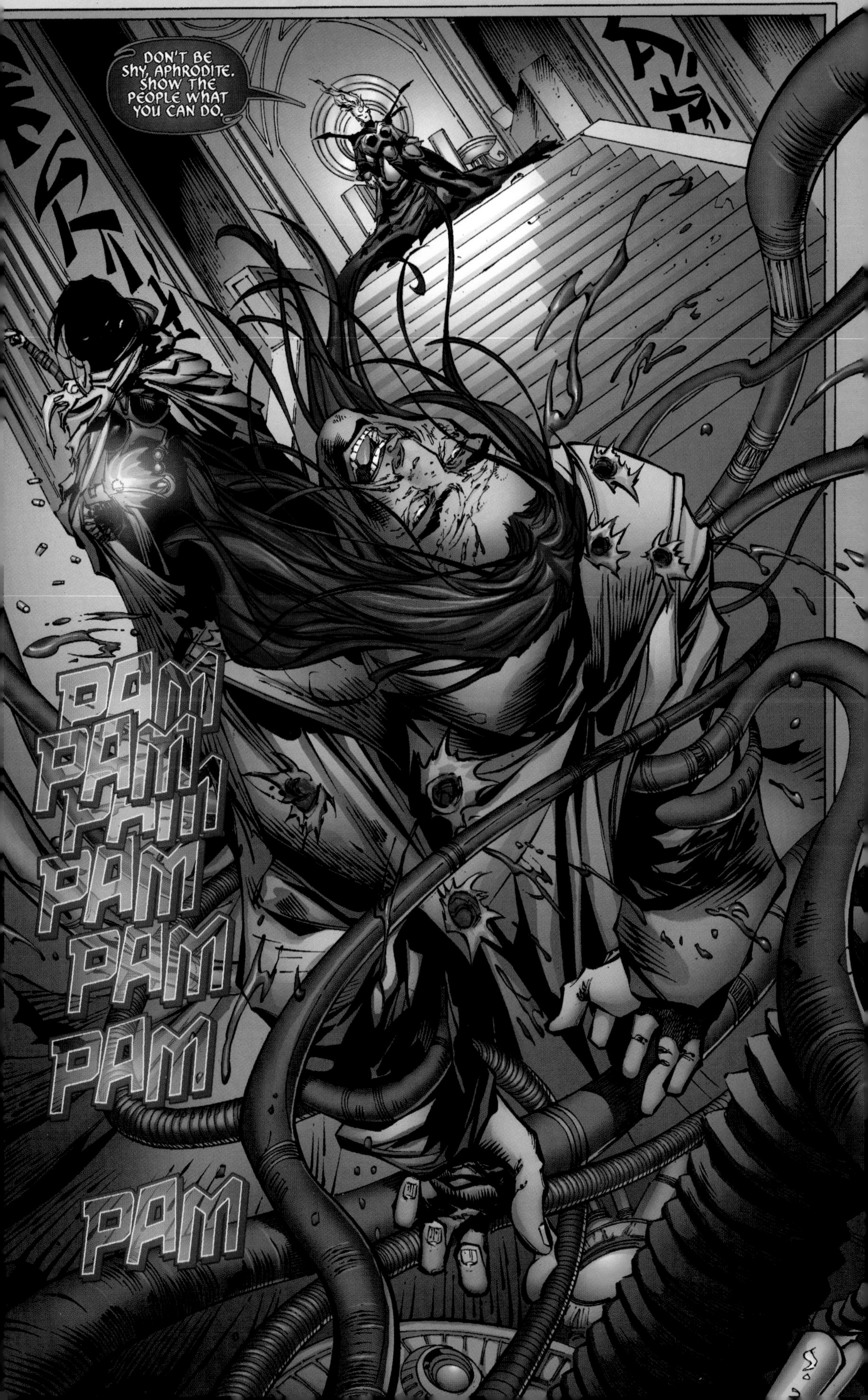

DON'T BE SHY, APHRODITE. SHOW THE PEOPLE WHAT YOU CAN DO.
PAM
PAM
PAM
PAM
PAM
PAM
PAM

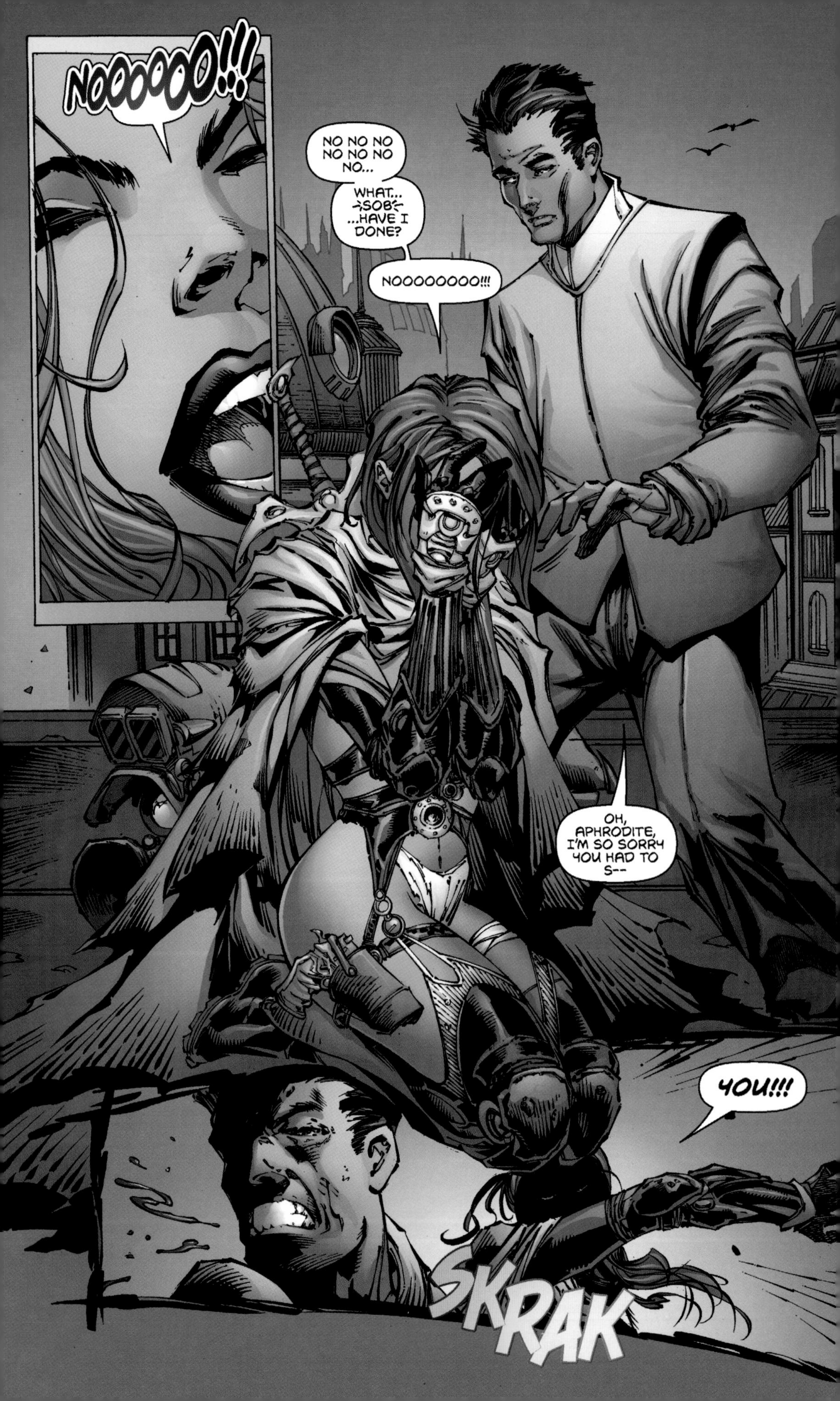
NOOOOOO!!!
NO NO NO
NO NO NO
NO...
WHAT...
-SOB-
...HAVE I
DONE?
NOOOOOOOO!!!
OH,
APHRODITE,
I'M SO SORRY
YOU HAD TO
S--
YOU!!!
SKRAK

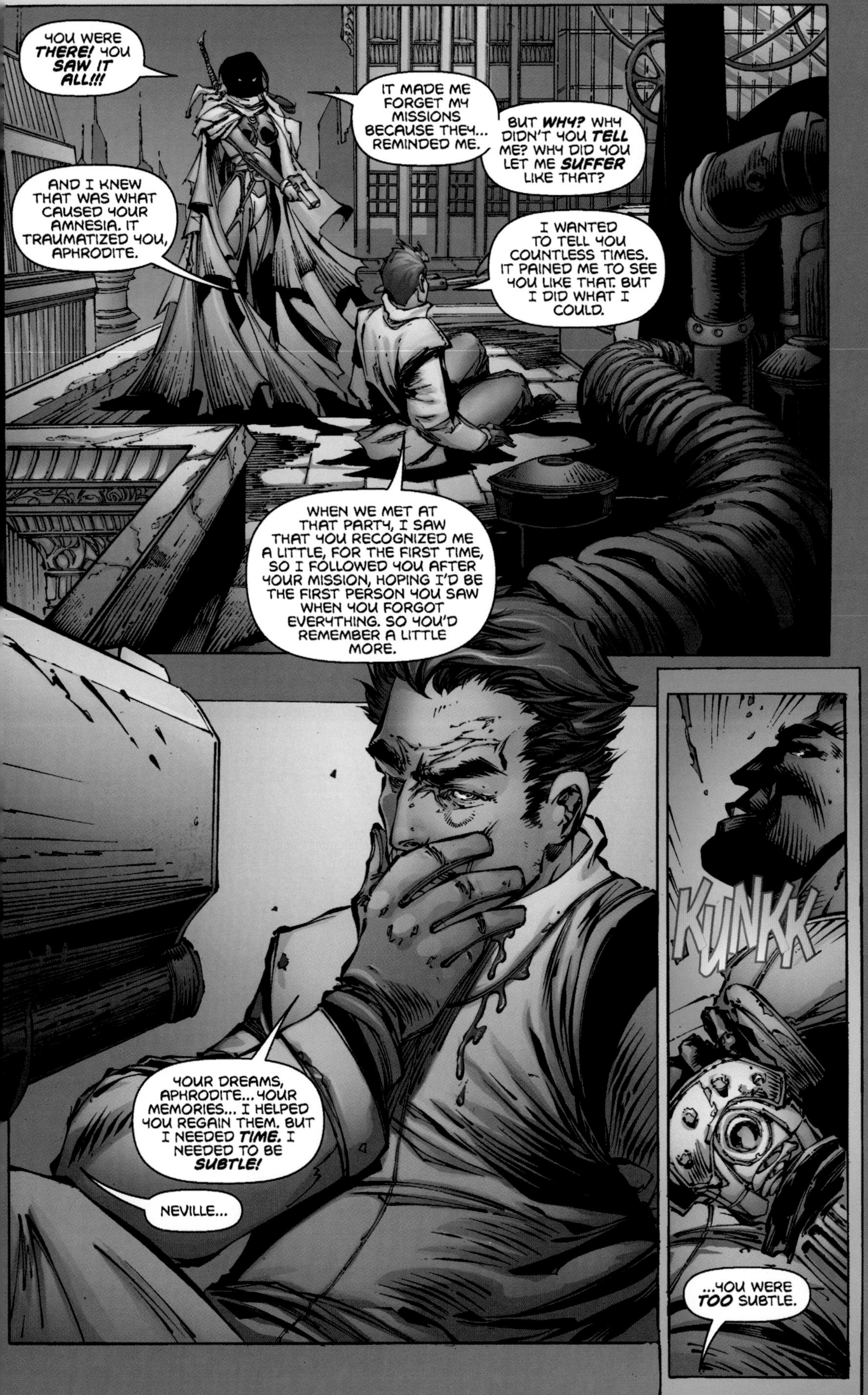
YOU WERE THERE! YOU SAW IT ALL!!!
IT MADE ME FORGET MY MISSIONS BECAUSE THEY... REMINDED ME.
BUT WHY? WHY DIDN'T YOU TELL ME? WHY DID YOU LET ME SUFFER LIKE THAT?
AND I KNEW THAT WAS WHAT CAUSED YOUR AMNESIA. IT TRAUMATIZED YOU, APHRODITE.
I WANTED TO TELL YOU COUNTLESS TIMES. IT PAINED ME TO SEE YOU LIKE THAT. BUT I DID WHAT I COULD.
WHEN WE MET AT THAT PARTY, I SAW THAT YOU RECOGNIZED ME A LITTLE, FOR THE FIRST TIME, SO I FOLLOWED YOU AFTER YOUR MISSION, HOPING I'D BE THE FIRST PERSON YOU SAW WHEN YOU FORGOT EVERYTHING. SO YOU'D REMEMBER A LITTLE MORE.
YOUR DREAMS, APHRODITE... YOUR MEMORIES... I HELPED YOU REGAIN THEM. BUT I NEEDED TIME. I NEEDED TO BE SUBTLE!
NEVILLE...
KUNKK
...YOU WERE TOO SUBTLE.

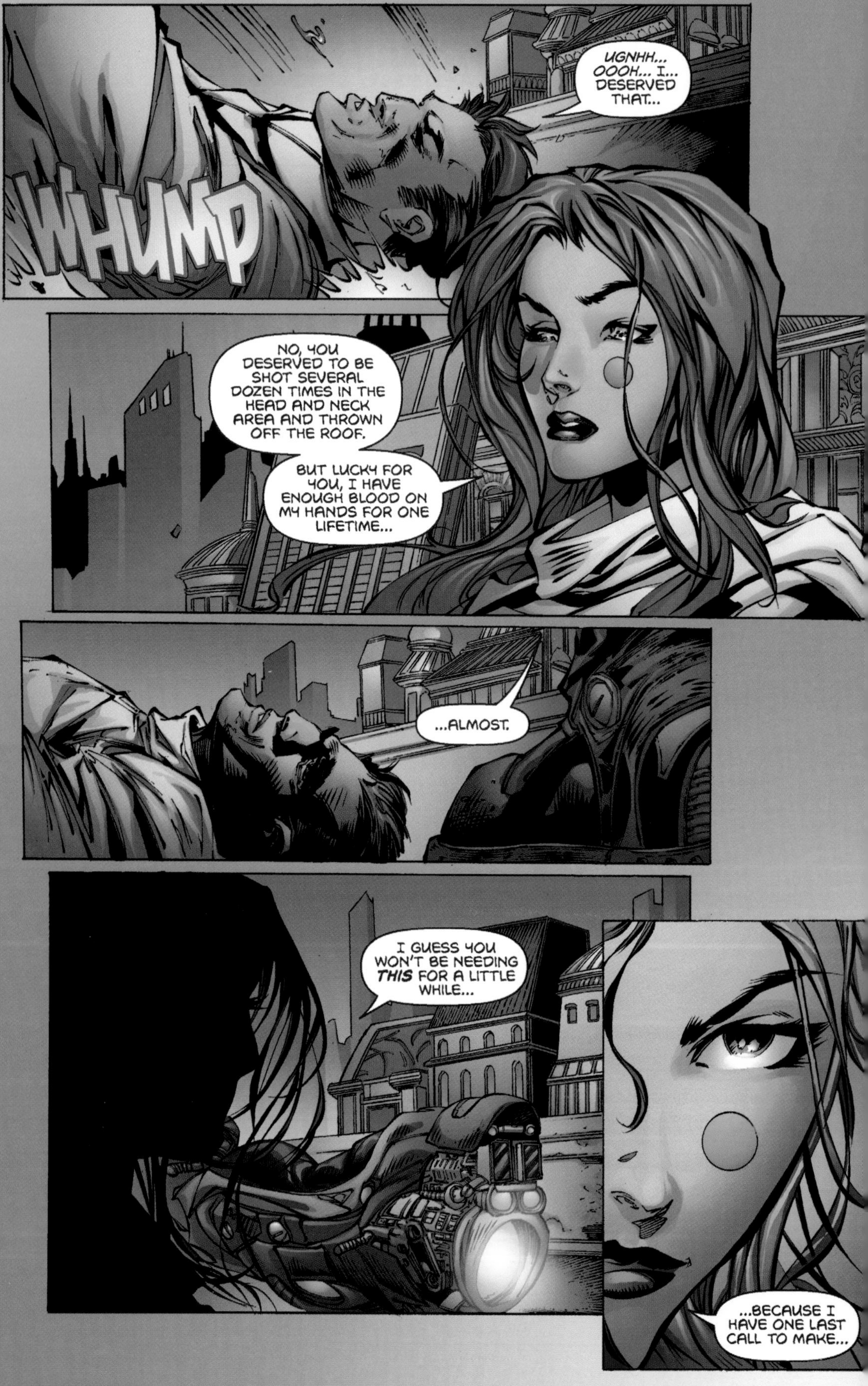
UGNHH... OOOH... I... DESERVED THAT...
WHUMP
NO, YOU DESERVED TO BE SHOT SEVERAL DOZEN TIMES IN THE HEAD AND NECK AREA AND THROWN OFF THE ROOF.
BUT LUCKY FOR YOU, I HAVE ENOUGH BLOOD ON MY HANDS FOR ONE LIFETIME...
...ALMOST.
I GUESS YOU WON'T BE NEEDING *THIS* FOR A LITTLE WHILE...
...BECAUSE I HAVE ONE LAST CALL TO MAKE...

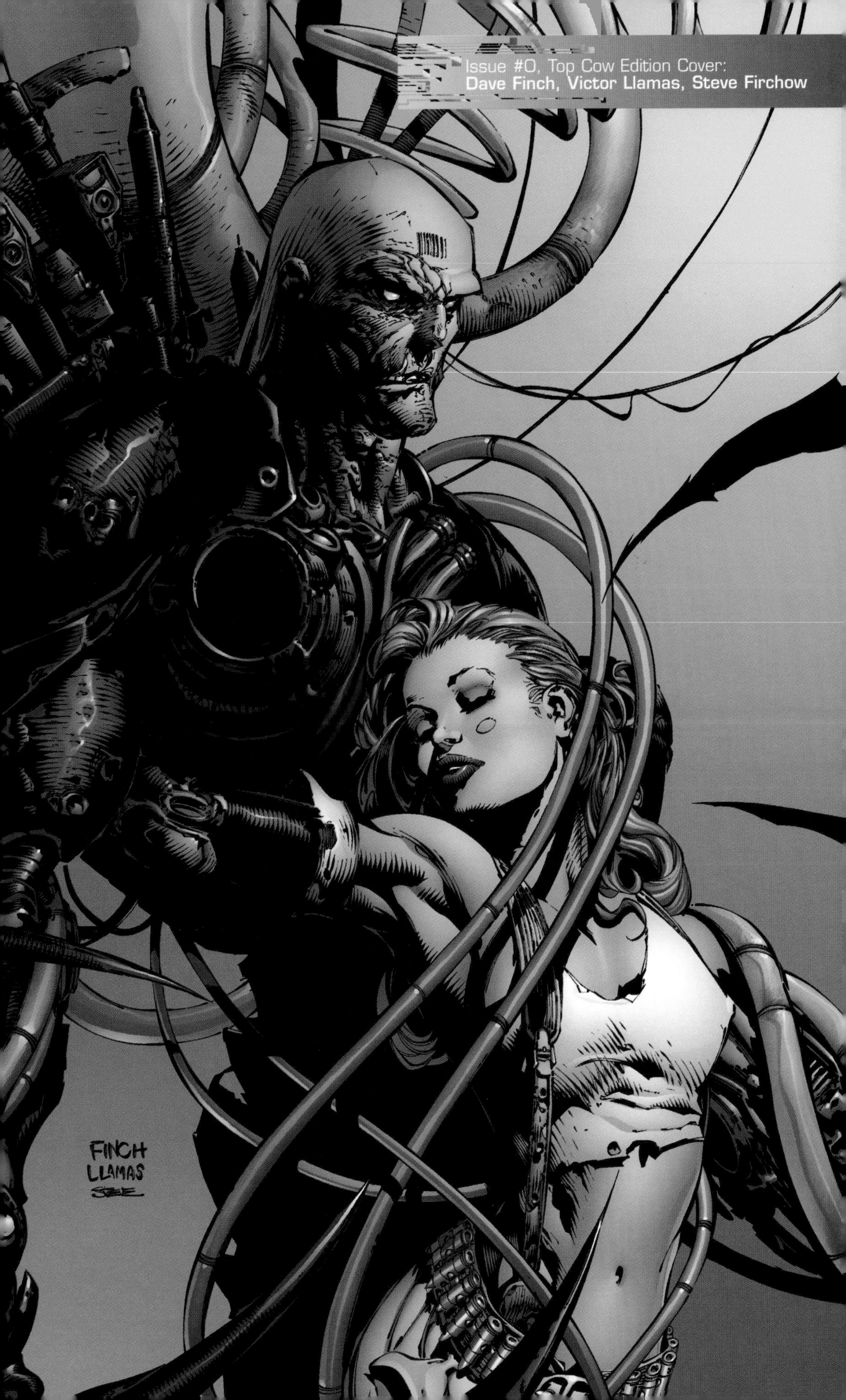
FINCH
LLAMAS

Issue #0, Top Cow Edition Cover:
Dave Finch, Victor Llamas, Steve Firchow

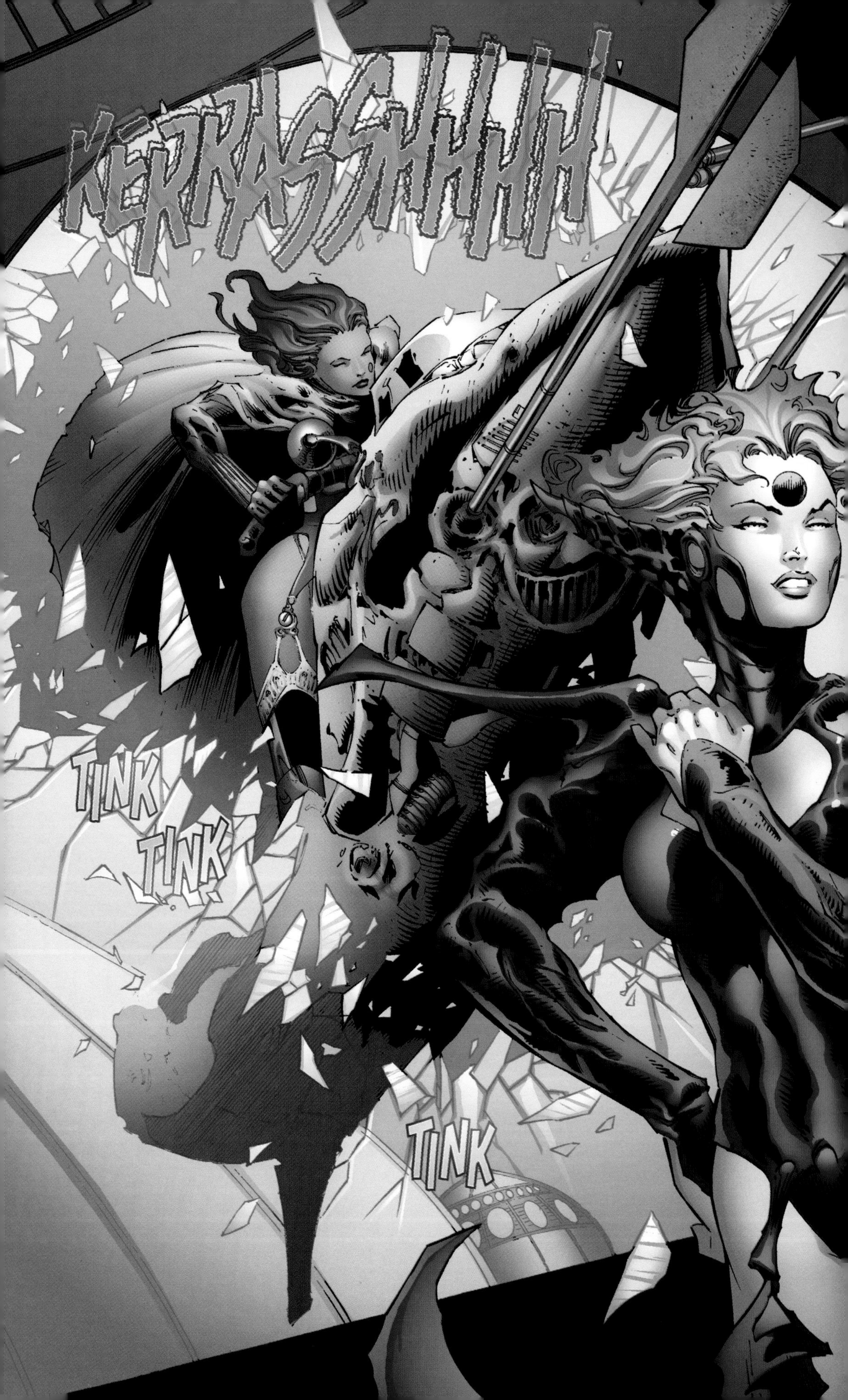
KERRASSHHHHH
TINK
TINK
TINK

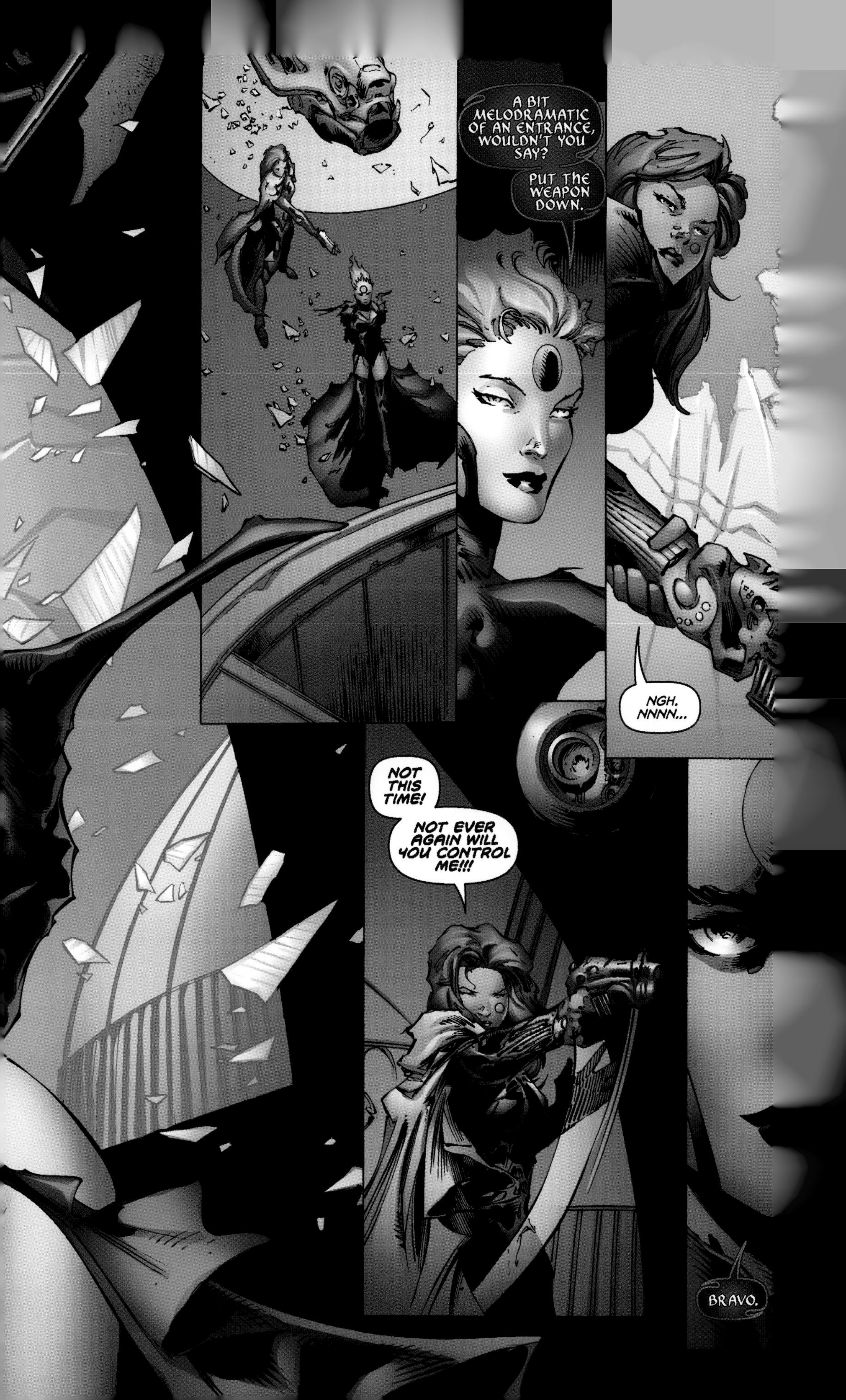
A BIT MELODRAMATIC OF AN ENTRANCE, WOULDN'T YOU SAY?
PUT THE WEAPON DOWN.
NGH. NNNN...
NOT THIS TIME!
NOT EVER AGAIN WILL YOU CONTROL ME!!!
BRAVO.

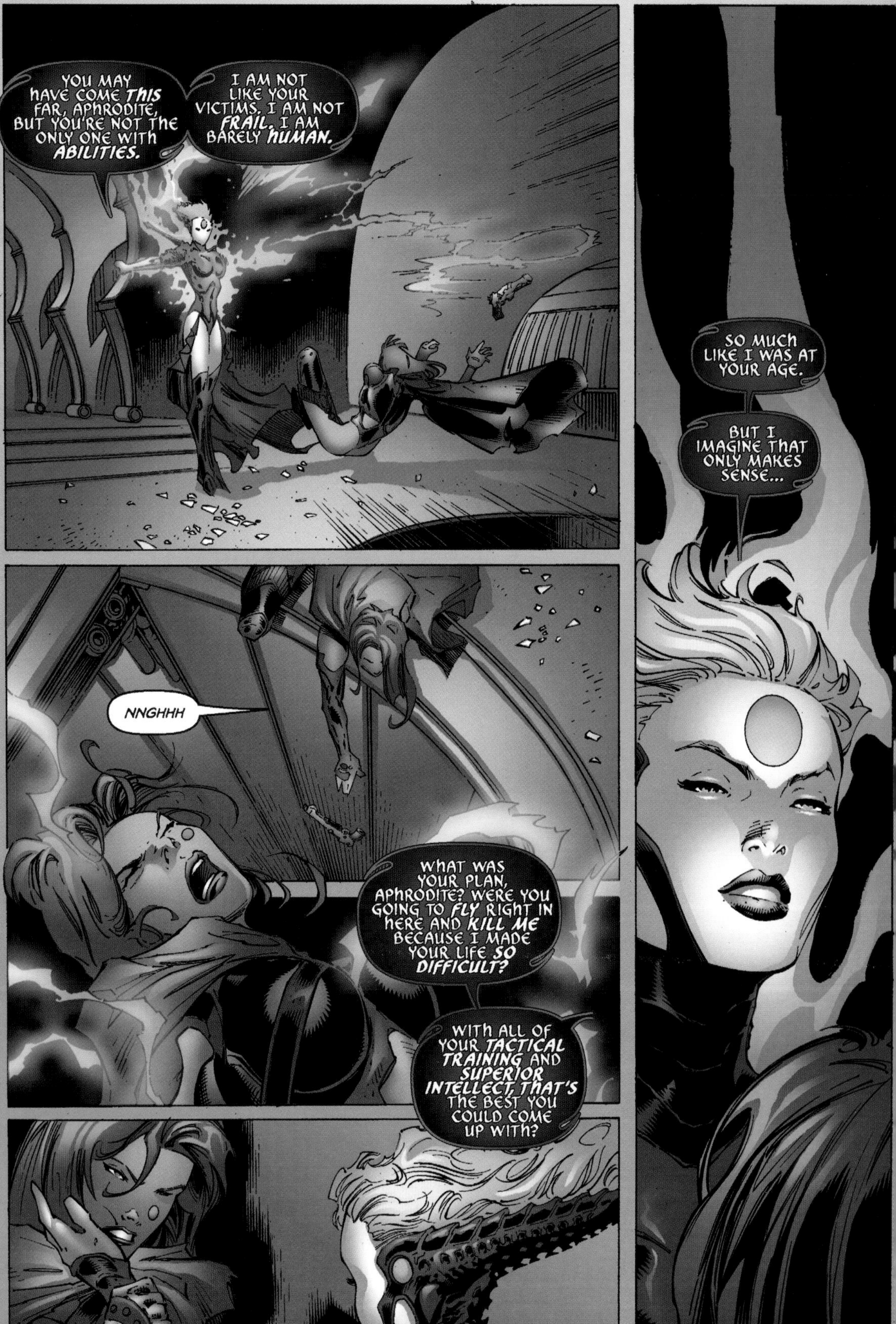
YOU MAY HAVE COME THIS FAR, APHRODITE, BUT YOU'RE NOT THE ONLY ONE WITH ABILITIES.
I AM NOT LIKE YOUR VICTIMS. I AM NOT FRAIL. I AM BARELY HUMAN.
NNGHHH
WHAT WAS YOUR PLAN, APHRODITE? WERE YOU GOING TO FLY RIGHT IN HERE AND KILL ME BECAUSE I MADE YOUR LIFE SO DIFFICULT?
WITH ALL OF YOUR TACTICAL TRAINING AND SUPERIOR INTELLECT, THAT'S THE BEST YOU COULD COME UP WITH?
YOU'RE QUITE SPECIAL, MY DEAR, BUT YOU'RE STILL SO BRASH.
SO MUCH LIKE I WAS AT YOUR AGE.
BUT I IMAGINE THAT ONLY MAKES SENSE...

Issue #1, Wizard World/Fandom Variant:
Dave Finch

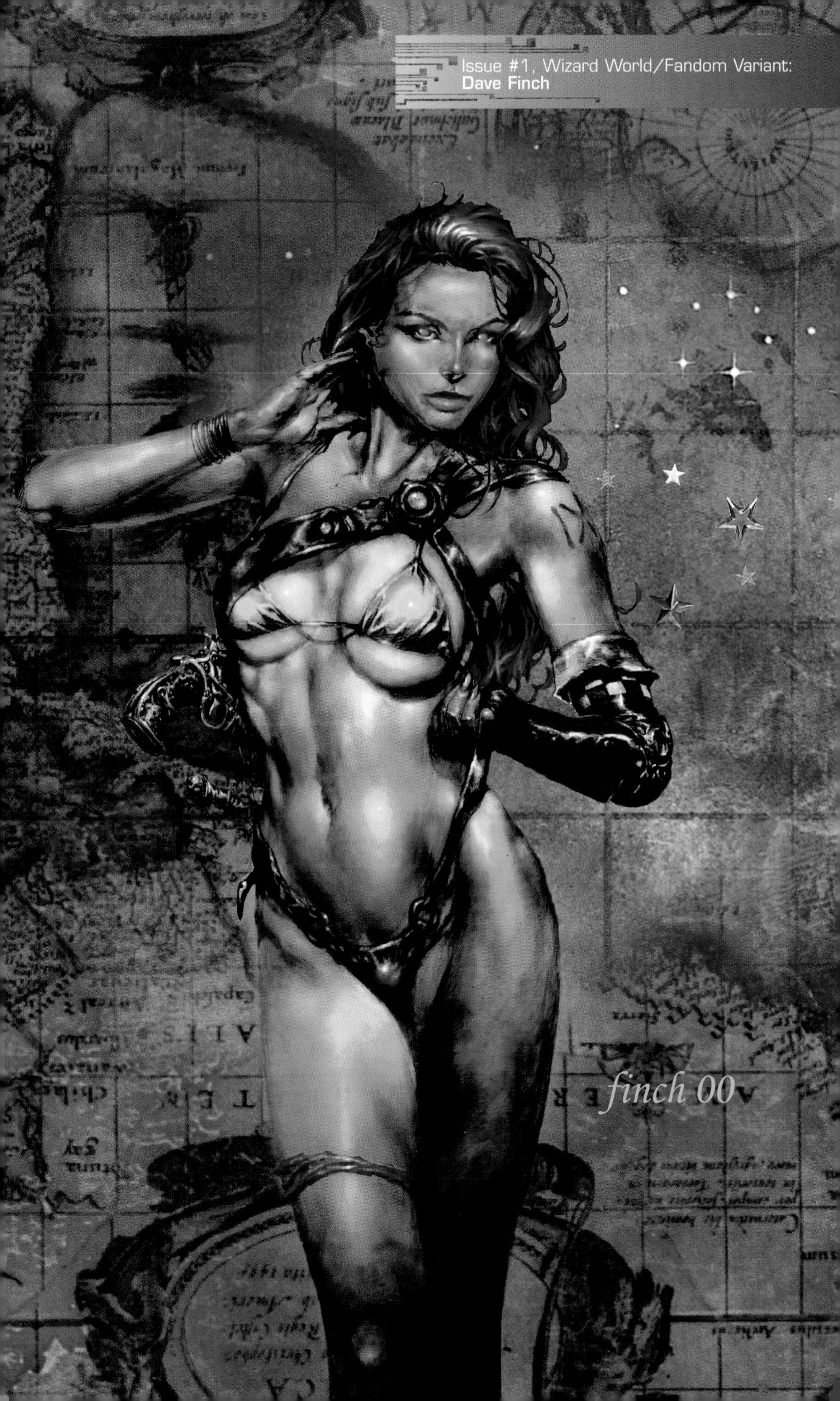
finch 00

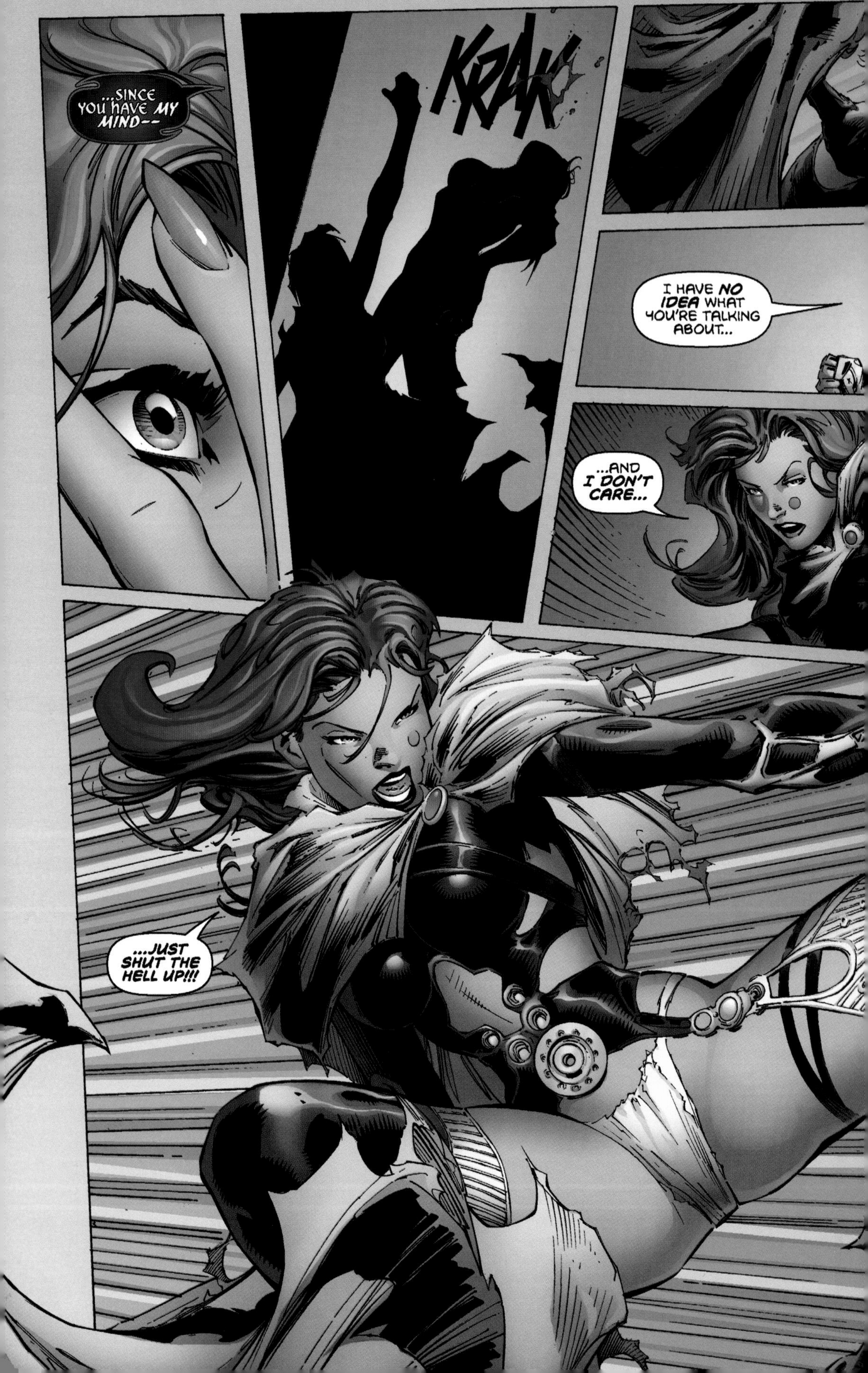
...SINCE YOU HAVE MY MIND--
KRAK
I HAVE NO IDEA WHAT YOU'RE TALKING ABOUT...
...AND I DON'T CARE...
...JUST SHUT THE HELL UP!!!

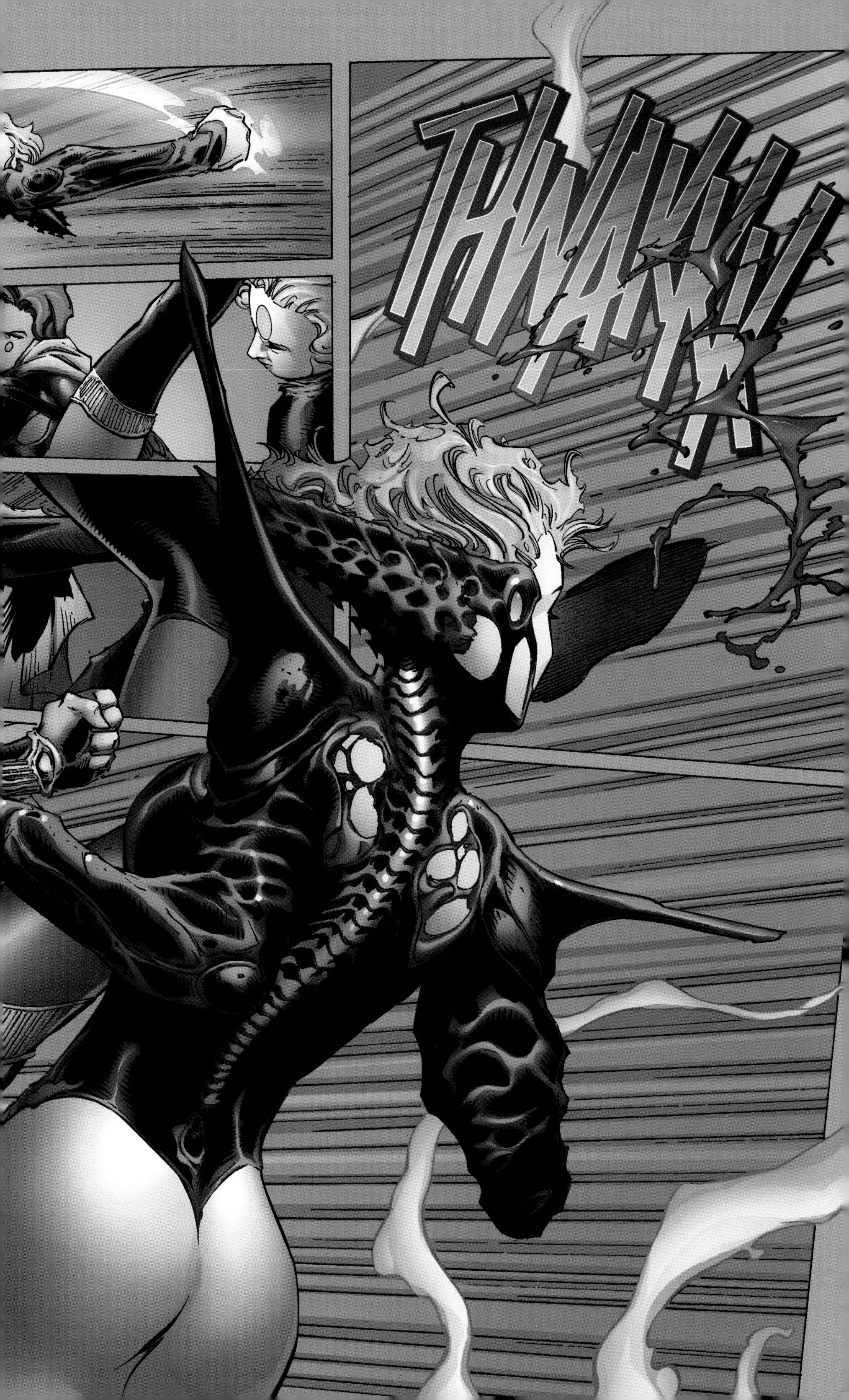
THWAKK!!

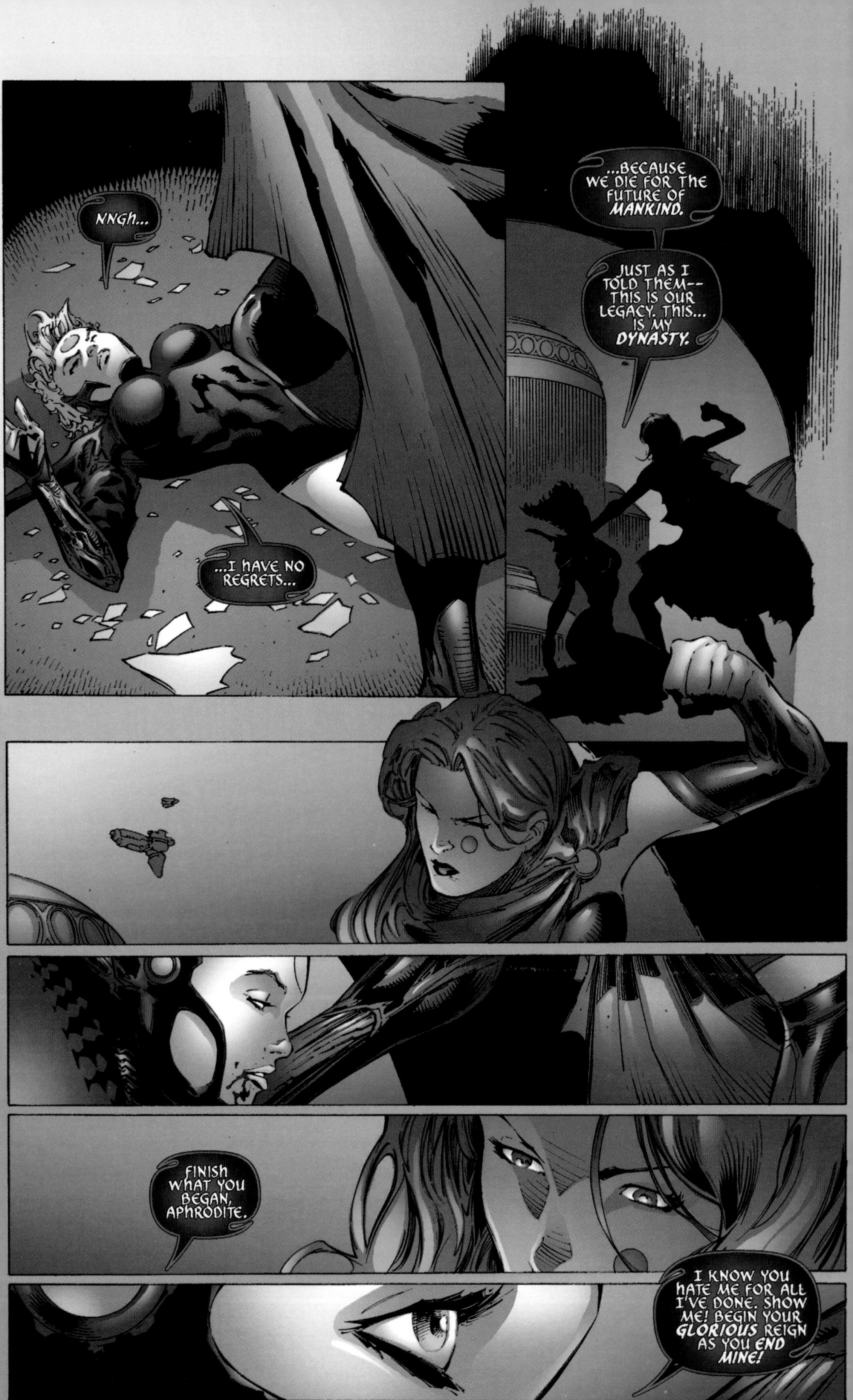
NNGh...
...I have NO REGRETS...
...BECAUSE WE DIE FOR THE FUTURE OF MANKIND.
JUST AS I TOLD THEM-- THIS IS OUR LEGACY. THIS... IS MY DYNASTY.
FINISH WHAT YOU BEGAN, APHRODITE.
I KNOW YOU hATE ME FOR ALL I'VE DONE. SHOW ME! BEGIN YOUR GLORIOUS REIGN AS YOU END MINE!

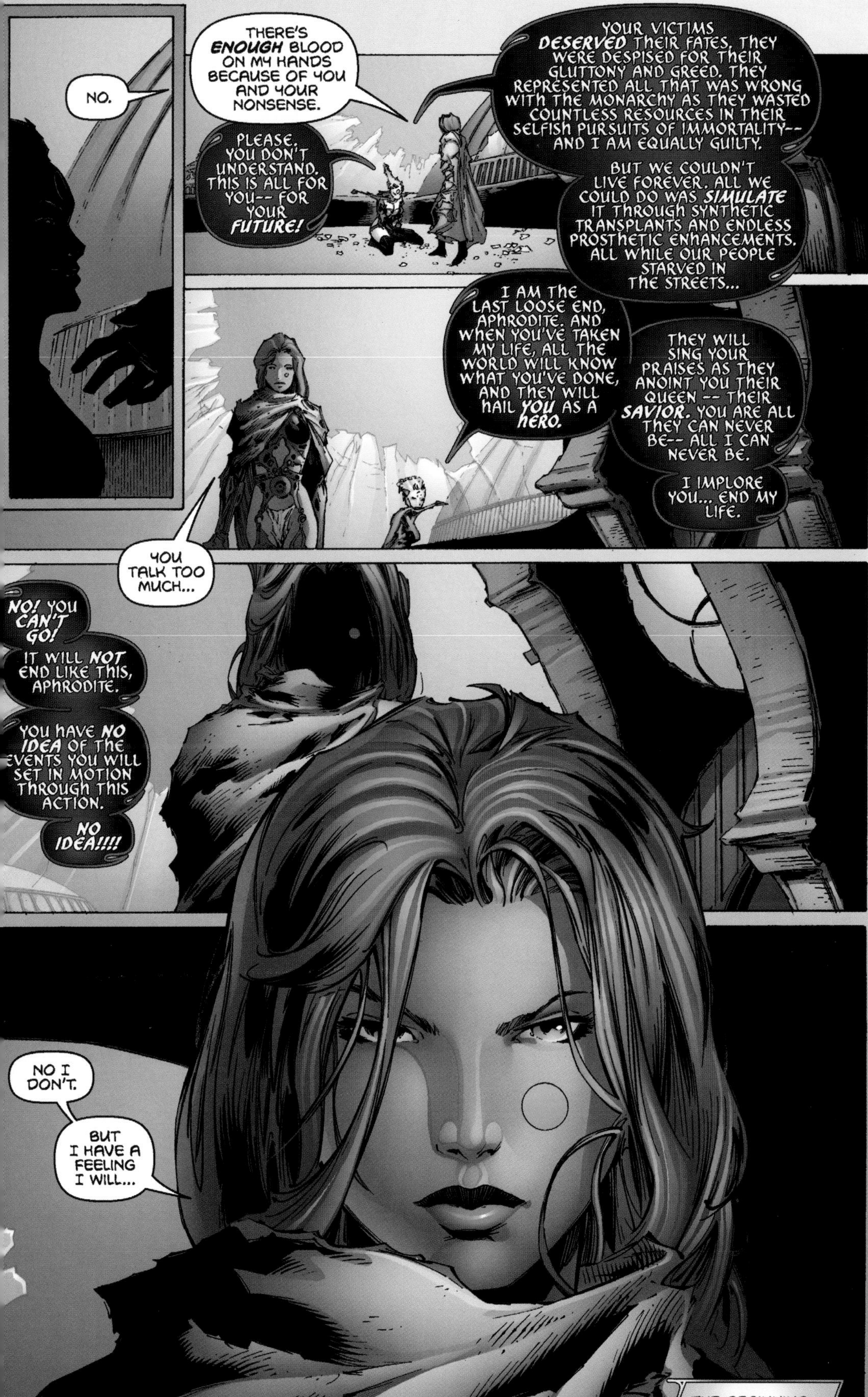
NO.
THERE'S ENOUGH BLOOD ON MY HANDS BECAUSE OF YOU AND YOUR NONSENSE.
PLEASE. YOU DON'T UNDERSTAND. THIS IS ALL FOR YOU-- FOR YOUR FUTURE!
YOUR VICTIMS DESERVED THEIR FATES. THEY WERE DESPISED FOR THEIR GLUTTONY AND GREED. THEY REPRESENTED ALL THAT WAS WRONG WITH THE MONARCHY AS THEY WASTED COUNTLESS RESOURCES IN THEIR SELFISH PURSUITS OF IMMORTALITY-- AND I AM EQUALLY GUILTY.
BUT WE COULDN'T LIVE FOREVER. ALL WE COULD DO WAS SIMULATE IT THROUGH SYNTHETIC TRANSPLANTS AND ENDLESS PROSTHETIC ENHANCEMENTS. ALL WHILE OUR PEOPLE STARVED IN THE STREETS...
I AM THE LAST LOOSE END, APHRODITE. AND WHEN YOU'VE TAKEN MY LIFE, ALL THE WORLD WILL KNOW WHAT YOU'VE DONE, AND THEY WILL HAIL YOU AS A HERO.
THEY WILL SING YOUR PRAISES AS THEY ANOINT YOU THEIR QUEEN -- THEIR SAVIOR. YOU ARE ALL THEY CAN NEVER BE-- ALL I CAN NEVER BE.
I IMPLORE YOU... END MY LIFE.
YOU TALK TOO MUCH...
NO! YOU CAN'T GO!
IT WILL NOT END LIKE THIS, APHRODITE.
YOU HAVE NO IDEA OF THE EVENTS YOU WILL SET IN MOTION THROUGH THIS ACTION.
NO IDEA!!!!
NO I DON'T.
BUT I HAVE A FEELING I WILL...
THE BEGINNING...

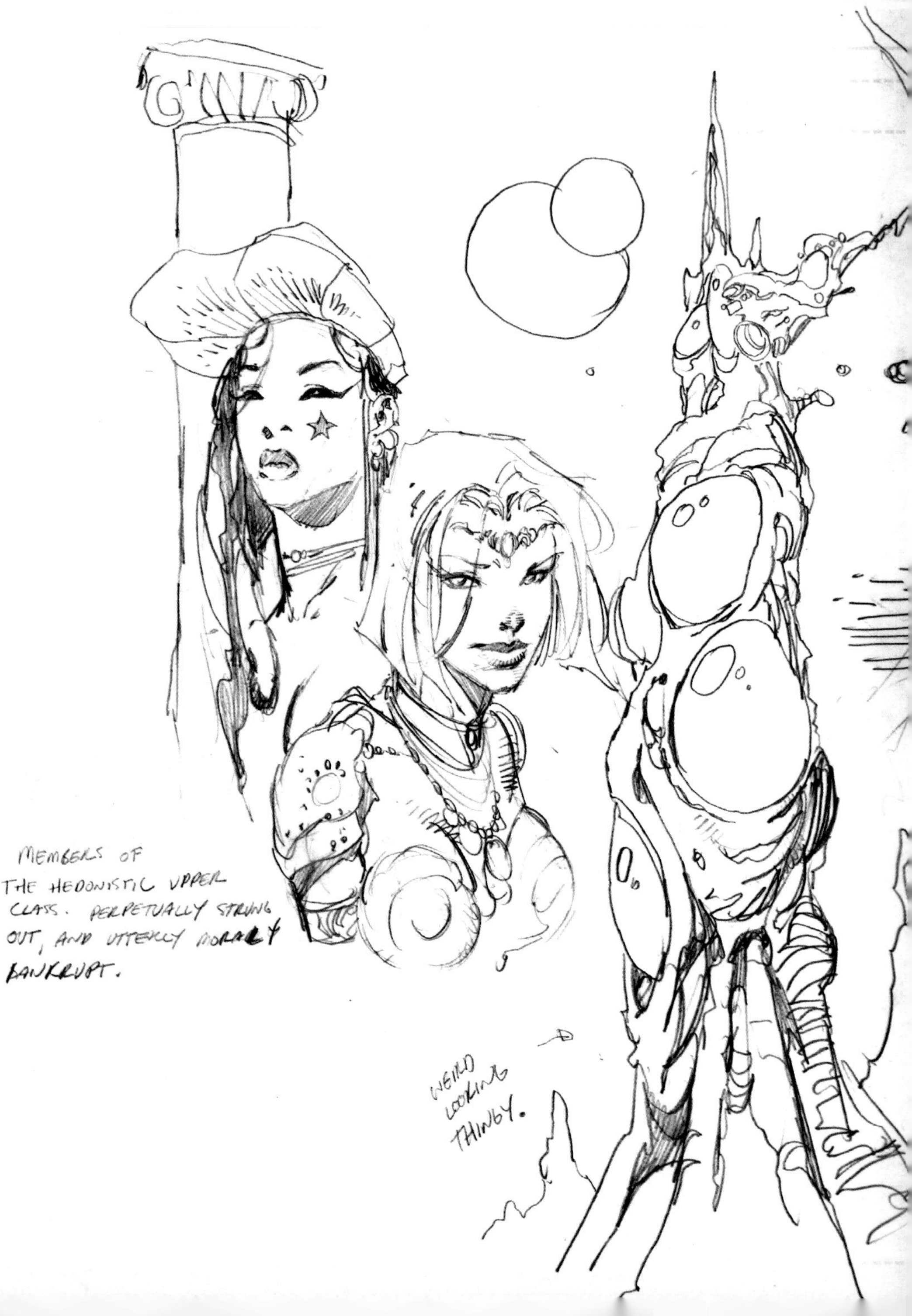
MEMBERS OF THE HEDONISTIC UPPER CLASS. PERPETUALLY STRUNG OUT, AND UTTERLY MORALLY BANKRUPT.
WEIRD LOOKING THINGY.

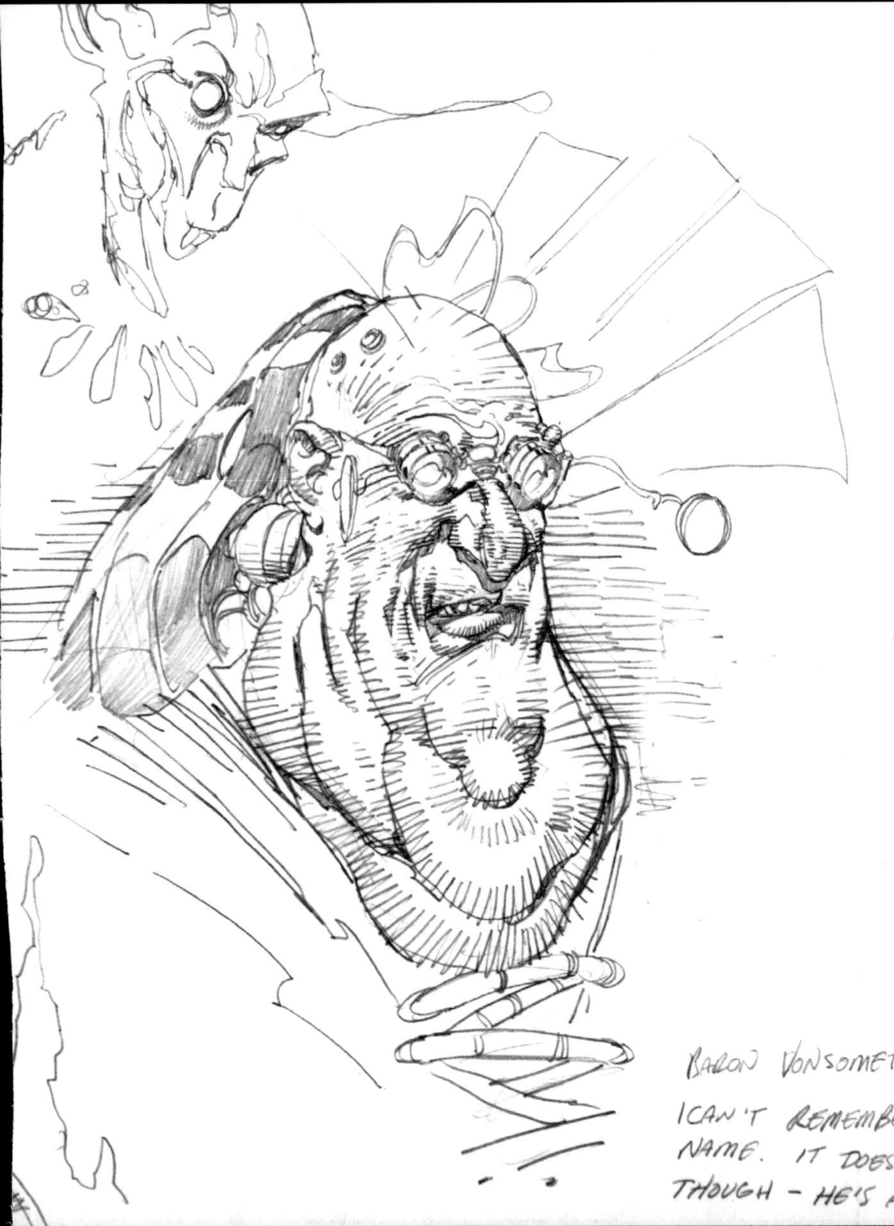

BARON VONSOMETHINGOROTHER

I CAN'T REMEMBER HIS NAME. IT DOESN'T MATTER THOUGH – HE'S ALREADY DEAD.

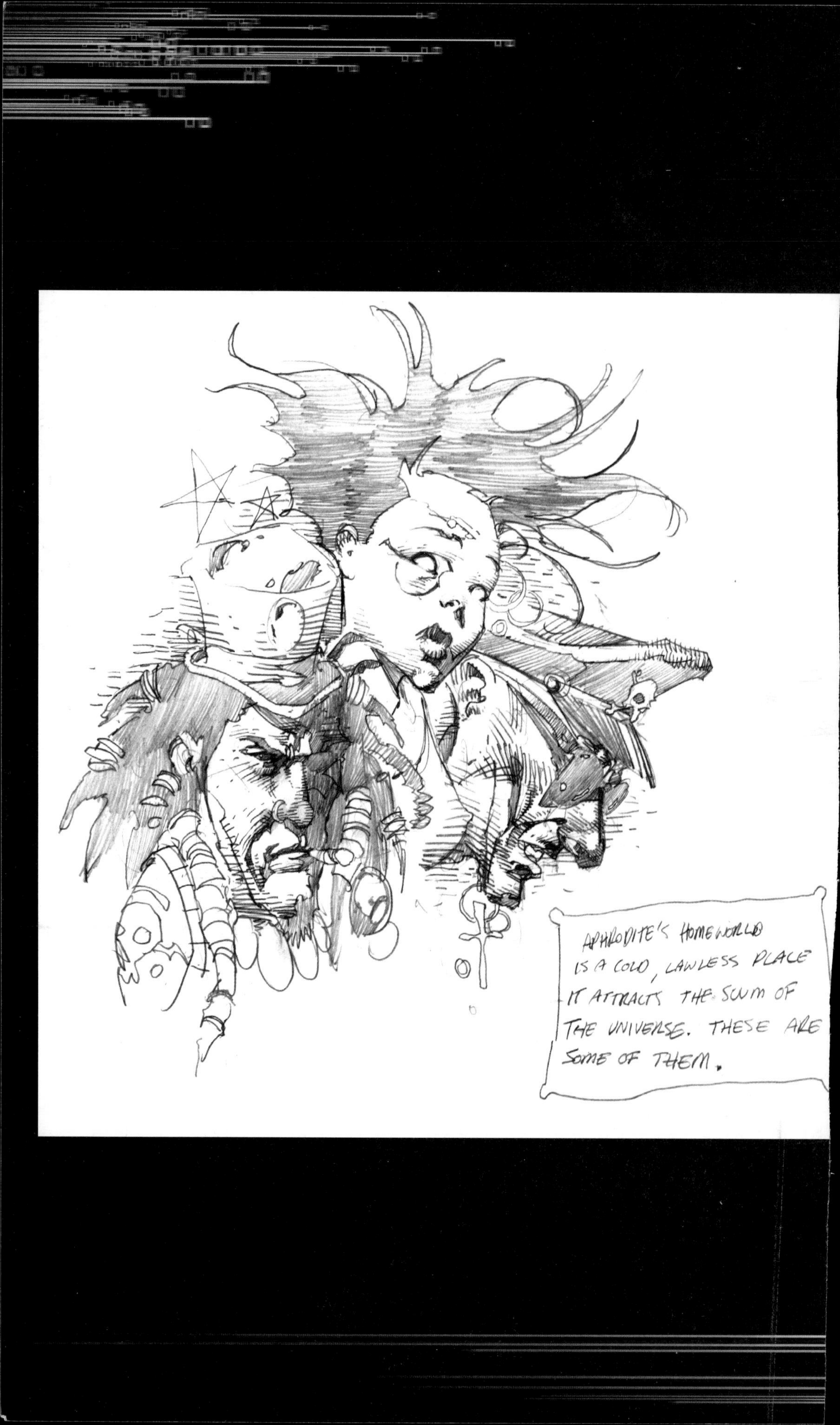
APHRODITE'S HOMEWORLD
IS A COLD, LAWLESS PLACE
IT ATTRACTS THE SCUM OF
THE UNIVERSE. THESE ARE
SOME OF THEM.